connecting science

■ Mark Edwards

■ Sue Hocking

■ Beverly Rickwood

PUPIL'S GUIDE

DYNAMIC LEARNING

Innovate · Motivate · Personalise

CD-ROM INSIDE

HODDER EDUCATION
PART OF HACHETTE LIVRE UK

Although every effort has been made to ensure that website addresses are correct at time of going to press, Hodder Education cannot be held responsible for the content of any website mentioned in this book. It is sometimes possible to find a relocated web page by typing in the address of the home page for a website in the URL window of your browser.

Hachette Livre UK's policy is to use papers that are natural, renewable and recyclable products and made from wood grown in sustainable forests. The logging and manufacturing processes are expected to conform to the environmental regulations of the country of origin.

Orders: please contact Bookpoint Ltd, 130 Milton Park, Abingdon, Oxon OX14 4SB. Telephone: (44) 01235 827720. Fax: (44) 01235 400454. Lines are open 9.00–5.00, Monday to Saturday, with a 24-hour message answering service. Visit our website at www.hoddereducation.co.uk

© Mark Edwards, Sue Hocking, Beverly Rickwood 2008
First published in 2008 by
Hodder Education,
Part of Hachette Livre UK
338 Euston Road
London NW1 3BH

Impression number   5 4 3 2 1

Year   2012 2011 2010 2009 2008

Cover photo NHPA Photo/Stephen Dalton
Illustrations by Oxford Designers and Illustrators Ltd
Typeset in 12/14pt ITC Officina Sans by Julie Martin Ltd
Printed in Italy

A catalogue record for this title is available from the British Library

ISBN: 978 0340 94598 8

Contents

Biology

Chemistry

Physics

Organs in the body

An organ is a part of a living organism. Each organ does a particular job. Organs are made up of tissues.

Brain The brain is a very complex organ. It controls body functions like breathing and heart rate, hunger and thirst, temperature and balance. It enables us to see, hear, taste and feel. Memories are stored here and we can think, solve problems, plan, and experience emotions.

Sense organs These include the eyes, ears, nose and tongue.

Liver The liver is a big organ that does many different jobs. It deals with toxins, such as drugs and alcohol.

Kidneys These filter the blood and remove waste. They also control the amount of salts and water in the body.

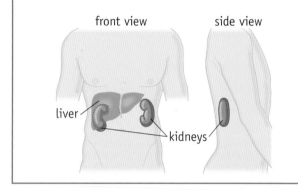

front view   side view

liver

kidneys

Small intestine This is where food is digested and absorbed into the blood.

Woman

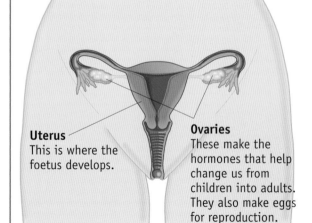

Uterus This is where the foetus develops.

Ovaries These make the hormones that help change us from children into adults. They also make eggs for reproduction.

Lungs The lungs link air and blood. We breathe air into the lungs where oxygen passes into the blood to go to body cells. The lungs also get rid of waste carbon dioxide.

Heart This is a double pump. It pumps blood around the body to give oxygen to all the body cells and take away carbon dioxide. It then pumps blood to the lungs to get rid of carbon dioxide and pick up more oxygen.

Stomach This is a muscular bag that holds food while it is being digested.

Large intestine This is where water from food is absorbed into the blood.

Don't forget that there are lots of other organs, like the main blood vessels and nerves and all the glands in the body.

It is impossible to say which organ is most important as they all have a job to do. If one organ fails it can affect all other parts of the body. However, you can live with one kidney or with half a liver.

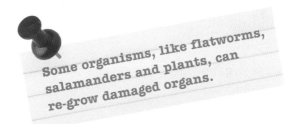

Some organisms, like flatworms, salamanders and plants, can re-grow damaged organs.

Skin The skin is the largest organ. It protects us from damage, entry of microbes and is waterproof. It also has nerve endings so we can feel heat or pain.

Man

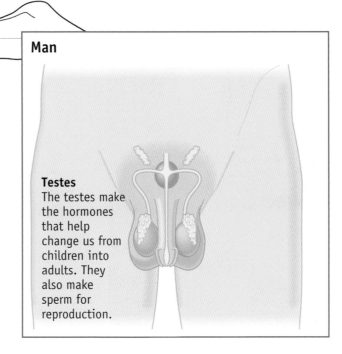

Testes
The testes make the hormones that help change us from children into adults. They also make sperm for reproduction.

3

Blood circulation and lungs

Groups of organs that work together form a system. The heart and blood vessels (arteries and veins) form the circulation system.

Blood carries oxygen and the products of digestion to muscles and other organs. The blood also carries away waste products from the organs, otherwise these would build up and poison the organs.

We breathe to get air into the trachea, then into the lungs.

Blood returns to the heart from the rest of the body.

The lungs and airways form the respiratory system. The lungs are where oxygen in the air can pass into the blood.

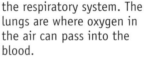

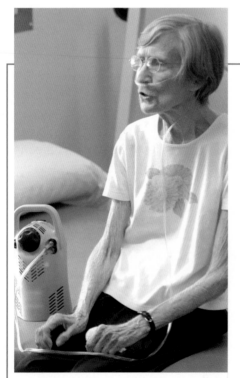

Lungs may be permanently damaged by cigarette smoke or dust. People with damaged lungs can't get enough oxygen into their blood and to their organs.

This means they may not even be able to walk across the room. They need to breathe from an oxygen cylinder.

Dust and smoke can also make the tubes of the airways to the lungs (trachea and bronchi) get narrow and inflamed. This can cause asthma or bronchitis.

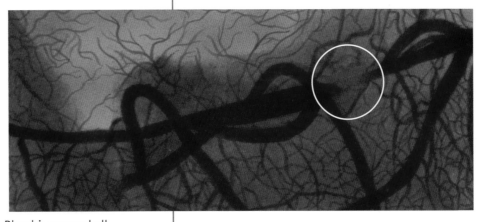

Blood is pumped all over the body.

The heart pumps the blood to the lungs, which remove waste and add oxygen.

Fatty deposits in an artery leading to the heart muscle can cut off the flow of blood and oxygen to the heart muscle. Part of the heart dies, causing a heart attack. Surgeons can use a piece of vein from an arm or leg and bypass the narrow or blocked artery. This is a coronary bypass.

The blood from the lungs then goes to the left side of the heart and is pumped all over the body.

The heart is a muscular pump.

Some people are born with a small hole between the left and right sides of the heart. This means they don't deliver quite enough oxygen to their organs and muscles and get tired very easily.

Both heart and lungs can be replaced with a transplant if they are damaged.

A machine can also take over the function of the heart and lungs. A heart–lung bypass machine removes waste and adds oxygen to the blood and pumps it to the rest of the body while an operation is being carried out.

There are fewer complications in a heart or lung transplant if the organs are kept together. If the person who receives the heart–lung transplant has a healthy heart it can be donated to someone else. So you could have a heart transplant and meet the living donor of your heart!

Where your food goes

The digestive system is where the food we eat is broken down so that it can be used by other parts of the body. Undigested food is passed out at the other end.

Many different organs make up the digestive system.

Oesophagus This is a muscular tube that starts at the back of the throat and moves the chewed food from the mouth down into the stomach.

Stomach The stomach is a muscular bag about the size of a coke can when empty. As food enters the stomach it mixes with digestive juices. Rings of muscle at either end then close and the stomach churns the food. Food stays in your stomach for about 2–6 hours.

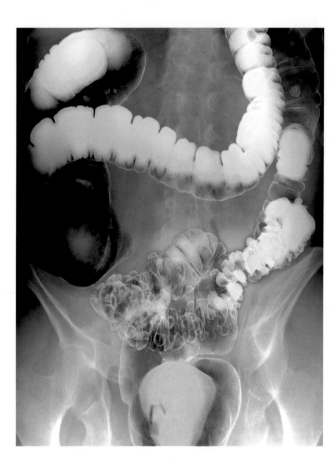

The stomach can be damaged by taking too much aspirin, which causes the stomach lining to bleed. It can also be damaged by ulcers, which may be a result of too much stomach acid and, in the majority of cases, a bacterial infection (*Helicobacter pylori*).

Doctors often use a barium meal to diagnose problems in the digestive system. Patients swallow the barium meal and then an X-ray is taken.

Mouth This is where digestion begins. Teeth chew the food into smaller pieces, the tongue mixes it with saliva and then it is swallowed.

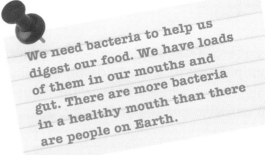

We need bacteria to help us digest our food. We have loads of them in our mouths and gut. There are more bacteria in a healthy mouth than there are people on Earth.

Small intestine Here, the food is completely broken down into its smallest parts. It is then absorbed into the surrounding blood vessels and transported by the circulation system to other organs in different parts of the body. There it can be used for growth, repair of damaged tissues, or as a source of energy.

Large intestine This is where water and minerals are absorbed into the blood vessels.

Rectum Undigested food is stored here before passing out of the anus.

Bladder Excess water absorbed into the blood, from the large intestine, and poisonous wastes from our food, need to be removed from the body. These are stored in the bladder as urine.

Anus

things to think about

Why do patients have to swallow a barium meal before their digestive system is X-rayed?

Reproductive organs and puberty

At puberty (age 11–14) your reproductive organs start to mature. From puberty to the beginning of adulthood (age 18–20) is adolescence, when you grow up. Your personality changes and you will also change physically, emotionally and psychologically.

Female

Ovary When girls are born they have millions of eggs in each ovary. After puberty begins, one of these eggs starts to mature each month and a girl's periods (menstrual cycle) start.

Halfway through the menstrual cycle (about two weeks after the last bleed and two weeks before the next period of bleeding) the egg bursts out of the ovary. This is ovulation. This is when a woman is most likely to become pregnant.

Mammary glands These are in the breasts, which develop in girls at puberty. During pregnancy they grow more so that after birth they can produce milk.

Womb (uterus) This is where the foetus (baby) develops. The uterus lining breaks down each menstrual cycle if the woman is not pregnant.

Oviduct Each month an egg passes along one of these from the ovary to the womb.

Cervix This is the entrance to the womb.

Vagina This is where sperm are deposited and where menstrual blood passes out of the body.

Bladder The bladder stores urine.

Urethra The urethra carries urine. In men it also carries sperm.

If a woman doesn't have her period when she expects it, she may be pregnant. When an egg is fertilised it travels to the womb and embeds in the lining. This causes the uterus lining to remain intact. A home pregnancy test kit can confirm pregnancy.

Male

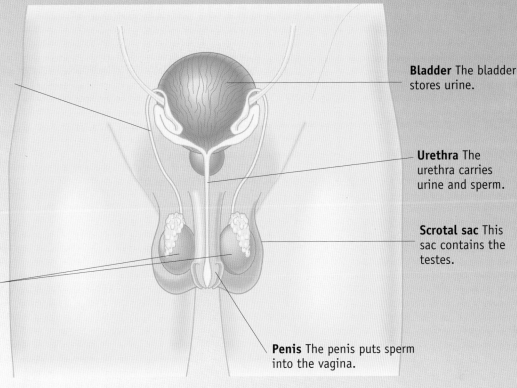

Sperm tube (vas deferens) This tube carries sperm from the testis to the urethra.

Testes Inside each testis are lots of coiled tubes. After puberty, millions of sperm are made in the testes every day.

Bladder The bladder stores urine.

Urethra The urethra carries urine and sperm.

Scrotal sac This sac contains the testes.

Penis The penis puts sperm into the vagina.

Some women can't get pregnant because they don't release eggs regularly, or at all. This problem may be treated with fertility drugs. Alternatively, eggs from a donor can be fertilised by sperm from the woman's partner and then placed into her womb.

Eggs can also be taken from a woman's ovaries, fertilised in a lab and inserted into her uterus. This is called IVF – In Vitro Fertilisation. The highly magnified picture shows injection of a sperm into an egg.

Some women may have lost their ovaries or womb due to cancer. Before their ovaries are removed their eggs can be taken and frozen. Later the eggs can be fertilised and put into the womb of a surrogate mother. This raises ethical issues as the surrogate mother then has to give up a baby she has carried for nine months. In the future, women who have lost ovaries or the uterus may receive transplants of these organs.

Some men have low sperm counts or have damaged sperm. Their partner's eggs can be fertilised by sperm from a donor.

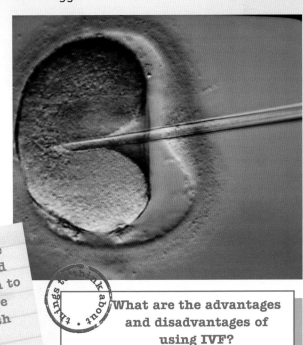

Early treatments with fertility drugs made women produce many eggs at a time and led to multiple births. Some women gave birth to eight babies. Now, when fertility drugs are prescribed, the eggs are fertilised in a dish and just two are put back into the womb.

things to think about **What are the advantages and disadvantages of using IVF?**

9

Sex and reproduction

Human females release one egg each month, around day 14 of the menstrual cycle. Once the egg is released it enters the oviduct. This is the time at which it is most likely a woman will become pregnant. If she has recently had sex, sperm from the male will have swum up from the vagina, through the uterus and into the oviduct. The egg may be fertilised if a sperm manages to reach it.

Fertilisation occurs when egg and sperm nuclei fuse together.

Each sperm has a tail so it can swim. Sperm are small as they don't need to have nutrients inside them. They swim in a fluid that contains nutrients. The sperm and this fluid together are called semen. Men produce lots of sperm, which increases the chance that one will reach the egg and fertilise it.

Many sperm surround the egg. When one has entered, the outside of the egg changes and no more sperm can get in.

The egg is much larger than a sperm because it has to have stored nutrients. These help it to survive until it implants in the uterus lining, about eight days after fertilisation.

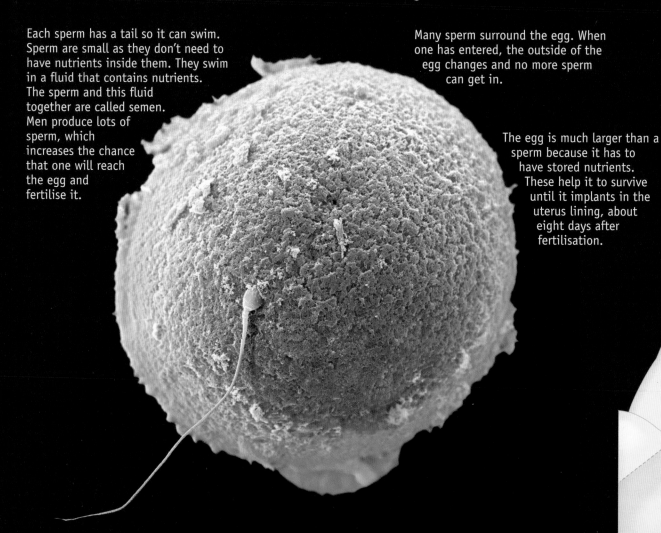

Humans, and other animals that live and breed on land, have internal fertilisation. The man has a penis which swells with blood when he becomes sexually excited. The penis becomes erect and he can insert it into the woman's vagina during sexual intercourse. When he ejaculates sperm are released into the vagina. They can swim through the cervix and uterus into the oviduct, where they meet the egg.

Many fish shed eggs and sperm into the water around them where sperm can swim to the egg.

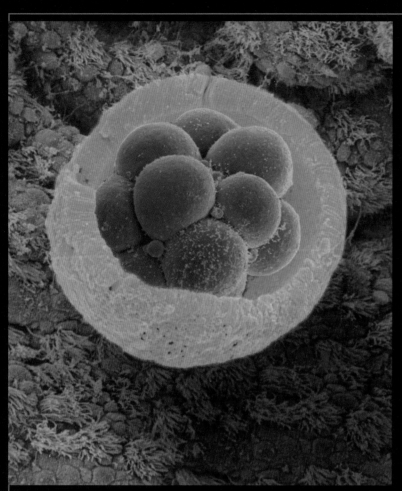

After an egg has been fertilised it travels down the oviduct over a period of about eight days. This fertilised egg is still inside the oviduct.

When it reaches the uterus it implants into the thick lining. This lining has been building up since the last menstrual period, ready to receive and protect a fertilised egg.

The implanted egg develops into a foetus. Over a period of nine months, the baby develops and grows inside the uterus.

Sometimes two eggs are released from the ovary at the same time. If both eggs are fertilised the woman can expect non-identical twins. Identical twins develop from one fertilised egg that has split into two.

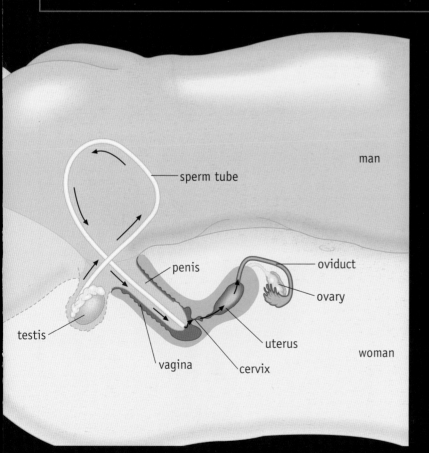

man

sperm tube

penis

oviduct

ovary

testis

uterus

woman

vagina

cervix

Sometimes one twin dies in the womb. Usually the body is broken down and reabsorbed by the mother. But sometimes the body of the dead twin is incorporated into the other twin's body. The small body of a dead twin was once found inside a boy. It had been mistaken for a growth.

Animals that have internal fertilisation produce far fewer eggs than those, such as fish, that have external fertilisation. Why do you think this is?

Pregnancy and foetus development

After an egg is fertilised it starts to form a ball of cells (an embryo). This implants in the uterus.

After eight weeks the developing being is about 4 cm long. From now on it's called a foetus. The organs of the foetus are in their final position but are not fully developed. A protective sac called the amnion has formed around the foetus. Inside the amnion is amniotic fluid. The foetus floats in the amniotic fluid so its weight is supported and it is protected from bumps.

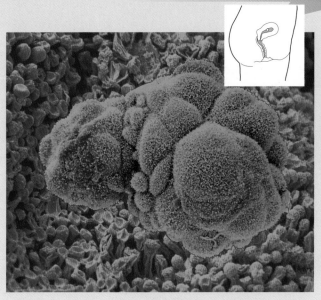

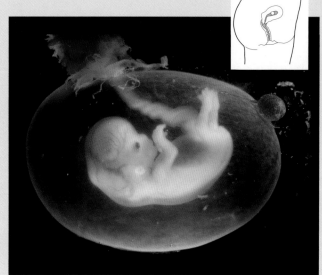

The placenta is a very important organ. It acts like a bridge between mother and baby. The umbilical cord is made up of hundreds of blood vessels and joins the foetus to the placenta. The blood vessels carry oxygen and nutrients from the mother's blood to the foetus. Waste, such as carbon dioxide, passes across the placenta from the foetus to the mother.

Because of the exchange across the placenta a pregnant woman should avoid alcohol and smoking. Harmful poisons from both cigarettes and alcohol can pass across the placenta to the foetus. These poisons can affect the development of the foetus and lead to low birth weight and other problems. The mother should also avoid other drugs, including some medicines.

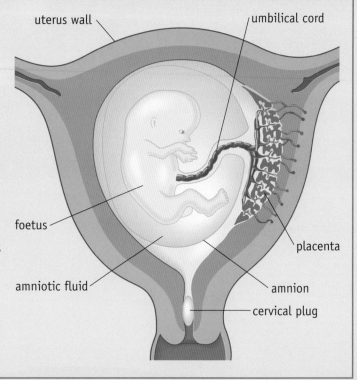

uterus wall

umbilical cord

foetus

amniotic fluid

placenta

amnion

cervical plug

By five months, the foetus has fully developed lips, eyelids, eyebrows, fingers and toes. The foetus is still growing and the brain needs to develop further.

Most foetuses under five months old cannot survive outside the uterus. Some babies are born a bit early – they are premature. They need to be in an incubator to keep them warm and they may be fed through a tube because they are not yet strong enough to feed on their own.

After 40 weeks the baby is ready to be born. This length of time is called gestation.

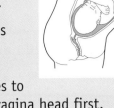

Just before birth the uterus muscles contract and the cervix dilates. The mother uses her abdominal muscles to push the baby out of the vagina head first.

The baby starts to breathe air, so the umbilical cord can be tied and cut. After a while the baby may take a feed of breast milk, made in the mother's mammary glands. The milk has just the right balance of nutrients and also helps protect the baby from infectious diseases.

Soon after the baby is born the placenta is also pushed out.

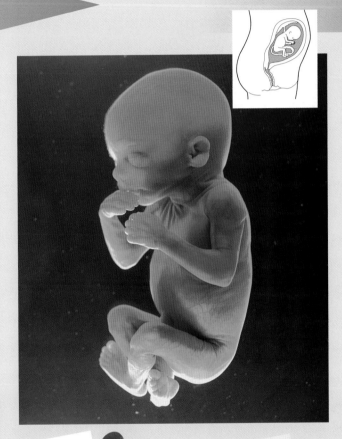

During pregnancy, a mother's health is carefully checked by the midwife. The development of the foetus is monitored by ultrasound scans. Doctors can now get a 3D picture of what the baby looks like in the womb.

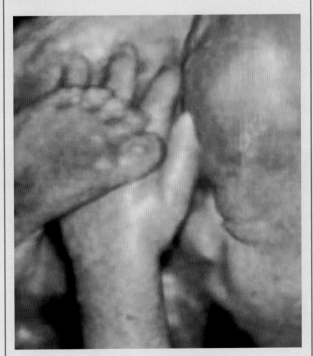

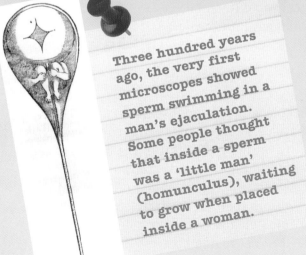

Three hundred years ago, the very first microscopes showed sperm swimming in a man's ejaculation. Some people thought that inside a sperm was a 'little man' (homunculus), waiting to grow when placed inside a woman.

Why do you think ultrasound scans are used, instead of X-rays, to see the developing foetus?

Absorbing nutrients

Food has to be broken down into smaller molecules so that the nutrients it contains can be absorbed from the small intestine into the blood.

Enzymes help break the food down quickly. Without enzymes it would take about 50 years to digest a meal in your stomach.

Enzymes are like tools. They get the job done (in this case breaking down the food) but they are not themselves changed by the process.

Different enzymes in our digestive system break down the different substances in our food.

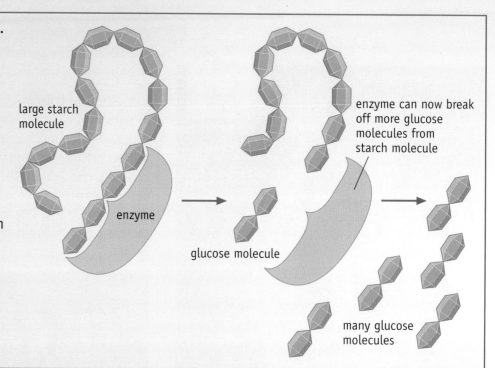

large starch molecule

enzyme

glucose molecule

enzyme can now break off more glucose molecules from starch molecule

many glucose molecules

After food has been digested in the stomach and intestine, the nutrient molecules diffuse through the cells in the intestine wall into the blood vessels. Blood carries the absorbed nutrients to other cells in different parts of the body, where they diffuse through cell membranes into the cells.

Early experiments on digestion were carried out when a Canadian trapper called Alexis St Martin was accidentally shot in the stomach. The wound left a hole in his side which led into his stomach. His doctor, William Beaumont, could take out partly digested food from his stomach.

People with coeliac disease do not produce the enzyme to digest foods that contain wheat. This means a chemical in the wheat, called gluten, can't be broken down and it damages the small intestine wall. Sufferers cannot absorb their food effectively. They become bloated and uncomfortable. Coeliac disease can be treated by avoiding wheat products.

Food molecules must pass through the wall of the small intestine into the blood. Every cell has a membrane that controls how things enter and leave the cell. We can investigate how the size of molecules affects their absorption through the cells in the intestine wall by using a model. A model doesn't have to look like the system it is modelling, but part of it may work in the same way.

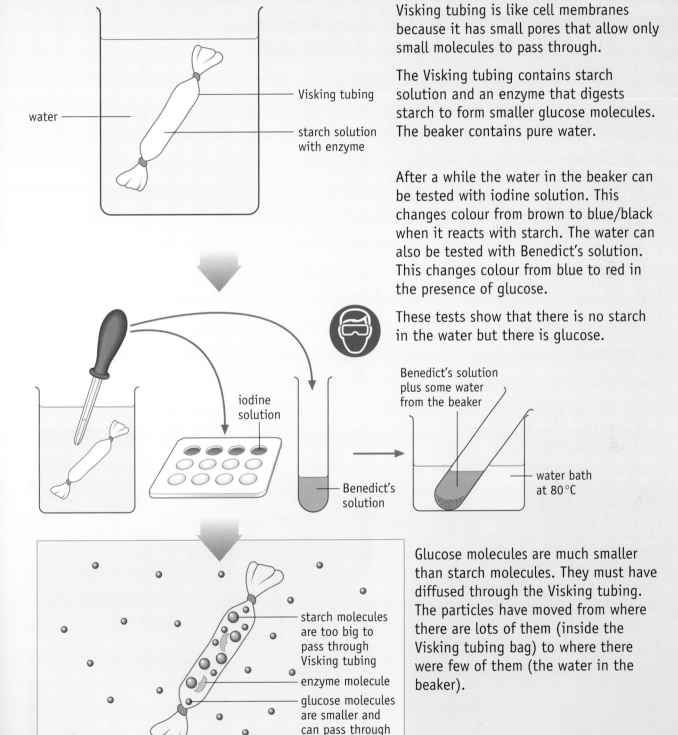

water

Visking tubing

starch solution with enzyme

iodine solution

Benedict's solution

Benedict's solution plus some water from the beaker

water bath at 80 °C

starch molecules are too big to pass through Visking tubing

enzyme molecule

glucose molecules are smaller and can pass through

Visking tubing is like cell membranes because it has small pores that allow only small molecules to pass through.

The Visking tubing contains starch solution and an enzyme that digests starch to form smaller glucose molecules. The beaker contains pure water.

After a while the water in the beaker can be tested with iodine solution. This changes colour from brown to blue/black when it reacts with starch. The water can also be tested with Benedict's solution. This changes colour from blue to red in the presence of glucose.

These tests show that there is no starch in the water but there is glucose.

Glucose molecules are much smaller than starch molecules. They must have diffused through the Visking tubing. The particles have moved from where there are lots of them (inside the Visking tubing bag) to where there were few of them (the water in the beaker).

things to think about

How could you use a Visking tubing model to investigate the effect of temperature on the speed of digestion by enzymes?

Specialised organs

We all start off as one cell – a fertilised egg. This cell divides again and again to form a ball of cells. Each of the cells in an embryo then becomes specialised to do a different job.

A group of similar specialised cells that do a particular job is called a tissue. A group of similar tissues that work together is called an organ.

The organs are all in place in an 8-week-old foetus. The graph shows the development of the brain and reproductive organs over the first 20 years of life.

The brain is very specialised. A newborn baby has a very undeveloped brain. The brain grows quickly in the first few years of life and certain areas become specialised to do certain tasks. By the time a child is 7 or 8 years old the brain is almost fully developed.

The ovaries and the testes are specialised reproductive organs. They don't grow very much until puberty, when they grow and develop very quickly.

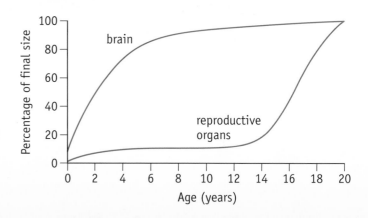

Groups of organs work together as systems to carry out specific jobs. In the lungs, gases must pass between the air and the blood. The lungs are specialised to do this job by having millions of tiny air sacs (alveoli).

The air sacs enclosed by this lung tissue, magnified about 400 times, are all connected to the tubes of the airways. There are capillaries (small blood vessels) surrounding each alveolus. The alveoli give a very large surface area for gas exchange.

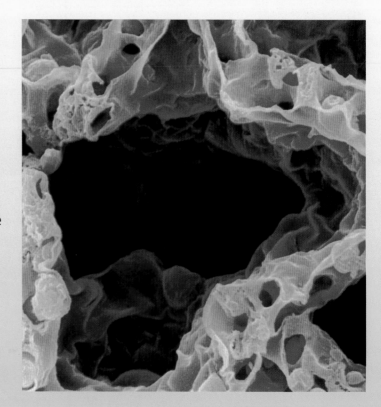

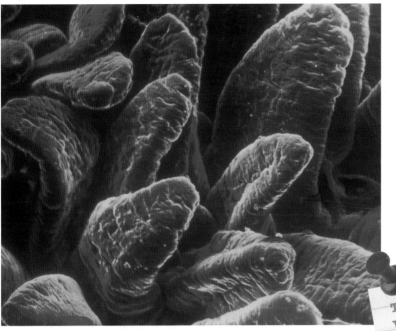

In the small intestine, digested food is absorbed into the blood to be taken to cells. The wall of the small intestine has lots of finger-like projections (villi). Inside each villus are capillaries. The large number of villi increases the surface area for absorption of food.

magnified about 400 times

The placenta is a unique organ. What makes it so unusual is that it is made partly from the uterus wall and partly from the foetus, so it is one organ made of cells and tissues from two different individuals.

Plants have organs too. Leaves are the organs that make food. Humans and other animals may eat the leaves.

Some plants live in places where the ground is poor in certain minerals. They have to get these minerals from digesting insects and small animals. The leaves of carnivorous plants are specialised to make fly traps or pitchers (jugs) to catch these animals.

things to think about

What parts or organs of plants need a large surface area?

Healthy eating

Eating a balanced diet is very important so that your cells absorb the right nutrients. Cells need energy from food so they can divide to make new cells so your body can grow. Cells have lots of other functions to carry out and these also need energy and certain chemicals.

You need carbohydrates, proteins, fats, vitamins and minerals. You also need fibre and water. You need them in the right amounts and your total energy intake should balance the energy you use.

About a sixth of your diet should be protein. Cells need protein to build their internal structures, and in turn to build and repair tissue such as skin, hair, muscles, bones and teeth. Babies and children are growing fast and making lots of new cells, so it is very important that they get enough protein in their diet. Enzymes are proteins and cell membranes contain protein.

You need to eat small amounts of vitamins regularly.

Vitamin C from fruit and vegetables is needed for healthy joints and blood vessels. It is needed to build something called connective tissue that supports and binds other body tissues. Lack of vitamin C causes an illness caused scurvy.

Vitamin D enables us to absorb calcium from our food. This keeps our bones hard. Oily fish and egg yolks contain vitamin D. Sunlight causes a fat under the skin to be changed to vitamin D.

Vitamin A is needed for eyes and skin and to help prevent infections. Liver contains vitamin A. Green and orange vegetables and fruits contain a substance that the body changes to vitamin A.

Vitamins in the B group keep nerves healthy and are used to help respiration, the release of energy from food.

Many military campaigns before the twentieth century were brought to a halt because the fighting force was weak from scurvy. In 1747 James Lind set about finding a cure for scurvy. He added various foods to sailors' diets and found that oranges and lemons prevented scurvy. Fifty years later lime and lemon juice was prescribed for all British sailors, who became known as 'limeys'.

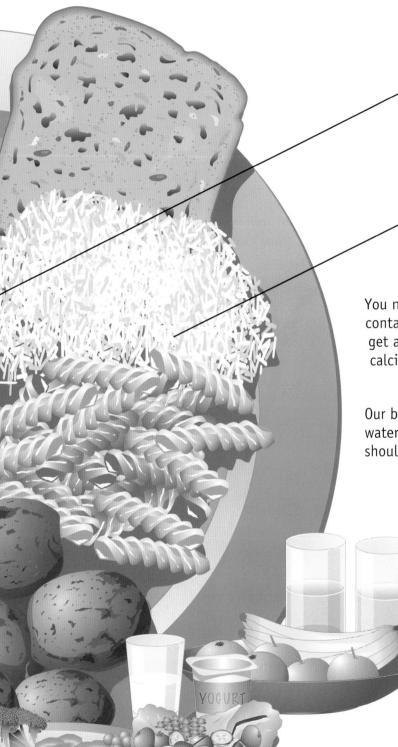

Just under as third of your diet should be fat or oil. Fat provides energy. We also store fat under the skin to help keep us warm and to protect us from knocks. Your cell membranes are made largely from fat.

Just over half of what you eat each day should be carbohydrate. Carbohydrates provide energy so cells can carry out all their tasks.

You need small amounts of minerals. Red meat contains iron for healthy blood so you don't get anaemia. Foods made from milk contain calcium for hard bones.

Our bodies contain a lot of water. We lose water in urine, sweat, tears and breath, so we should drink several glasses of it each day.

Fibre doesn't give us energy but stops us getting constipated. If you eat at least five (ideally eight to ten) portions of fruits and vegetables each day, some wholemeal bread and some cereal, you will get your fibre as well as vitamins and minerals.

things to think about

Pregnant women are often advised to supplement their diet with folic acid (vitamin B6) but to avoid taking too much vitamin A. Why can too much of some vitamins be a bad thing?

Microorganisms and disease

Microorganisms are small organisms that can only be seen with a microscope. Microorganisms are also called microbes. They include bacteria, viruses, some fungi and some protoctists.

Bacteria, fungi, protoctists and viruses can sometimes cause disease, but certain types of bacteria and fungi are also very useful.

Diseases caused by such microorganisms are said to be infectious diseases.

- Microbes can be transmitted (passed) from person to person.
- Once a microbe has entered our body, it can multiply and destroy tissues or create toxins, making us ill.

We can reduce the chance of being infected or infecting others by practising good hygiene. For example, we should wash our hands after going to the toilet and before and after preparing food.

Doctors and nurses use hand gels containing alcohol to help to prevent the transmission of infections in hospitals. Patients and visitors should also use the hand gels. The alcohol in the gel kills most microbes, but not *Clostridium difficile*.

Fungi are multicellular microorganisms. Some are used to produce antibiotics. Others are eaten or used in the production of food such as blue cheese or Quorn™.

Certain fungi can infect us and cause diseases such as thrush and athlete's foot. This micrograph (magnified 400 times) shows vaginal cells (pink) infected with the fungus (dark) that causes thrush.

This person has a thrush infection on the tongue.

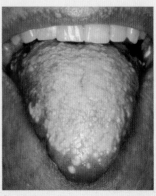

Bacteria are small, single-celled organisms. Some bacteria can make us ill but most of them don't harm us and many can be useful. Bacteria in our gut help digest our food. Other bacteria are also used in industry to make yogurt, cheese, insulin and gasohol – a biofuel for vehicles.

Viruses are even smaller than bacteria. Viruses have to enter cells to reproduce and in the process they kill those cells.

Human diseases caused by viruses include flu, measles, cervical cancer and HIV/AIDS. These are all serious illnesses that can kill.

Staphylococcus bacteria (magnified here 11 800 times) live on our skin and don't normally harm us. If they get into a deep wound, for example during surgery, they can make us very ill. This means it is very important for surgeons to operate under sterile conditions (no microbes present).

This coloured micrograph shows a blood cell (green) infected with HIV (red), magnified 6000 times. There is no cure for the disease caused by the HIV virus. The virus is transmitted in blood, semen and vaginal fluids. Condoms can prevent its spread.

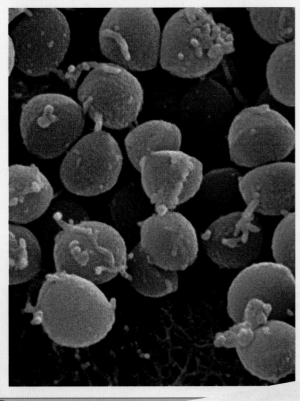

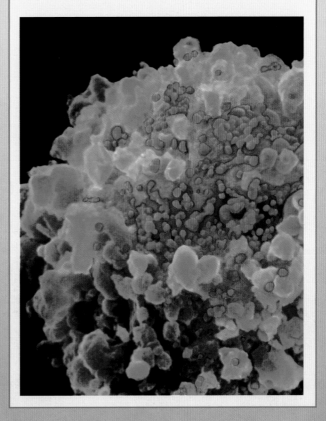

The combined mass of all bacteria on Earth adds up to more than the combined mass of all other living creatures. The bacteria in your gut add up to a tenth of your mass and there are more of them than there are cells in your body. In your mouth there are more bacteria than there are people on Earth.

things to think about • Some fluorescent dyes can be used to detect bacteria. The dye sticks to bacteria and glows when ultraviolet light is shone over them. How might these dyes be useful to prevent the spread of infectious disease?

Defences against disease

We have three barriers against infectious diseases:

- Our skin is a physical barrier that stops microorganisms entering.
- If the skin is cut then microbes can enter. To prevent this the blood clots and seals the wound with a scab.
- The stomach lining makes acid that kills microbes on food.

If microbes get past these defences, white blood cells attack them. Some engulf the microbes and then break them down. This white blood cell is attaching to and engulfing bacteria (blue).

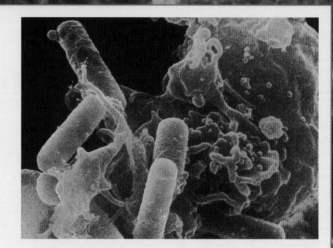

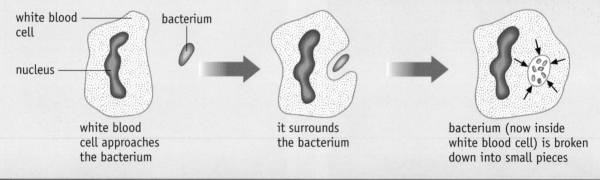

white blood cell

bacterium

nucleus

white blood cell approaches the bacterium

it surrounds the bacterium

bacterium (now inside white blood cell) is broken down into small pieces

This type of white blood cell makes special chemicals called antibodies. These chemicals cover the microorganisms and stop them entering cells. It also helps the other white blood cells to engulf them.

Some of this type of white blood cell stays in the blood after the infection. If the same type of microorgansism infects the body again, these white blood cells are ready to act quickly and you don't get any symptoms. You are immune.

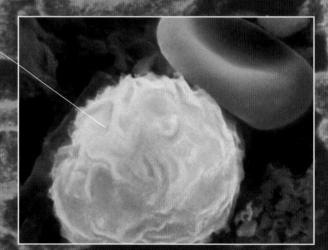

Smallpox was a terrible disease that killed most of its victims. In 1796 Edward Jenner noticed that milkmaids who had had cowpox (a mild illness) did not get smallpox. He put pus from someone with cowpox into a scratch on a boy's arm. The boy caught cowpox. A few weeks later he injected the boy with pus from someone with smallpox. The boy didn't get smallpox.

Cowpox pus was used for many years to make people immune to smallpox. No one knew how this worked until much later. We now know that antibodies the body makes to destroy cowpox viruses also work against the smallpox virus.

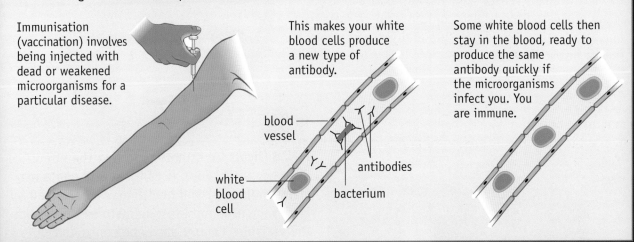

Immunisation (vaccination) involves being injected with dead or weakened microorganisms for a particular disease.

This makes your white blood cells produce a new type of antibody.

Some white blood cells then stay in the blood, ready to produce the same antibody quickly if the microorganisms infect you. You are immune.

blood vessel

white blood cell

antibodies

bacterium

Children in Britain are usually immunised against diseases such as measles, mumps and rubella (MMR vaccine), and other diseases such as polio and tetanus.

Some parents chose not to have their children vaccinated with the MMR vaccine after one doctor suggested it could cause autism. No other studies have produced evidence to support this claim.

Because not as many children have been vaccinated, there has recently been an increase in cases of mumps.

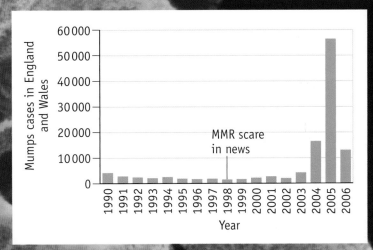

MMR scare in news

What could be the most likely reason for parents not having their children vaccinated?

The virus that causes cancer of the cervix is sexually transmitted. There is a vaccine, and the spread of all sexually transmitted diseases can also be prevented by *always* using a condom or femidom. These are physical barriers, a bit like the skin, and prevent the transmission of microbes.

Millions of people – most of them children – die each year in developing countries from infectious diseases that are preventable with vaccines. However, the diseases that cause the greatest problems (TB, cholera, malaria and HIV) do not have effective vaccines.

23

More on healthy eating

Ready-made meals may save time but most contain chemicals added during manufacturing. Some additives increase shelf-life. Fat is often added to improve taste, give texture and provide bulk, but too much fat increases your risk of heart disease. Many processed foods also contain a lot of salt. Too much salt raises blood pressure and increases your risk of heart disease.

It is difficult for scientists to test the effects of different diets. Food is complex and contains many chemicals, and health may be affected by environmental and lifestyle factors. This means the variables cannot easily be controlled.

Additives are allowed in food only after they have been fully tested. Scientists compare the health and behaviour of animals that have been fed food containing the additive with that of a control group fed the same food but without the additive. However, the way an additive affects a rat or mouse could be quite different from how it affects humans. Measuring behaviour such as hyperactivity is very difficult.

Some foods have additives for specific health purposes. Stanol is added to some margarines to reduce blood cholesterol levels. Trials on groups of humans have produced evidence that these additives work.

You may read other health claims for food. Sometimes the scientific evidence is unclear and different scientists may have different views because they:

- evaluate and criticise the research method
- use the same data but come to a different conclusion
- find different evidence that may refute the claim.

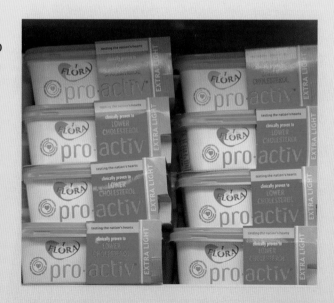

Dietary advice is usually based on analysing diets of groups of people that have a high incidence of a certain disease. However, new information from the Human Genome Project is changing scientific understanding about how our diet affects us. Scientists are finding out how genes interact with specific foods.

Some chemicals in food can switch on or off the genes that control metabolism and growth. Nutrigenomics is a new interdisciplinary science to study how an individual's unique genome can affect how their body responds to nutrients.

In the future we may all have a recommended tailor-made, personalised diet to reduce our personal risk of heart disease and cancer.

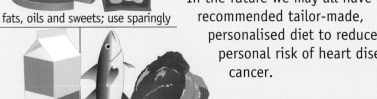

fats, oils and sweets; use sparingly

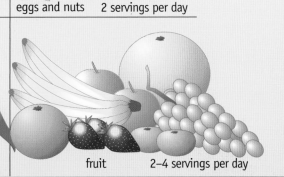

milk, yogurt and cheese
2–3 servings per day

meat, poultry, fish, dry beans, eggs and nuts   2 servings per day

vegetables   3–5 servings per day

fruit   2–4 servings per day

bread, cereal

potatoes

rice and pasta

carbohydrates   6–11 servings per day

In the meantime we all need to follow a balanced diet with foods from each food group. If we want to lose weight, we should eat less and move more. There's no such thing as good or bad food, only good and bad diets. It's all a question of balance.

Doctors advise us to eat a diet with lots of colourful food. Red tomatoes are high in lycopene, an antioxidant that may reduce the risk of certain cancers and heart disease. But you would need to eat nearly an entire 200 cm^3 (ml) bottle of tomato ketchup a day to get a daily lycopene intake of 30 mg.

things to think about

How could you design an investigation to see if yogurt reduces blood cholesterol? Think of the pros and cons for our each having a personalised diet plan.

Respiration

Respiration is the release of energy from food. It happens in the cells. All cells need energy to function, and for growth and repair.

Aerobic respiration needs oxygen.

The respiration reaction in cells takes place in lots of little steps, but this equation summarises the process.

glucose + oxygen $\longrightarrow$ energy + carbon dioxide + water

$$C_6H_{12}O_6 + 6O_2 \longrightarrow energy + 6CO_2 + 6H_2O$$

The lungs connect the air outside the body with the circulation system. Air enters the lungs when we breathe in.

Inhaled air contains about 20% oxygen and about 0.04% carbon dioxide. The blood entering the lungs doesn't have so much oxygen in it. As there is more oxygen in the lungs than in the blood, oxygen diffuses into the blood.

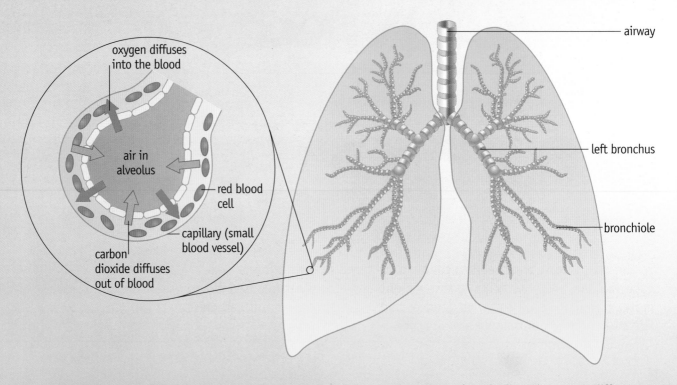

oxygen diffuses into the blood

air in alveolus

red blood cell

capillary (small blood vessel)

carbon dioxide diffuses out of blood

airway

left bronchus

bronchiole

Oxygen is carried in the blood from our lungs to the heart and then to the organs of our bodies. The oxygen diffuses from the blood into the cells of those organs.

The carbon dioxide that cells produce during respiration is carried to the lungs by the blood. So the blood in the lungs contains more carbon dioxide than the air in the lungs. Carbon dioxide diffuses from the blood to the air sacs (alveoli) in the lungs and is breathed out. Exhaled air contains about 4% carbon dioxide and about 16% oxygen.

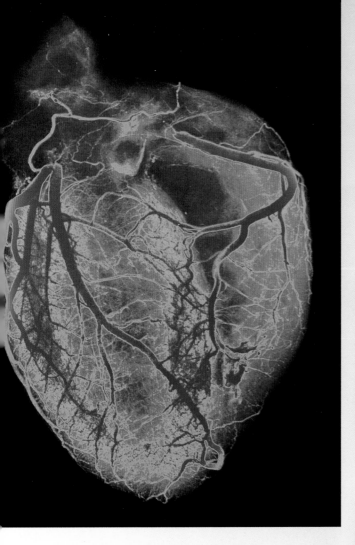

The lungs and all other organs need a good blood supply to deliver oxygen and nutrients and carry away waste carbon dioxide.

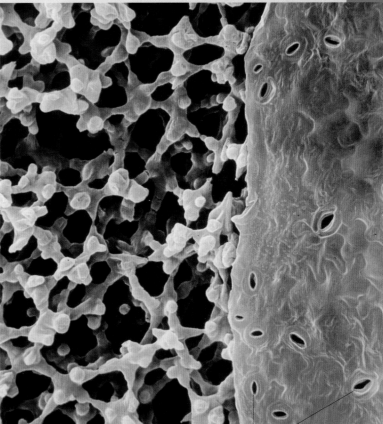

leaf surface removed to show cells inside the leaf

stomata

Plants also use aerobic respiration in their cells to release energy. The energy is used for their cells to function; and for growth, reproduction and movement.

Plants don't have lungs. Oxygen goes into the leaves through tiny pores (stomata) in the leaf surface. The leaves are thin and flat so the oxygen diffuses easily to all the cells. The carbon dioxide produced by respiration comes out through the same pores.

Combustion is very similar to respiration. Fuels need oxygen to burn and they produce carbon dioxide (and water), as well as energy – usually in the form of heat.

When we burn coal or oil, carbon that has been locked inside these fuels for millions of years is released into the air as carbon dioxide. Because we burn such a lot of fossil fuel, the amount of carbon dioxide in the air is increasing.

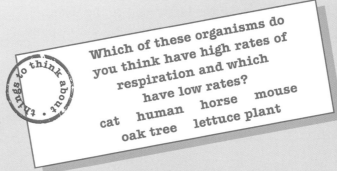

things to think about •

Which of these organisms do you think have high rates of respiration and which have low rates?

cat   human   horse   mouse
oak tree   lettuce plant

Fitness

Fitness is the ability to do physical activity or exercise.

Regular exercise strengthens the heart muscle and muscles in walls of arteries, and improves blood circulation (cardiovascular fitness). Exercise also keeps the immune system, bones, joints and muscles strong, and helps prevent obesity. When you exercise you make chemicals in the brain (endorphins) that make you feel happy, so exercise is also good for mental health.

Every person should exercise for at least 30 minutes each day, doing something that increases the pulse rate.

When you start to exercise, your muscle cells use more glucose, so they need more oxygen. Your breathing rate and heart rate increase to meet this demand, but they can't increase quickly enough. Until the muscle cells get all the oxygen they need, they respire anaerobically (without oxygen) as well as aerobically.

Anaerobic respiration produces lactic acid. After exercise, your heart rate stays high while the blood clears the lactic acid from your tissues. Your breathing rate also stays high for a while. This helps to take the lactic acid to the liver, where it may be changed to glucose and respired aerobically.

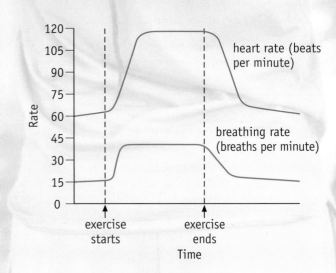

The time from finishing exercise until heart and breathing rates get back to normal is called the recovery time. The fitter you are, the shorter the recovery time. Fitter people also have lower resting pulse rates.

To measure fitness, measure:

- normal resting pulse
- the pulse at the end of the exercise
- how long it takes for the pulse to get back to normal.

It's also useful to see if your fitness is improving by finding if your recovery times are getting shorter as you train.

Other fitness measures that sports scientists use are strength, suppleness, stamina, speed and agility.

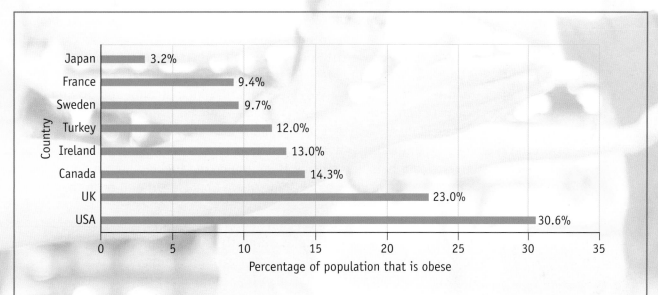

The proportion of overweight or obese individuals in the population can tell us about the nation's cardiovascular fitness. Since the 1980s the proportion of overweight and obese people in the UK has doubled. Now 63% of men and 53% of women are overweight or obese. Obesity in children is also increasing.

things to think about

What possible reasons are there for the differences in obesity rates between countries such as the UK and Japan or Canada?

Obesity is partly due to lack of physical exercise and partly due to increased food intake. The reasons for reduced exercise and increased food intake are complex.

Children today tend to watch TV or play on computers rather than playing outdoors. Some parents fear that their children are at risk if they play outdoors. People tend to eat while watching TV – often junk food containing lots of fat. Many children are driven to school because they live too far from their school to walk and parents may perceive it is dangerous for them to cycle.

Research shows that if you have overweight friends you are more likely to become overweight. It seems that the culture of eating wrong foods or not exercising can spread from person to person, so perhaps we really do have an obesity epidemic.

Drugs and health

A drug is a chemical that alters the way your cells, and therefore tissues and organs, work. Because drugs affect nerve and brain cells, they also affect behaviour.

Drugs include:
● medicines such as painkillers and antibiotics
● caffeine (in tea, coffee and cola), tobacco and alcohol
● illegal substances such as marijuana (cannabis), heroin and solvents (like glue)

Different types of drugs have different effects on the brain and body.

● Stimulants increase the speed at which impulses (messages) are carried across the gaps (synapses) between nerves. This makes you feel more alert. Caffeine and nicotine are stimulants.
● Depressants reduce the speed at which impulses are carried across synapses or along nerves. This slows thinking and reactions. Alcohol and some painkillers are depressants. Drinking alcohol and driving can be very dangerous, so there is a legal limit for drinking and driving.
● Hallucinogens such as LSD and marijuana alter the brain's perception. Driving under the influence of hallucinogens is very dangerous.
● Opiates are painkillers made from opium and include heroin and morphine. Painkillers block some nerve impulses to and from the brain.

Nicotine in tobacco is a stimulant drug. It is very addictive so many smokers get hooked and find it hard to give up. Being addicted and so using the drug more often may lead to a long-term effect on health by damaging organs permanently.

The chemicals in tobacco smoke make the small airways in the lungs constrict so it is harder to breathe in and out. Nicotine and tar interfere with the cleaning mechanism of the lungs so debris can build up in the lungs and smokers may be more prone to chest infections. There are other chemicals in tobacco smoke, such as tar, which cause cancer.

People who smoke may have fertility problems and find it more difficult to conceive a baby. Smoking during pregnancy can also lead to miscarriage, or affect foetal development and lead to low birthweight babies.

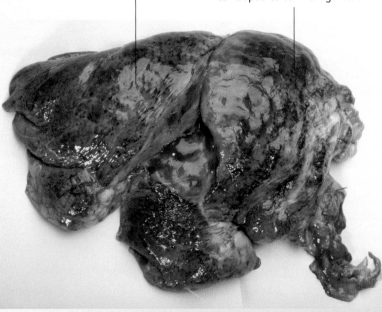

lung tissue damaged by smoke

tar deposits turn lungs black

Drugs can enter the body by being:

- injected
- inhaled
- ingested
- infused into the blood (an intravenous drip).

Alcohol relaxes you and removes inhibitions so at first it seems to stimulate, but it is a depressant. It also interferes with balance, co-ordination and judgement. Some people become addicted to alcohol. Alcohol poisons cells. The liver breaks it down but long-term drinking causes liver damage, brain damage and reduces mental ability.

Cannabis has been used as a painkiller in the Far East for about 6000 years and the Romans used to fry and eat cannabis seeds.

Cannabis alters your mood, co-ordination, ability to think and your self-perception. Some studies have shown that some people who use cannabis develop mental health problems such as anxiety, hallucinations, paranoia (an irrational fear that people are trying to harm you), depression and problems with memory. Some people become addicted to it.

However, cannabis can also relieve pain. Some people want it legalised so that multiple sclerosis sufferers can use it. They would not smoke it, as the tar from it can cause cancer. There are clinical trials in Canada to see how effective spraying cannabis extract under the tongue is for pain relief.

things to think about

Why would scientists need to choose volunteers carefully for taking part in clinical trials on cannabis?

Brain and spine

The brain and spinal cord are organs that make up the central nervous system (CNS).

The CNS responds to an impulse from a sense organ by sending impulses to other organs, such as the muscles in our arms or legs, to bring about a response. These impulses travel in both directions along most nerves.

Messages travel from a sense organ to the CNS and back to the muscles by electrical impulses at 80 m/s. Nerves are much shorter than 80 m, so the message takes a very short time to go from sense organ to CNS and back to a muscle. The time for this round trip is called our reaction time. Our reaction time slows down as we get older. When you reach 70 you have to reapply for your driving licence to make sure you can still drive safely.

Damage to the spinal cord or nerves can often result in paralysis because the brain can't communicate with other parts of the body. Damage to the brain may cause epilepsy. Strokes can cause brain damage.

Scientists used to think that damaged nerves couldn't regrow but we now have evidence that they may.

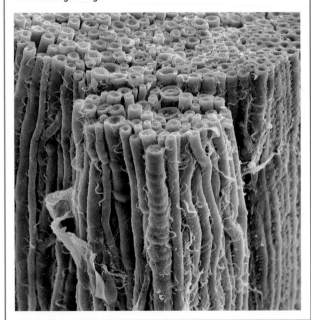

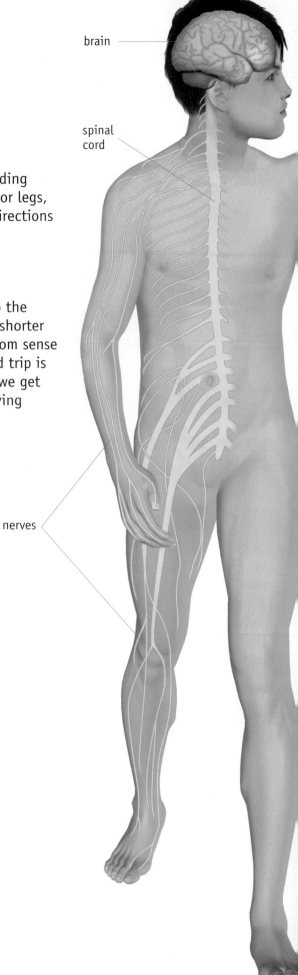

brain

spinal cord

nerves

The CNS controls body systems. It receives impulses from the sense organs: the eyes, ears, nose, tongue and skin. Each impulse is caused by a stimulus, which is a change to the environment that is detected by a sense organ.

The brain allows us to feel pain in other parts of the body but it can't feel pain in itself. So some brain surgery is carried out while the patient is conscious!

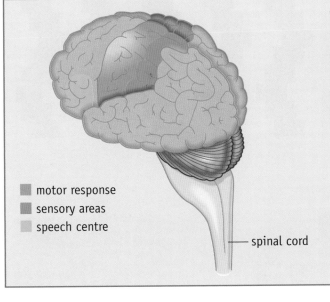

The crinkly bit of the brain is where the processing and thinking happen. Different areas of the brain have special functions, such as for speech, interpreting impulses from sense organs about what we see, hear, taste, smell and feel; and controlling body organs. The brain also houses our memories.

motor response

sensory areas

speech centre

spinal cord

We still have a lot to learn about how the brain works. Early studies measured electrical waves produced by the brain. We now use other techniques including magnetic resonance imaging (MRI) scans.

MRI scans measure blood flow to different parts of the brain. This technique can be used to find out which areas of the brain are used when we are asked to think about specific things or actions. MRI scans can also be used to diagnose problems, such as a brain tumour, or to assess brain damage after a stroke.

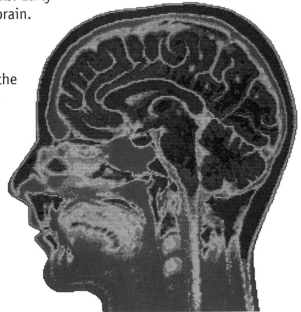

Perception and the brain

Perception is when the brain receives sensory stimuli and interprets them. For example, the eyes send nerve impulses to the brain and the brain interprets these. So it is really the brain that sees. Sometimes it tricks us.

Sometimes the brain misinterprets the information that reaches it from the eyes. This causes optical illusions.

Richard Gregory noticed this pattern of tiles on a café in Bristol. The tiles are arranged in parallel rows, but the thickness and brightness of the mortar between them, plus the fact that the tiles are offset, creates an illusion.

Pain usually results from a tissue damage stimulus being interpreted by the brain as pain. Scientists still have a lot to learn about phantom limb pain, where people who have had limbs amputated can still feel pain in those absent limbs. Maybe the stimulus comes from the stump and the brain interprets it as pain in the non-existent limb. Whatever is happening, the pain is real because it is the same pain that would be felt if the limb existed.

We have an area of the brain devoted to recognising faces. In the rare brain disorder called prosopagnosia, people can't recognise faces – even their own in the mirror. After a car accident, Lincoln Holmes was left with damage to this part of the brain. Once, he went to the cloakroom at a conference and saw a friend of his. He spoke and got no response. Then he realised he was in front of a mirror, and must be looking at himself.

In some people the parts of their brains that interpret different senses get confused. They may hear or taste colours, and see sounds. This is called synaesthesia.

Using functional magnetic resonance imaging (fMRI) scientists have proved that it is a genuine phenomenon but they don't yet have a convincing explanation. It could be that signals intended for one part of the brain are carried to another part. Many people remember associating days of the week or numbers with different colours when they were children, so maybe babies are synaesthetes and some people don't 'grow out of it'.

In the same way that optical illusions work because the brain is tricked and this alters our perception, we may confuse real events with other similar events that happened at another time or with events we have read about. However, we think we are accurately recalling the events.

Eyewitness accounts are not always reliable as the brain fills in memories after the event. Sometimes leading questions asked by lawyers can suggest these memories to eyewitnesses.

When samples of people were shown a film of one car hitting another some were asked 'Did you see the broken glass?' and some were asked 'Did you see any broken glass?'

How do you think the style of questioning affected the answers given?

Psychologists and neuroscientists design experiments and carry out surveys to develop and test ideas and explanations about perception. Often the participants are tricked into thinking the experiment is about something else so that their responses aren't altered by their expectations.

These investigations may measure misperception but they don't necessarily explain it. In any experiment to test a hypothesis, a correlation between two variables does not mean that one causes the other. It is also very hard to design proper controls for perception experiments, since different people may perceive things differently. There are still a lot of questions about the nature of perception that we can't yet answer.

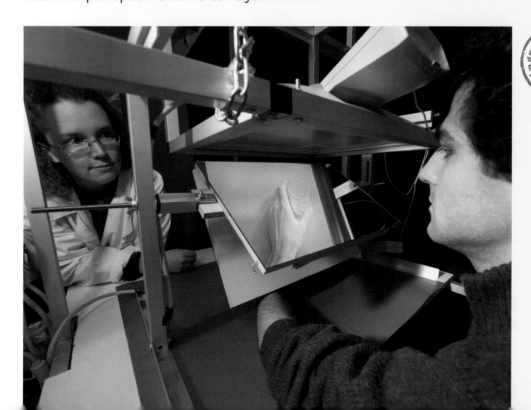

things to think about •

How could you design an experiment to find out if synaesthesia is a failure to develop beyond a normal phase of infancy?

Behaviour and the brain

Living organisms respond to stimuli. This is called behaviour. Scientists who study animal behaviour in the wild are called ethologists. Other scientists study animal behaviour in laboratories. Psychologists and neuroscientists study human behaviour.

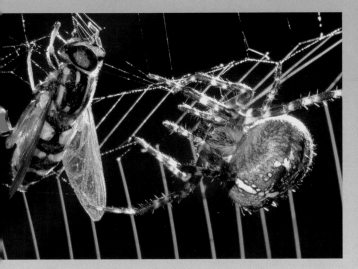

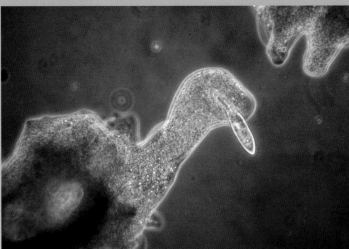

Simple organisms have short life spans and limited ability to learn. They show innate behaviour only.

Spiders instinctively know how to spin webs to trap prey.

The single-celled amoeba above can move towards or away from a stimulus. It engulfs and feeds on a smaller paramecium by altering its shape to flow around its prey.

More complex animals have larger brains with memories and can learn from experience, as well as responding instinctively to stimuli. Other internal factors that influence behaviour are genes and brain chemistry.

There are lots of different chemicals in the brain. The billions of nerve cells in the brain use these chemicals to communicate with each other across the gaps between them (synapses).

A behaviour that increases survival will become common as those with the behaviour survive and pass it on (through genes or teaching) to their offspring.

Nerve gases developed as chemical weapons block nerve transmission at synapses and cause muscle spasm.

Males and females show some behaviour differences. There are structural differences between male and female brains but also differences in social expectations – the way that boys and girls are brought up. Our behaviour is a result of both genes and environment.

Adolescent behaviour, such as a tendency to take many risks, may also be due to structural or chemical changes taking place in the maturing brain.

Our brains with their memories and abilities are what define us – our personalities. We need to look after the brain. Good nutrition is important. Vitamin B is essential for nervous system development and some foods are said to boost concentration.

In 1953 a 20-year-old RAF engineer (Ronald Maddison) volunteered for what he thought was a trial for a cold cure. He died from Sarin nerve gas. A secret inquest said his death was an accident but in 2004 after a 64-day inquest the ruling was that he had been unlawfully killed. A report said that some of the nerve gas research was unethical.

Drugs can interfere with perception and behaviour. Alcohol removes inhibitions, gives false confidence and interferes with sleep patterns. Some people act more violently when they are drunk. Long-term abuse may cause brain damage, affecting learning and memory. Ecstasy can cause permanent damage to the part of the brain that stores memories. It can also affect emotions.

Sleep is essential for the brain to process information received during the day. Sleep deprivation can affect memory and concentration. Sleep is also important in brain development. Babies and children who do not get enough sleep may develop behaviour problems, permanent sleep disruption and loss of brain mass.

We still have a lot to learn about brains and behaviour. Some investigations, such as child development tests, tell us about how we behave in certain situations but don't explain why we behave in that way.

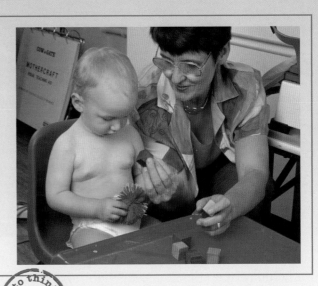

Some behaviour disorders with a neurobiological cause, such as schizophrenia, can be treated with drugs. Depression may be caused by changes in brain chemistry. Antidepressants can help. Cognitive behaviour therapy to help people get rid of negative thoughts can also help, as thoughts influence our emotions and behaviour.

things to think about • **Why do you think it is difficult to prove a theory that adolescents tend to be over-emotional because emotion processing moves to a different brain area during brain maturation?**

Behaviour and environment

Plants respond to stimuli in their environment – they show behaviour.

These seedlings are growing towards the light. This is an example of positive phototropism.

The root of this germinating wheat grain grows down, in the same direction as the pull of gravity. The shoot grows in the opposite direction. These are geotropic responses.

Some plants respond to touch, like ivy growing on a wall.

Day length influences flowering in some plants. Tobacco plants flower when days are shorter, towards the end of summer.

All these are examples of plant behaviour. Plants don't have a nervous system but they make chemicals that can be transported to different parts of the plant. These chemicals control the responses that plants make.

All organisms on Earth have a circadian (daily) rhythm. In humans it determines our sleeping and feeding patterns.

The rhythm is controlled by a biological clock – an area in the brain just above where the optic nerves (between eyes and brain) cross over. It is called the SCN (suprachiasmatic nucleus). This internal mechanism has its own 24-hour rhythm but is affected by environmental stimuli such as light and temperature.

Changes in exposure to day and night lengths can affect our moods and body functions. Some people suffer jet lag after travel, or SAD (seasonal affective disorder), a type of depression, during the short days of winter. This affects astronauts too. The treatment is to be exposed to artificial periods of day and night, using bright light.

Even bacteria have a circadian rhythm, possibly to restrict DNA replication to dark periods when it won't be damaged by ultraviolet light.

Apart from feeding and mating – behaviours that favour survival – animals also communicate and co-operate with each other. They have a social environment. Animals also teach each other. When one chimpanzee learnt to peel an orange, the behaviour spread very quickly to other chimpanzees.

Jane Goodall was the first to observe chimpanzees making and using tools and she worked out the complex social system within the troupe. She also observed chimps waging war on neighbouring groups. Although she lived with the chimps, she had to be objective and not biased. Ethologists can't interfere and must try to avoid making subjective interpretations. They record observations and data.

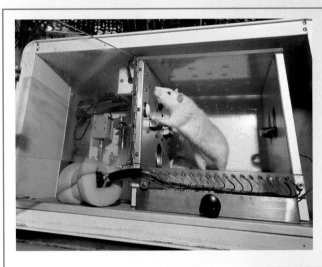

Some learned behaviour is the result of conditioning. Animals can be trained by being rewarded when they show the desired behaviour, like this lab rat. The reward acts as a reinforcement and the animal repeats the behaviour. Some scientists study animal behaviour in labs using controlled experiments. However, the animals' behaviour may be modified by being in this unnatural situation, so the results may not be valid. Also, there may be limits in extrapolating animal behaviour to human behaviour.

Children's behaviour can be regulated by reward and punishment. Social learning theory suggests that children also learn by watching how others behave, mimicking behaviour that is rewarded in others.

things to think about •

How do you think some **TV** programmes or films may adversely affect children's behaviour?

Variation in living things

You will have noticed that all humans are very similar. At the same time, each of us is unique and you can recognise people as individuals.

How are we different from each other? We have different blood groups, different shaped noses and ear lobes, and some of us have disorders such as cystic fibrosis. For each of these differences we can identify a few categories. Each of us has a particular blood group, such as A, B, AB or O. Some of us can smell freesias and some can't. We have free or attached ear lobes. We either have cystic fibrosis or we don't.

These are examples of discontinuous variation. There are no in-betweens.

You could ask a large number of people what their blood group is. We represent discontinuous data using bar graphs.

When carrying out such a survey you need to collect data systematically. This means you need to plan carefully how to collect and record your data.

When carrying out a survey you also need to ask a large number of people. This gives you a large sample. If you only asked a few people they might all give the same response and you would not see any variation. The bigger the sample, the more likely it is to represent the whole population.

blood group	tally	total
A	ⅢⅢ ⅢⅢ ⅢⅢ Ⅲ	18
B	ⅢⅠ	6
AB	Ⅱ	2
O	ⅢⅢ ⅢⅢ ⅢⅢ ⅢⅢ	20

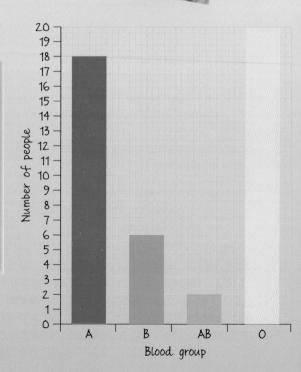

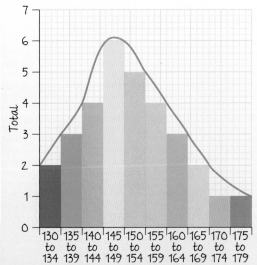

height to nearest cm	tally	total
130–134	II	2
135–139	III	3
140–144	IIII	4
145–149	⌦IIII I	6
150–154		

We are all different in height, weight, hair colour and skin colour. These are examples of continuous variation. A continuous variable can have any numerical value. If we measure the heights of a large number of people of the same age, we would get continuous results that can be plotted as a frequency graph or histogram.

In this group, people aren't tall or short. There is a range of heights. Most are in the middle of the range and there are a few at each end of the range. Data that are not representative of the sample cannot be used to make a valid conclusion. If you only measured a few people, they might just happen to be at the ends of the range and not representative of most people of that age group.

things to think about

Doorways and beds were a lot smaller in Tudor times, which tells us that the average human height has increased over time. How can we explain this?

Inherited variation

You will notice that people who are related to each other usually look alike. Many children look very like one or both of their parents and some brothers and sisters look very similar. Identical twins are so alike that it is often very hard to tell them apart.

We inherit features from our parents. The variation caused by inheriting features is called inherited variation.

Offspring are always similar to their parents but never identical. This is because at fertilisation a sperm joins with an egg. Half the information for the child comes from the father's sperm and half comes from the mother's egg.

Some diseases can be inherited. This family tree shows how haemophilia (a disease that increases the time for blood to clot after an injury) has been passed down through the generations of the Royal Family since Queen Victoria.

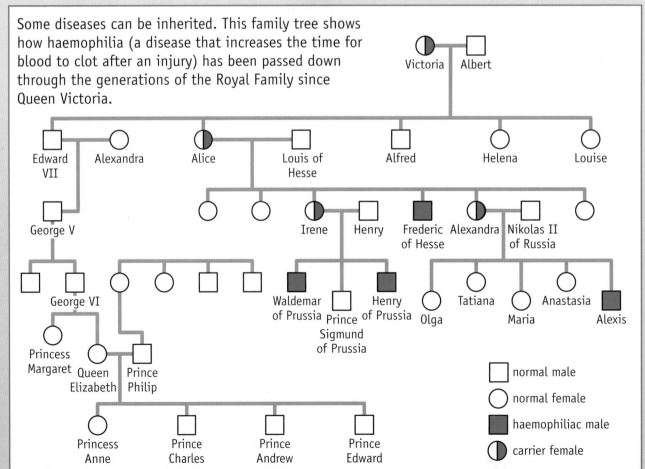

Other animals all show inherited variation. These kittens are all from the same litter. They have inherited some fur features from their mother and some from their father. They are similar to their parents, but not identical.

Farmers use inherited variation to ensure they have animal stocks of a high quality. They will breed animals with useful characteristics, such as good muscle tone, that will mean more meat and a higher price for the animals when they are sold.

Plant breeders also use inherited variation to produce seed that will give crops with high yields.

things to think about • In some families, parents and children have similar strengths in subjects such as engineering, medicine or music. Do you think these abilities are inherited or nurtured by the environment the children are brought up in, or perhaps a bit of both? How could scientists investigate this phenomenon?

43

Non-inherited variation

Not all variation is due to inheritance. Variation caused by environmental factors is called environmental variation.

Piglets from the same litter have the same parents but there are often size differences between them. This is not solely an inherited variation. The womb was their environment before they were born. Some piglets may have got more food and grown faster when they were in the womb environment.

Both these crops were grown from seeds of the same parents. The variation in height is due to the conditions in which the plants were grown. The taller, stronger plants got more minerals from the soil and this produced healthier growth.

You would expect these twins to look exactly the same because they have inherited the same genetic information from their parents. However, one may have received less food or oxygen while in the womb. So there is some variation that is not inherited.

things to think about

The colour of some flowers can be changed by growing the plants in acid soils. If you grew plants in acid soil, and then collected seeds from them, would their offspring have the same colour flowers as the parent plants?

Disease and diet are other environmental factors that can cause variation.

This child is very small for her age because she has been severely undernourished (not enough food).

A heart defect like a hole in the heart can also affect the height to which a child may grow, as it may reduce the amount of oxygen and nutrients delivered to tissues. People with tuberculosis (TB) are often shorter than average, because the disease interferes with lung function and may reduce oxygen supply to tissues.

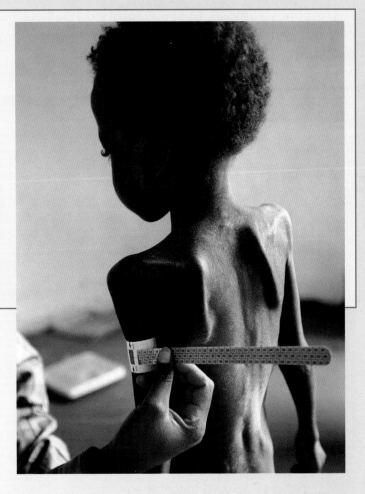

Some children are much better than others at maths or at learning a foreign language. They may have inherited the potential to develop these skills from their parents but environmental factors, such as diet, allow some of them to develop those skills more. A good diet helps your brain to develop.

Intellectual ability is an example of continuous variation and is the result of inherited and non-inherited variation – nature and nurture – working together.

All children inherit the ability to learn language. However, they need to be brought up in a learning environment where parents talk to them. This usually needs to happen by the time the child is 2 years old. This is when the brain is most receptive to learning language.

Feral children, who have been brought up by animals, show behaviour like that of their 'foster parents'. They often have few or no human language skills when they are found by humans.

Your sex was determined the moment the egg and sperm joined. This is not the case for alligators, crocodiles and turtles that lay their eggs on land.
Eggs incubated at the cooler temperature of 30 °C become females. Those incubated at 34 °C become males. Here, the environment determines the sex of the babies.

Microscopes

Microscopes allow us to see magnified images of objects that are too small to see with the naked eye. Cells are so small we need to use microscopes to study them.

1 Place the slide on the stage of the microscope so that the specimen is directly above the hole in the stage. Clip it into place.

2 Adjust the position of the mirror so that light reflected from the lamp passes up through the specimen.

3 Rotate the nosepiece so that the smallest (lowest power) objective lens is directly over the specimen.

4 Turn the coarse focus knob and bring the stage up as far as it will go.

5 Use one eye to look down the eyepiece. Slowly turn the coarse focus knob to focus the image.

6 Use the fine focus knob to get a clear, sharp image.

7 If you want to use a higher magnification, make sure that the object is in the centre of your field of view. Rotate the next size objective lens into place. Readjust the focus, using the fine focus knob.

Take care not to move the objective lens too far down or you will crack the slide.

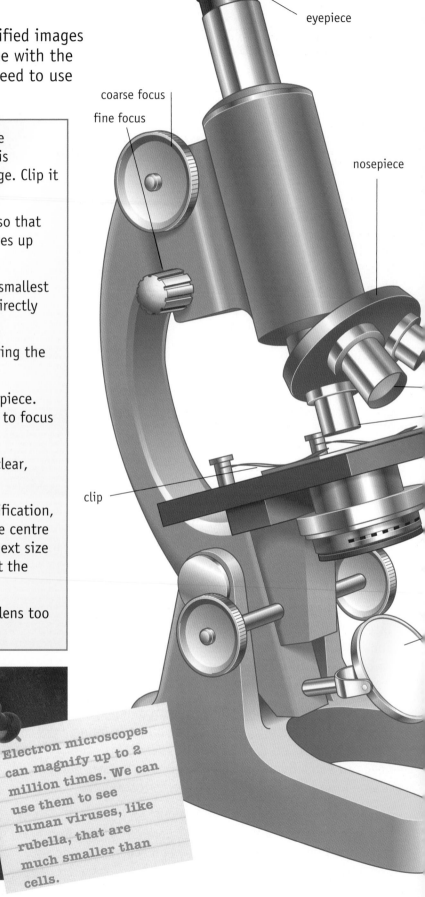

eyepiece

coarse focus

fine focus

nosepiece

clip

Electron microscopes can magnify up to 2 million times. We can use them to see human viruses, like rubella, that are much smaller than cells.

Magnification is the number of times greater the size of the image is compared to the size of the object. If something is magnified ×40, it means that the image you see with a microscope is 40 times longer and 40 times wider than the actual object.

The formula for magnification is:

$$\text{total magnification} = \text{objective lens magnification} \times \text{eyepiece magnification}$$

If your eyepiece lens magnifies ×10 and the objective lens ×4, then the total magnification is 10 × 4 or ×40. We write the magnification on drawings made from microscope images.

Microscopes have objective lenses. You may have up to three of these on your microscope for different magnifications. Each lens focuses light rays from the specimen on the slide and produces a bigger image of the object. The eyepiece objective lens then magnifies this image again.

stage

mirror

lamp

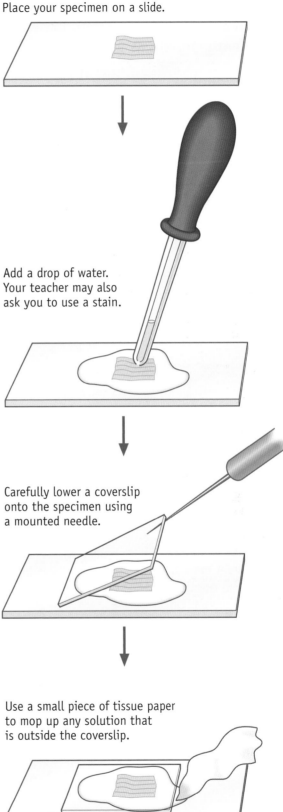

Place your specimen on a slide.

Add a drop of water. Your teacher may also ask you to use a stain.

Carefully lower a coverslip onto the specimen using a mounted needle.

Use a small piece of tissue paper to mop up any solution that is outside the coverslip.

Cells

You and many other living organisms are made up of organs. Each organ is made of tissues that work together. These tissues are made of smaller cells. Living organisms made of many cells are described as multicellular.

Some living organisms consist of only one cell. They are described as single-celled. *Amoeba*, *Euglena*, *Paramecium* and all bacteria are single-celled.

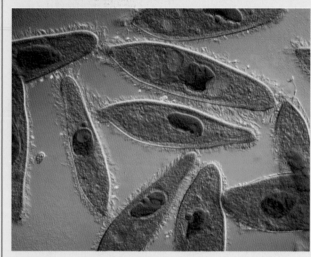

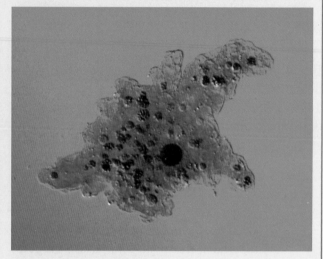

Paramecium, about 0.2 mm long. Each single cell is covered in cilia (microscopic hair-like structures) that help move the cell.

Amoeba, about 1 mm long

Cells are too small to see with the naked eye so we use microscopes to see and study them.

Both plants and animals are made of cells and their cells have some things in common: they both have a membrane around the outside and jelly-like cytoplasm inside. Both types have a nucleus.

There are differences though.

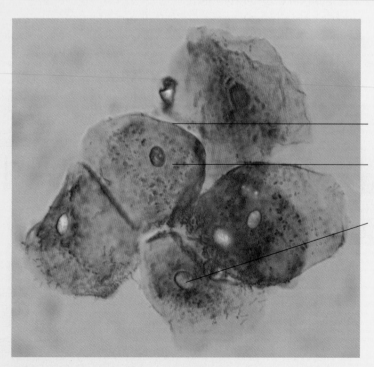

The membrane controls how things enter and leave cells.

The cytoplasm is where some chemical reactions go on.

The nucleus contains chemicals that control everything that goes on in the cell.

animal cells – magnified about 1000 times

Cells are the smallest parts of living organisms that can function and live on their own.

All the functions to sustain life go on inside the cell.

There are smaller structures inside the cell, each doing different jobs. These smaller parts are made of many molecules. Molecules are much smaller than cells and aren't themselves alive, as cells are.

Viruses aren't made of cells. They are very small and don't have cytoplasm, a membrane or a nucleus. This is why they aren't classified as living. However, they invade cells of other living organisms and then they can make copies of themselves. Weird!

In the 1950s a doctor took some cancer cells from Henrietta Lack. Cancer cells don't die and keep on dividing. Her cell line, HeLa, is used in labs all over the world and there are now more of her cells than were in her body. They have been used in many medical labs and she has been recognised for her contribution to science.

things to think about

Henrietta Lack's cells were taken and used without her permission. Her husband was told after her death. In a later court case it was ruled that she did not own her cells. What do you think about this ruling?
One biologist, Leigh Van Valen, says that HeLa cells have evolved into a single-celled life form and suggests that they be classified now as a separate species *Helacyta gartleri*. Other biologists disagree with him. What do you think?

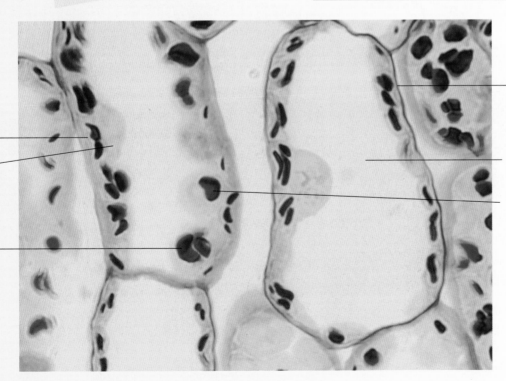

plant cells – magnified about 1000 times

The plant cell wall (outside the membrane) keeps the shape of the cell and protects it.

The big fluid-filled vacuole also keeps the cell firm.

The chloroplasts have chlorophyll that traps sunlight.

49

Growing from one cell

We all begin as one cell, formed when a sperm fertilises an egg in the oviduct. As this cell moves down the oviduct, towards the womb, it divides into 2, then 4, 8, 16 and so on.

Growth is an increase in the number of cells. As an embryo grows, the individual cells do not get bigger. The picture on the far right shows a ball of cells on a pin head.

After the fertilised egg has divided ten times there are 1024 cells (1, 2, 4, 8, 16, 32, 64, 128, 256, 512, 1024). By the twelfth day after fertilisation, the embryo has about 2000 cells.

There are probably about 100 million million cells in an adult human and about a quarter of these are red blood cells. If you counted each cell at a rate of two per second, and didn't stop to eat, drink, pee or sleep, it would take you 1.5 million years!

Counting cells is not an effective way of measuring the growth of a foetus or a child. Instead, we measure changes in height or weight. As children grow taller they usually become heavier, although an increase in weight could just be the result of the child becoming fatter.

Age of foetus (weeks)	Body length (mm)
6	5
9	25
12	65
16	120
20	160
24	300
28	350
36	450
40	500

Children will all grow taller at slightly different rates due to inherited and non-inherited variation. Nutrition, physical activity and disease also influence how we grow. These are all non-inherited factors.

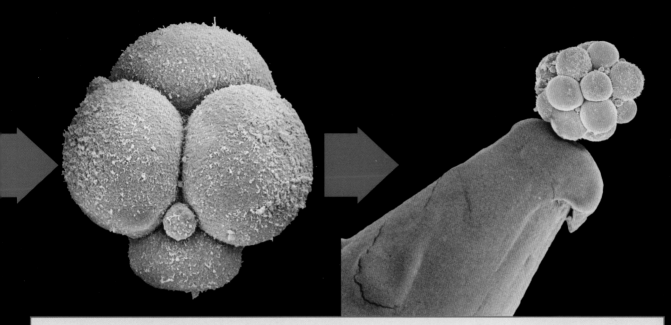

If we measure the heights of a large number of children of different ages from birth to adulthood we can see the range in height at each age. We can then work out average (mean) height at each age by dividing all the heights in the age group by the number in the group.

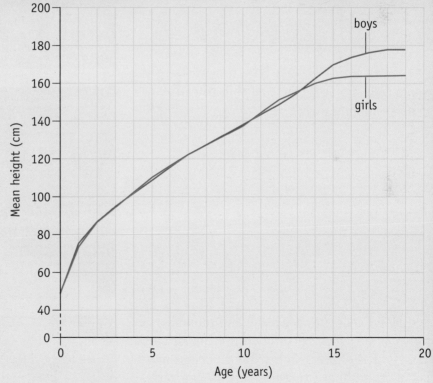

things to think about

Why do you think many girls aged 12 are taller than many boys aged 12?

You can see from the graph that children grow very quickly during their first year, then more slowly and steadily until puberty, when they grow quickly again. After that growth spurt they grow steadily until growth stops. For girls this is usually around 16–17 years and for boys around 18–20 years.

The charts that doctors use show a range of heights at each age as some children are shorter or taller than the mean, depending on the genes they inherited.

Charts like this are only reliable if many individuals have been measured and there are sufficient data.

Specialised cells

Once the egg is fertilised it starts dividing into a ball of cells. By the time a human embryo is 8 weeks old all its organs are formed. Some cells have become different from others – lung cells are different from heart cells and red blood cells are different from white blood cells.

Cells in an embryo are somehow 'told' what type of cell to become. The cells differentiate and become specialised to do special tasks. A group of specialised cells form a tissue and groups of tissues form an organ.

Cells aren't two-dimensional. They have a three-dimensional shape which varies according to the type of cell and its function.

Skin cells are flattened to form a protective layer. As they are so closely packed they prevent microbes from entering us.

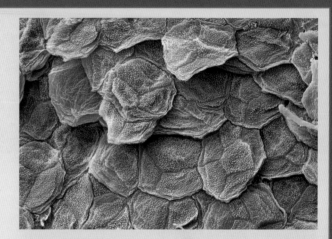

Nerve cells are very long and thin to carry impulses a long way.

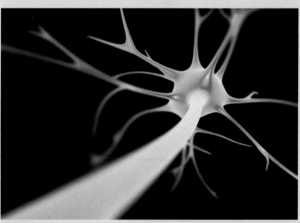

Red blood cells are very small and round so they can be squeezed through the tiniest blood vessels. They have also lost their nucleus and many other inner structures so they can carry more oxygen.

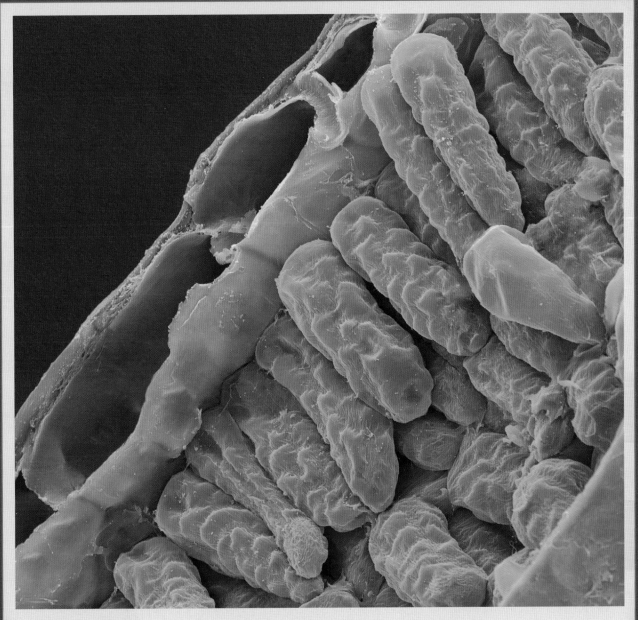

Plants also contain cells. Leaves are organs and their function is to make food.

Cells below the surface of plant leaves are long and cylindrical so that many can pack together (like pencils in a case) but with spaces between them for gases to move.

These cells also contain chloroplasts. Chloroplasts are made up of a green pigment called chlorophyll that traps sunlight energy for photosynthesis.

Sex cells are also specialised. Eggs are fairly big cells because they need stored food to nourish the embryo while it travels from the oviduct to implant in the uterus. Sperm cells are much smaller with a long tail for swimming to the egg.

The biggest cell in the world is an ostrich egg. It is fertilised inside the mother and then laid so it has to contain enough food and space for a baby ostrich to develop in.

Genes

Genes are the units of inheritance for characteristics. They are found on chromosomes in the nucleus. The chromosomes are visible in these root cells.

Each chromosome is a long length of DNA. Specific areas of DNA within each chromosome are called genes.

Genes control the characteristics of an organism because they contain instructions to make proteins. Some of those proteins are enzymes. Enzymes regulate all reactions going on in cells.

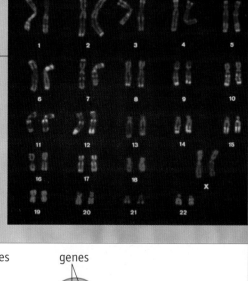

Humans have two sets of chromosomes in each cell nucleus, one from the mother and one from the father. Knowing this helps us to understand how features are inherited from both parents in sexual reproduction.

- The chromosomes are in the nucleus of cells.
- Each chromosome contains many genes.
- We normally have two copies of each gene in the nucleus of our cells because we have two copies of each chromosome (two sets of chromosomes).
- But each egg and sperm has only one set of chromosomes.
- So, at fertilisation, the two single sets of chromosomes and genes join to produce a new cell with the full complement of chromosomes and their genes. Half of the genetic information in the fertilised egg cell is from the father and half is from the mother.
- This fertilised cell then divides to make an embryo which develops into a foetus. After the baby is born it grows into an adult.
- Hence, we each have half of our genes from each parent.

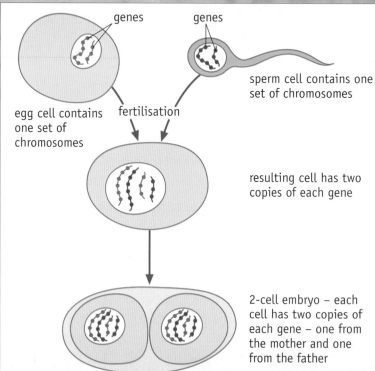

egg cell contains one set of chromosomes

fertilisation

sperm cell contains one set of chromosomes

resulting cell has two copies of each gene

2-cell embryo – each cell has two copies of each gene – one from the mother and one from the father

Cells in the developing embryo become specialised and differentiated when some of the genes are switched off or on. Although all of the cells in an organism contain all the genes (the genome), only a small proportion of them are active in each type of cell. This allows certain cells to do particular jobs.

Scientists didn't always know about genes.

- Cells had been discovered when microscopes were used in the 1600s and by the early 1800s scientists said all living things were made of cells.
- In the 1860s Gregor Mendel did experiments on inheritance in peas. He suggested that there were things in cells that acted as units of inheritance and passed from one generation to the next.
- By 1910 the term 'gene' had been introduced and fruit fly chromosomes were being mapped to see where genes were on them.
- By the 1940s scientists knew that DNA, found in cell nuclei, was the chemical of inheritance.
- In the 1950s Watson and Crick with Wilkins and Franklin, worked out that the structure of DNA was a double helix, like the one shown in this picture. In the 1970s the first gene was sequenced and in the 1990s the Human Genome Project began, which was to sequence all human genes.

things to think about

Red blood cells don't have a nucleus so that there is more space for oxygen to be carried. When red blood cells are first made in bone marrow they have a nucleus and before they go into circulation the nucleus breaks down. Do red blood cells in your blood have any genetic information?

Humans have about 20 600 genes in each cell. A mouse has 29 000 genes.

Selective breeding

Genes are inside the nucleus of our cells and they control our features. An organism that has adaptations that enable it to survive in its environment is more likely to live long enough to breed and pass on the versions of the genes that give these adaptations to the next generation.

Usually nature (the environment) selects the organisms that survive to reproduce. Nature selects the best-adapted organisms – those with the best-suited features – to survive. This is called natural selection.

Both prey and predator animals need to be well camouflaged like the stone-mimic grasshopper in the picture above.

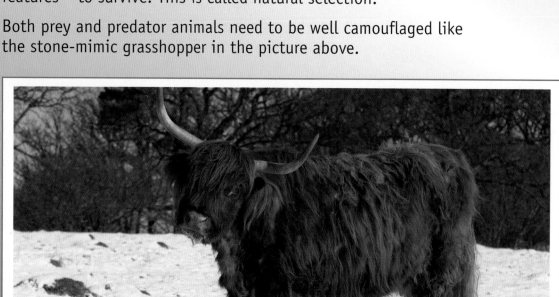

Humans can interfere with nature to select animals or plants with desirable characteristics and breed from them. Selective breeding increases the chance of certain variations of genes passing from parent to offspring. This is called artificial selection.

People have been using selective breeding since we started farming about 10 000 years ago. Farmers selected plants that grew well and gave the highest yield and tasted nice. They selected animals that gave lots of milk or meat and were also docile and easy to manage. Some animals were selected to do work, like pulling a plough or carrying humans.

Highland cattle are bred for the cold climate as they have thick coats.

Many crop plants such as rice, corn and wheat have been developed over thousands of years from their wild ancestors. As selective breeding produced plants and animals that gave more food, the human population could increase.

More recently agricultural scientists have selectively bred crops to give a bigger yield or better disease resistance and so provide us with more food for the same area planted. A type of emmer wheat (right) is still grown, but has a lower yield than modern varieties.

How do you think that climate change may influence crop selective breeding programmes?

These dogs are all members of the same species. They have been bred to look and act differently.

In natural selection, nature selects which organisms survive and breed. In artificial selection, humans select the ones to survive and breed. The characteristics we want from them may actually give the organisms a disadvantage if they were returned to the wild.

Dogs were domesticated to be companions and to help humans hunt. Because dogs are looked after they stay puppy-like in many ways and are less aggressive than their wild wolf ancestors. Humans have selected which characteristics get passed on in the dogs, but if these dogs had to return to the wild they probably would not survive.

Genetic engineering

Selective breeding is a slow process. It takes many generations to obtain the useful characteristics we want in an animal or plant.

We can speed up the process by obtaining genes from one organism and putting them into another organism. This is called genetic engineering.

Because genes can be transferred from one organism, such as an animal or bacterium, to a different organism like a plant, scientists can achieve genetic changes that would not be possible through selective breeding.

The gene we want to introduce into one organism has to be obtained from the nucleus of another organism's cells. It can be snipped out using special enzymes. The gene is then inserted into the other cell at the fertilised egg stage so that as the cell divides, all the cells of the genetically modified organism have the new gene.

gene for desired characteristic

fertilised egg cell

nucleus of cell from first organism

chromosome with the desired characteristic

chromosome in nucleus of organism we want to modify

all cells in the organism have the modified gene

Genetic modification of animals can be used to produce medical treatments. Some sheep are genetically modified to produce milk that contains a human protein. This protein (an enzyme inhibitor) can then be extracted from the sheep's milk. The protein is used to treat people with hereditary emphysema, preventing the disease from progressing.

Sheep that are genetically modified using genetic engineering are called transgenic sheep. A gene has been taken from human cells and put into sheep cells.

Genetically modified (GM) plants have many agricultural benefits. Drought-resistant varieties of crops have been produced by genetic engineering and could improve food production in arid regions of the world.

Golden rice is a variety of rice that has been genetically modified to contain vitamin A. It was developed to be used in areas where the normal diet is lacking in vitamin A. Eating golden rice could prevent 500 000 cases per year of permanent blindness caused by vitamin A deficiency among children in Africa and Asia.

- Farmers often save seed from their crop to plant next year. However, most genetically engineered seed is sold with a contract that means the farmers can't save seed and have to buy more.

- Some people think that eating genetically modified plants is unsafe because the proteins produced in the plant by the inserted gene might be dangerous. To test GM crops scientists plan and carry out trials – controlled experiments – to see if these novel foods have toxins in them. To date there have been no known cases of poisoning from commercially grown GM crops.
  We need to remember than many crops produced by traditional selective breeding, notably potatoes and tomatoes, contain toxins. People eat these without harmful effects.

- Some people think that eating genetically modified plants and animals is unsafe for the environment. Trials are also carried out to see if genes from GM crops can get into nearby wild plants.

things to think about • Some critics of GM crops say that insecticide-resistant crops mean fewer insects on the crops, which will mean fewer birds in that ecosystem. Do you think biodiversity would increase or stay the same if we grow non-GM crops?

In the US some Amish people, who follow a very traditional lifestyle, plant GM disease-resistant crops. This means they don't have to use chemical pesticides and expose their farmers to harmful chemicals.

Stem cells

Cells must become specialised to carry out particular functions. Groups of specialised cells make up tissues, which make up organs.

Stem cells are unspecialised cells that have the ability to develop into any kind of specialised cell, such as nerve cells or liver cells. Stem cells can divide and multiply many times while still unspecialised and then differentiate into different types of specialised cells.

There are three types of stem cell:

- embryonic stem cells – taken from early embryos. These can develop into any kind of cell.
- umbilical cord blood cells. These can differentiate into many types of cell but not as many as embryonic stem cells.
- adult stem cells – found in some types of adult tissues. These can divide and repair the tissues in which they are found.

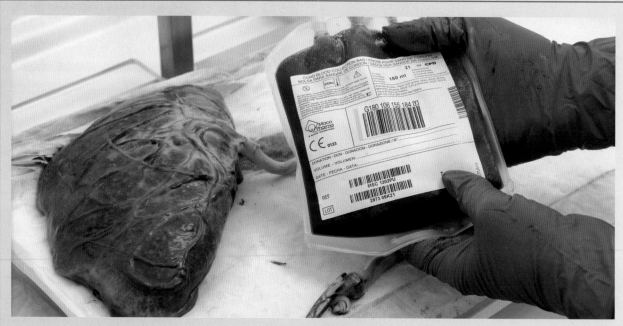

Some parents ask doctors to collect the placenta and umbilical cord blood when a baby is born. This is so the umbilical stem cells can be collected and cryogenically stored (frozen) in case their baby or a family member ever needs it.

Adult stem cells, in the form of bone marrow transplants, have been used for a long time to treat leukaemia and other blood or bone cancers.

Use of embryonic stem cells is the most controversial as it has led to embryos being discarded. However, it seems to be possible to take one cell from a small ball of cells (the early embryo at 4–5 days old) and produce a cell line from this cell. The embryo can still survive this process.

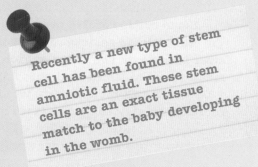

Recently a new type of stem cell has been found in amniotic fluid. These stem cells are an exact tissue match to the baby developing in the womb.

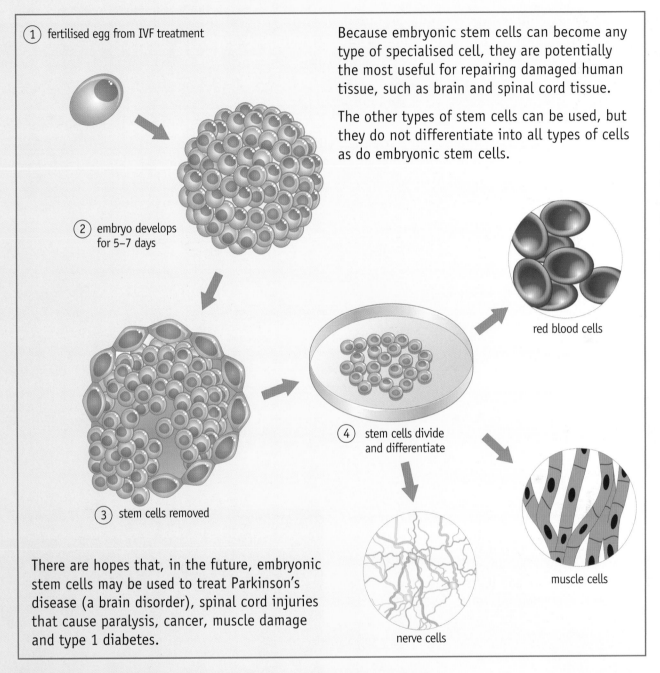

① fertilised egg from IVF treatment

② embryo develops for 5–7 days

③ stem cells removed

④ stem cells divide and differentiate

red blood cells

muscle cells

nerve cells

Because embryonic stem cells can become any type of specialised cell, they are potentially the most useful for repairing damaged human tissue, such as brain and spinal cord tissue.

The other types of stem cells can be used, but they do not differentiate into all types of cells as do embryonic stem cells.

There are hopes that, in the future, embryonic stem cells may be used to treat Parkinson's disease (a brain disorder), spinal cord injuries that cause paralysis, cancer, muscle damage and type 1 diabetes.

IVF fertility treatment leads to many spare embryos that are usually discarded. Scientists may be able to use these embryos but Pro-Life groups say that all embryos should be protected.

Stem cell research raises ethical questions about the rights of an embryo and of people suffering from brain and spinal cord damage. Our society should consider the advantages and disadvantages of stem cell research before making an informed decision about whether it is morally acceptable.

things to think about

What might be the advantages or disadvantages of using cells from amniotic fluid as opposed to cells from an embryo?

Life cycle of plants

All flowering plants have special organs for reproduction – the flowers. Flowers have both male and female reproductive organs. Their final products are seeds. Seeds grow into new plants. This is how plants reproduce sexually.

The female parts of the flower are the stigma, style and ovary. Inside the ovary are ovules, each of which contains a female sex cell. The stigma is sticky so that pollen grains stick to it.

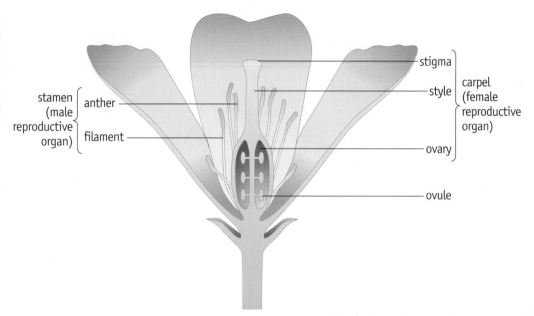

stamen (male reproductive organ) — anther

filament

stigma

style

carpel (female reproductive organ)

ovary

ovule

The male parts of the flower are the stamens.

Each consists of a long stalk called the filament, which has an anther at the top where pollen is made. Each pollen grain contains one male sex cell.

In 1991 the frozen body of a man was found in the Alps. Scientists found pollen inside the man. Pollen from each type of plant is distinct and the scientists could work out that he died 5300 years ago as he travelled through a hornbeam forest in summer.

Insects are attracted to flowers because of the scent or colours. They can carry the pollen within a flower, from flower to flower on the same plant, or between plants. In some plants wind blows the pollen.

When pollen lands on the stigma:

1 A pollen tube grows out of each pollen grain and down through the style.

2 One male sex cell is carried in each tube to the ovary.

3 In the ovary, fertilisation happens when a female sex cell inside one ovule and a male nucleus from a pollen grain join.

Many pollen tubes grow down to the ovary, where there are many ovules. This is like sperm swimming to the egg in humans.

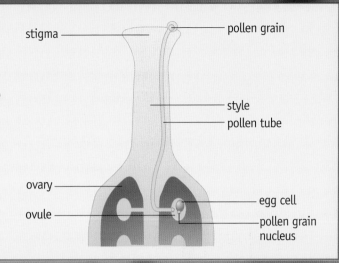

stigma — pollen grain
style
pollen tube
ovary
ovule
egg cell
pollen grain nucleus

Each fertilised ovule develops into a seed. Inside each seed is an embryo and a food store. The ovary with seeds becomes a fruit.

When the seeds are ready they are scattered away from the parent. Seeds are dispersed by the wind or by animals that eat them.

Some seeds stay dormant over winter. In the spring, when there is warmth and water, they germinate and grow into a new plant. The plant produces flowers, and the cycle starts all over again.

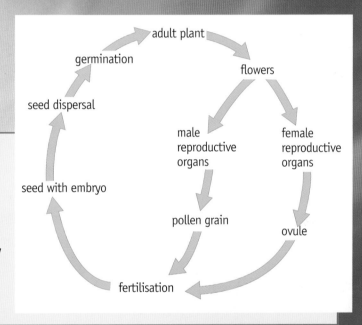

adult plant
germination
flowers
seed dispersal
male reproductive organs
female reproductive organs
seed with embryo
pollen grain
ovule
fertilisation

Not all plants reproduce sexually. Some reproduce asexually – without the fertilisation of a female sex cell by a male sex cell. Spider plants reproduce asexually by producing runners with small plantlets on the end. These plantlets can root and become separate individuals. The new plants are all genetically exactly the same as the parent so they are clones of the parent.

Plant growth

Each plant starts from one cell which is inside the seed. The seed also contains stored food.

The plant grows by cell division. The single cell divides and becomes an embryo. Cells in the embryo become specialised into root, shoot and what will eventually become leaves.

Eventually the seed germinates. The root and shoot break through the seed's coat and a new plant grows. The energy for the cell division has come from the seed's food store.

Plants are multicellular organisms. They are made of many cells that are grouped into tissues (a group of cells that carry out a particular function). Many tissues are grouped into plant organs, such as roots, stems and leaves.

Each plant organ has a specific function.

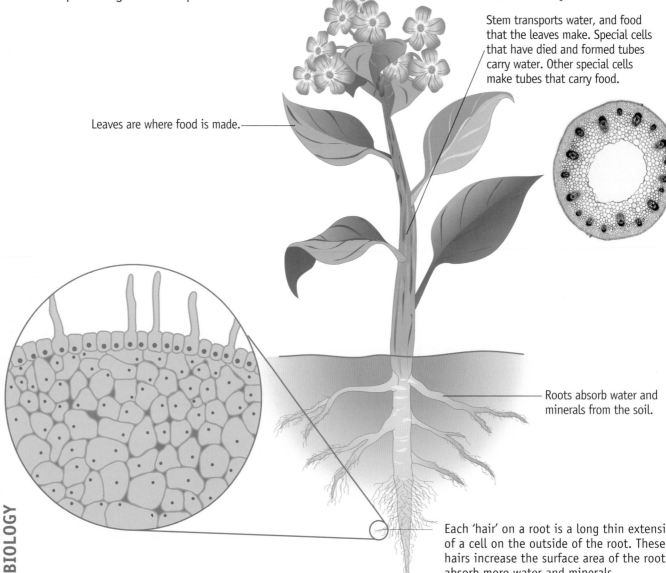

Flowers are for sexual reproduction after which they make seeds.

Stem transports water, and food that the leaves make. Special cells that have died and formed tubes carry water. Other special cells make tubes that carry food.

Leaves are where food is made.

Roots absorb water and minerals from the soil.

Each 'hair' on a root is a long thin extension of a cell on the outside of the root. These hairs increase the surface area of the root to absorb more water and minerals.

Plants take up water and minerals from the soil but they don't get their food from the soil. Plants make their own food, in a process called photosynthesis. They need water as a raw material for this process. They also need light. If the plant can carry out photosynthesis it will make food and grow.

For healthy growth a plant needs small amounts of minerals from the soil. Plant growers add fertiliser to the soil so that plants have all the minerals they need.

Other environmental factors that affect growth include water, light intensity, temperature, soil pH and pollutants or toxins in the soil or air.

Scientists can investigate the effect of one of these variables on plant growth. They grow two large batches of the same type of plant and only change the variable being investigated whilst growing the plants in a controlled environment.

You can measure plant growth by measuring the height or mass of a plant. Dry mass gives us more reliable data than just the mass as the water content of a plant can vary.

To gather data systematically (in a planned and orderly way), at timed intervals randomly take ten plants from each batch and measure their heights to find the mean height.

The table shows some data for growth of seedlings. Some were grown at 10 °C and some at 20 °C.

Day	Mean height (mm)	
	Grown at 10 °C	Grown at 20 °C
1	8	10
3	15	24
5	30	40
7	35	55
9	40	69
11	50	75
13	55	90

The data can be graphed on the same set of axes. We can't make assumptions about biological data, so the points should be joined with straight lines and we don't extrapolate.

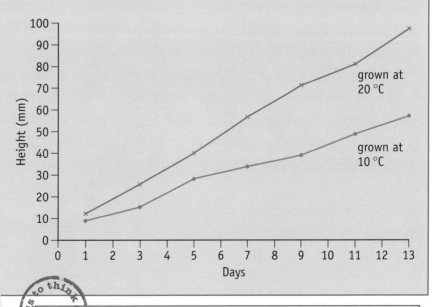

Some poplar trees can grow 27 m (about the height of 11 football goalposts) in 6 years. In the US there are plans to grow these as a crop to produce biofuel.

Why do you think the seedlings' speed of growth varied throughout the investigation?

Photosynthesis

Plants can make their own food because they have chlorophyll – this is what makes leaves green. Chlorophyll traps light energy and turns it into chemical energy. Carbon dioxide and water are the other raw materials that plants need to make food.

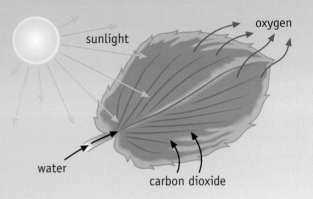

We can represent photosynthesis with an equation:

$$\text{carbon dioxide + water + energy from sunlight} \xrightarrow{\text{in presence of chlorophyll}} \text{glucose + oxygen}$$

Plants can turn the glucose made by leaves into useful materials such as starches, fats or proteins and DNA.

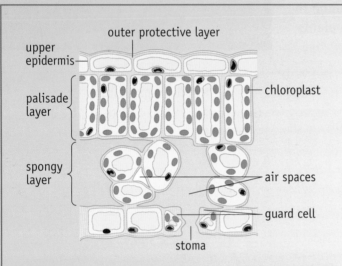

Leaves are organs that are specialised for photosynthesis. Different specialised cells within the leaf do different jobs.

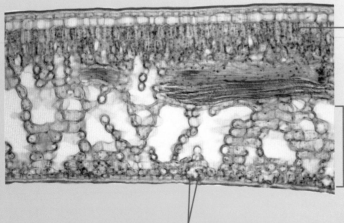

Cells inside the leaves (palisade cells) have chloroplasts. Chloroplasts contain chlorophyll to trap light energy. So photosynthesis actually takes place in the chloroplasts. A layer of cells with more space between them lets gases diffuse to and from the palisade cells.

On the underside of leaves there are pairs of specialised cells called guard cells. These have pores (gaps) between them called stomata. The pores allow carbon dioxide from the air to enter the leaf and the oxygen made during photosynthesis to pass out of the leaf.

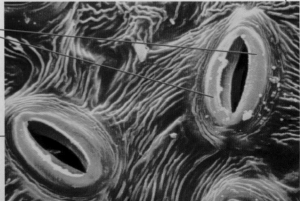

Because plants make food they are called producers. Nearly all food chains begin with plants. Without plants we would have no food. Food like pizza bases, bread, chips, pasta and rice are all made from plants such as wheat, potatoes and rice.

The total mass of living material (biomass) of the plant and animal populations in a food chain can be shown in a diagram called a pyramid of biomass. The diagram looks like a pyramid because a lot of plants (large total mass) are eaten by animals that have a smaller total mass, which in turn are eaten by predators that have an even smaller total mass.

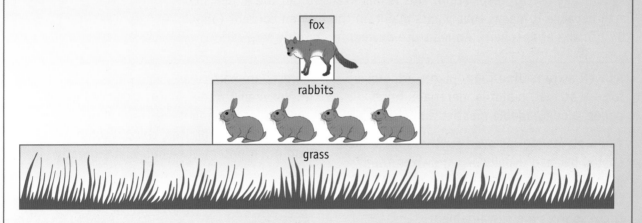

Biomass is measured in kilograms. Scientists measure the biomass as the total dry mass of a population of plants or animals. Dry mass is more reliable than wet mass as the water content of a plant can vary. However, plants and animals are killed when they are dried.

Another difficulty is that the sample taken of an organism might not be representative. The plants or animals could be suffering from disease and so have a lower than average biomass.

things to think about • In some places on the sea bed, below 2–3 km of water, there are thermal vents where magma erupts and water comes out of the vents at temperatures of up to 400 °C. Why were scientists totally surprised to find a community of giant tube worms, clams and mussels around these hot springs, and what could be the start of the food chain for this marine ecosystem?

Respiration and photosynthesis

The sunlight energy that plants capture during photosynthesis is used to make glucose. To obtain energy from the glucose or other types of stored food made from the glucose, plants respire. They can use the energy for growth and for reactions that go on in their cells.

Plants usually respire aerobically, using oxygen and producing water and carbon dioxide as waste products.

glucose + oxygen ⟶ energy + carbon dioxide + water

Plants can only photosynthesise when it is light, but they respire all the time.

Plants produce oxygen as a waste product of photosynthesis. The amount of oxygen they produce by photosynthesis is greater than the amount of oxygen they use for respiration. This is important for all the animals on Earth because it means that plants maintain the oxygen content (about 20%) in the atmosphere. Animals use oxygen for aerobic respiration.

As well as providing food, plants are grown for use as fuel, building materials, fibres, paper, biodegradable plastics and chemicals.

When plants are removed for these uses, more should be, and usually are, grown in their place. If this happens then the oxygen content of the air should be maintained and the resources are sustainable.

Forests are particularly valuable at maintaining the oxygen content of air. When humans remove large amounts of tropical rainforest to build roads and houses, the oxygen produced and other potential resources are greatly reduced.

The table shows the world biomass per year for some different ecosystems. It varies in the different habitats due to lots of factors – temperature, rainfall, soil type, size of plants growing, day length and light intensity.

Ecosystem	Area (million km^2)	Biomass (billion tonnes per year)	Biomass per million km^2 (billion tonnes per year)
Tropical rainforest	17.0	37.4	2.20
Deciduous forest	7.0	8.4	1.20
Savannah	15.0	13.5	0.90
Cultivated land	14.0	9.1	0.65
Marine	361.0	54.9	0.15

The biomass in each ecosystem is proportional to the amount of photosynthesis going on in these areas – more photosynthesis means more plant growth. The biomass is therefore also proportional to the amount of oxygen produced.

You can see that tropical rainforest is most important as a producer of biomass and therefore of oxygen.

Rainforest also takes a lot of carbon dioxide out of the air. Preserving the rainforest and planting more trees could help to offset the increased carbon dioxide added to the air by burning fossil fuels. Deforestation contributes to global warming.

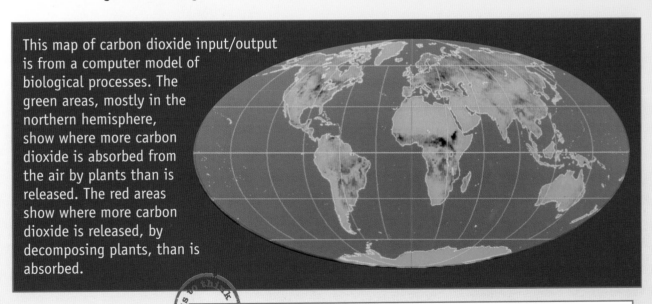

This map of carbon dioxide input/output is from a computer model of biological processes. The green areas, mostly in the northern hemisphere, show where more carbon dioxide is absorbed from the air by plants than is released. The red areas show where more carbon dioxide is released, by decomposing plants, than is absorbed.

Many square kilometres of deciduous forest have been removed in Britain. Some of the cleared land has been used for housing and roads and the rest has been used for farming. How do you think that this has affected oxygen production?

69

Classifying organisms

Living organisms can be grouped according to their similarities and differences. If organisms look similar, have similar body functions and behaviour and can interbreed to produce fertile offspring then they are classified as members of the same species. Members of the same species are not all identical – there is variation between individuals.

By observing the characteristics of living things, biologists first classify organisms into groups called kingdoms. Each kingdom is then divided into smaller and smaller groups, according to how closely biologists think the organisms are related to one another.

We can classify a gorilla in the following way

kingdom	Animalia	(all animals)
phylum	Chordata	(all the vertebrates)
class	Mammalia	(all mammals)
order	Primates	(also inludes monkey, marmoset, human)
family	Pongidae	(also includes chimpanzee, bonobo, orangutan)
genus	*Gorilla*	
species	*gorilla*	

The gorilla (*Gorilla gorilla*) is the only species in the genus.

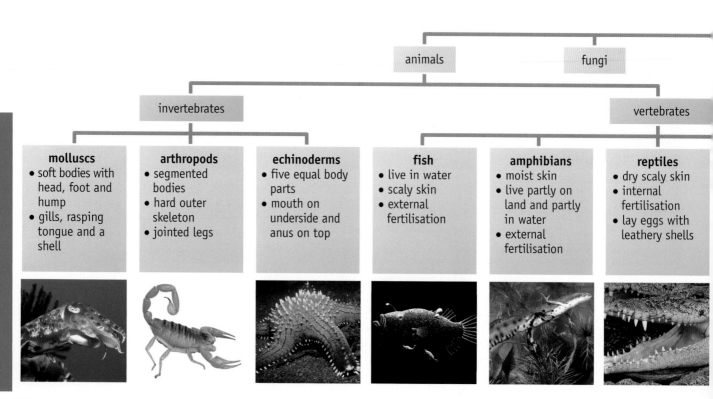

animals — fungi

invertebrates — vertebrates

molluscs
- soft bodies with head, foot and hump
- gills, rasping tongue and a shell

arthropods
- segmented bodies
- hard outer skeleton
- jointed legs

echinoderms
- five equal body parts
- mouth on underside and anus on top

fish
- live in water
- scaly skin
- external fertilisation

amphibians
- moist skin
- live partly on land and partly in water
- external fertilisation

reptiles
- dry scaly skin
- internal fertilisation
- lay eggs with leathery shells

As scientists learn more they have to change their ideas. Biologists used to think that all living organisms belonged to one of two kingdoms – animals or plants. Using this system, fungi were classified as plants because they seemed totally unlike animals. We now know they aren't like plants either, so they have their own kingdom. The same is true of bacteria. These were once classified as plants but now have their own kingdom.

There are still many organisms that are difficult to classify. These are all put into a group of 'odds and ends' called the protoctists.

In 1938, a strange fish was caught off the coast of South Africa. The local museum curator identified it as a fish, the coelacanth, thought by scientists to have been extinct for 70 million years!

things to think about

Scientists often discover new species in exotic places such as rainforests. Will we ever be able to say how many species of living organisms there are on this planet?

Sometimes we need to find out what an organism is. Keys are written by biologists to help us to identify plants and animals or to help us put them in the correct group. Keys are made up of a series of questions.

You could use a key to identify an animal caught in a stream, or a flower growing on grassland.

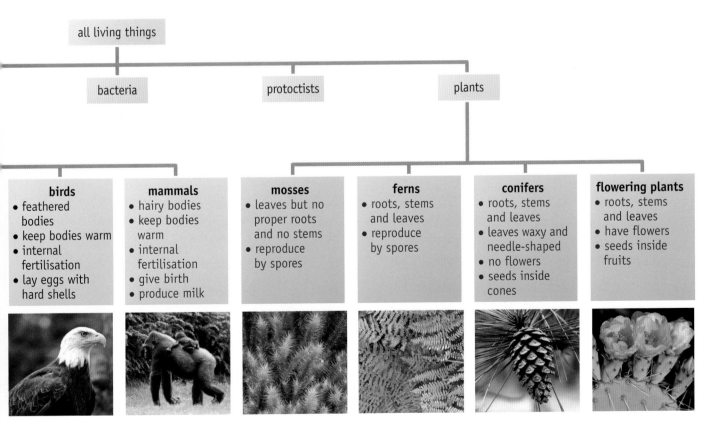

all living things

bacteria   protoctists   plants

birds
• feathered bodies
• keep bodies warm
• internal fertilisation
• lay eggs with hard shells

mammals
• hairy bodies
• keep bodies warm
• internal fertilisation
• give birth
• produce milk

mosses
• leaves but no proper roots and no stems
• reproduce by spores

ferns
• roots, stems and leaves
• reproduce by spores

conifers
• roots, stems and leaves
• leaves waxy and needle-shaped
• no flowers
• seeds inside cones

flowering plants
• roots, stems and leaves
• have flowers
• seeds inside fruits

71

Food chains and webs

An ecosystem is the physical features of a particular area together with the organisms that live there.

An ecosystem could be a coral reef, savannah or marshland, as seen here, or a desert, ocean, river, tundra, tropical rainforest, woodland, farmland or garden, together with all the organisms that live there.

There are food chains within all ecosystems. Plants use sunlight energy for photosynthesis to produce food. Plants are called producers.

Animals that eat plants or eat plant-eating animals are called consumers. Those that eat other animals are also known as predators. The animals they eat are prey. Some animals (like humans) eat both plants and animals.

Plants are important because they make energy from sunlight available to animals. The energy in plants passes to the consumers that eat them. This energy then passes to any predator that eats the consumer.

A food chain shows how energy from sunlight passes from producers to consumers.

An example of a food chain in a garden is:

lettuce (producer) → snail (consumer) → thrush (consumer/predator) → cat (consumer/predator)

The arrows show the direction in which energy is transferred.

During its lifetime, one snail can eat lots of lettuce, one thrush will eat many snails and a cat will eat more than one thrush. We can show this information in a pyramid of numbers.

The numbers of organisms in an ecosystem depend on many factors. The type of soil (how much water and amount of nutrients it contains) and climate (temperature, rainfall and hours of daylight) determine the numbers and types of plants that grow. This affects the numbers and types of animals that eat the plants. In turn, this affects the numbers and types of predators in the ecosystem.

The organisms at each point of a food chain depend on the resources available. Plants need resources such as sunlight, water, soil and space. Animals need resources such as food, space and shelter.

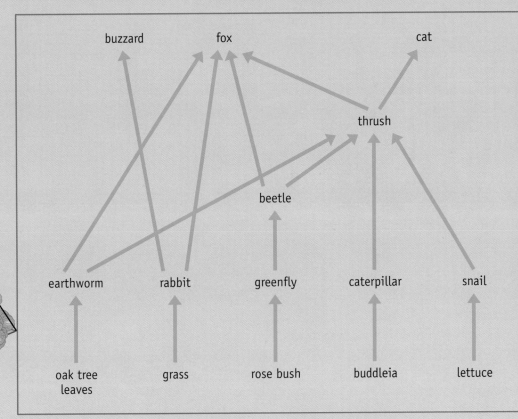

There are many food chains in any one ecosystem. These different food chains all interact to form a food web. Some species eat more than one type of food. For example, a thrush eats earthworms, beetles, caterpillars and snails. We cannot show all this information in a food chain.

Less than 1% of the original energy from sunlight caught by plants will reach you when you eat a beefburger!

things to think about •

If the greenfly on the roses in a garden were killed by the gardener, how would this affect the other animals in the garden?

73

Where organisms live

The place where an organism lives is called its habitat. A habitat provides the resources that an organism needs to survive, such as food, shelter and a place to nest.

The number of organisms in a habitat depends on the resources available. More light, water and minerals means more, or bigger, plants which can feed more species.

Different habitats provide different environmental factors such as light, temperature range or water availability, and will therefore be home to different types of organisms. A compost heap and a beech tree are two such habitats that provide different kinds of resources.

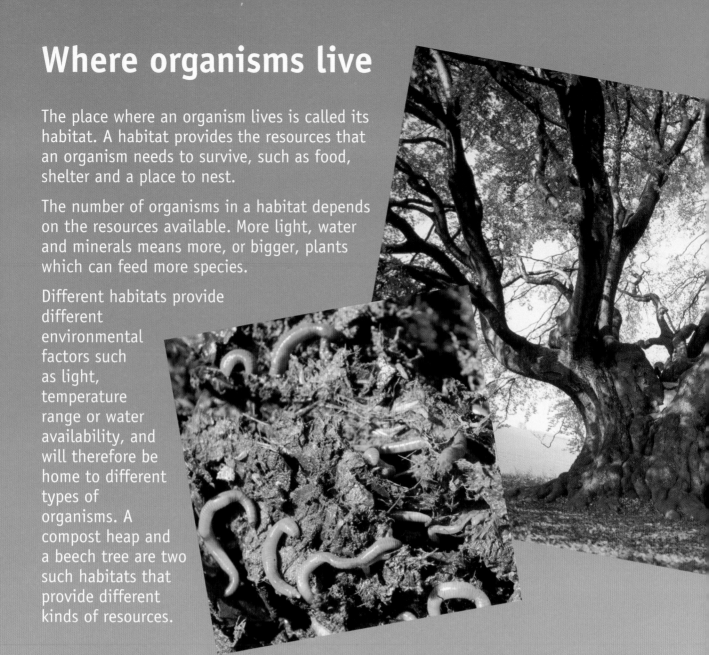

Ecologists study habitats. They can measure variables such as temperature, light intensity or moisture. They also use sampling techniques to collect data on the type of species living in a habitat. With square frames, called quadrats, ecologists count the number of each separate species within several quadrats placed randomly in the habitat. They can estimate the sizes of populations of various species within the whole habitat. If they carry out these surveys regularly they spot changes in populations and can investigate why these changes are happening.

Ecologists may study local (gardens, parks), national (moorland, fenland, chalk downs) or global (ice caps, tropical rainforest) habitats.

Polar bears live on the Arctic sea ice. They swim and hunt under the ice or in the sea. They are very well adapted for living in their habitat. They can walk on ice because the soles of their feet are hairy. Thick white fur insulates and camouflages them. They are strong with sharp claws and teeth to catch seals and walruses. Their keen senses of smell and hearing help them find their prey.

Some organisms can live in a range of habitats. If one habitat disappears they can move to another. Foxes are found in both country areas and in towns.

Other organisms are so well adapted to their habitat that if it shrinks their numbers will fall. The giant panda eats mainly bamboo and is found only in mountains of eastern Tibet and southwest China. Many new roads are being built in China, leaving less space for bamboo to grow. This means the number of giant pandas is decreasing and they are in danger of becoming extinct.

Some animals are adapted to the daily or yearly changes in their habitat. During the winter months in Britain there is less food available. Many small mammals hibernate – they go into a deep sleep and their body temperature drops so they don't lose so much heat.

Some birds migrate to a warmer place. Swallows fly to South Africa in the autumn and return to the UK the following spring.

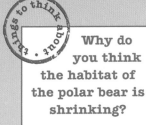

things to think about

Why do you think the habitat of the polar bear is shrinking?

Competition and co-operation

Living things interact with each other and with their environment. The availability of resources, such as light, water, minerals and space, affects populations of organisms and the sizes of individuals within these populations.

Competition and co-operation also affect populations. Some organisms compete and some co-operate.

As the number of individuals in a population increases they compete for resources. The size of the individuals decreases. The cress on the right-hand side was planted with more seeds in the pot. Many of the seedlings are very small.

The size of a plant population influences the size of the population of animals that feeds on it. This in turn influences the size of the population of predators. The size of population of predators can also influence the population size of the prey organisms.

Any ecosystem can only support a certain number of organisms within a population. Once the maximum population size is reached it should stay relatively stable, with some fluctuations.

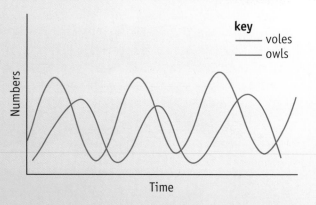

key
— voles
— owls

Numbers

Time

To maintain the population size each pair of organisms should produce two surviving offspring. Most organisms produce far more young than this. Resources are always limited so there is competition between living organisms for them.

Some individuals within a population just happen to be better adapted than others to their environment to better catch or find food or escape predation.

In a population of reindeer, those that have very broad, flat and deeply cleft hooves will be best able to run on snow and icy ground. It is these that will escape their wolf predators.

Birds of prey, such as eagles, hunt singly. Those with the sharpest claws and beaks and keenest eyesight will be more successful at capturing prey.

Some animals co-operate with each other in order to obtain food.

Wolves prey on animals much larger than them, so they work together. They live and hunt in packs. Sometimes half the pack pursues the prey while the other half cuts off the prey's escape route. Only one pair of wolves in the pack produce young each year. The other females in the pack help rear these young so that the lead female can still hunt.

Humans can use predators to try to control populations of crop pests. Whitefly damage tomato plants by feeding on the underside of leaves and tapping into the sap. To reduce the number of whiteflies and the damage they do to tomato plants, tomato growers introduce *Encarsia* wasps into the greenhouses. These wasps lay their eggs in the whitefly larvae so the wasp eats the larva from within and kills it.

This is an example of a food chain.

tomatoes ➡ whitefly ➡ *Encarsia* wasp

Encarsia wasp hatches out of the dead whitefly larva

Introducing predators to control populations can go wrong. The Indian mongoose was introduced to Jamaica to control the rat population. However, these mongooses preferred to eat the eggs of local birds and reptiles instead. At least five Jamaican species are now extinct due to the mongoose.

things to think about •

What other animals co-operate with each other to increase their chances of survival?

Human impact on habitats and food chains

The human population has grown very fast over the last 200 years. This population increase means that we take up more space for houses, roads, factories, trade areas, schools and hospitals. We also have to grow more food. This means that many habitats for wildlife have been destroyed.

Tropical rainforests are shrinking. Forests and woodland in Britain have also been replaced by farmland. All of this means that food sources and shelter for many animals have been reduced. Trees are important in many food chains and they are also habitats that house a variety of animals.

The farmland that replaced forests creates new habitats, such as hedgerows between fields. However, modern farming techniques use big machinery and need big fields, so many hedges have been removed. This is a physical change that has caused the destruction of a habitat.

The population of house sparrows in the UK has declined by more than half since the 1970s. We do not yet fully understand the reasons although these factors could be important.

- Hedgerow and meadow habitats for insects that sparrows feed on have been lost.
- House sparrows often nest in roofs, but modern house designs have sealed roofs.
- Cat numbers in towns have increased.

During the last 60 years farming has become more efficient. Modern farming uses fertilisers, pesticides and herbicides to increase crop yield. However, maximising food production for humans can significantly affect other animals and plants.

● Chemical changes can reduce the number of other plants (weeds) and so reduce food available for some consumers.
● Rain can wash nutrients from fertilisers into rivers. This makes algae grow faster, which blocks light for water plants. The plants die and are decomposed by bacteria that use oxygen, so many fish also die.
● Some weeds are a habitat for small insects, so weedkillers can also destroy habitats.
● Pesticides kill many insects, not just pests, and so reduce food available for birds.
● Some of these chemicals remain in the environment and may accumulate in animals that eat plants, and in animals lower in the food chain.
● Some chemicals may remain on the food we eat and so enter the human food chain.

Modern farming and industry use machinery that is powered by fossil fuels such as petrol and diesel. Electricity is also used, for example to heat animal houses and for milking machines or to make fertilisers. Some of this electricity is generated in oil-fired or coal-fired power stations.

Sulphur dioxide emissions from burning fossil fuels can cause acid rain. Pollution from industrial waste can also affect habitats directly by damaging trees and can affect food chains by killing organisms in rivers and lakes.

In 1900 the population of the world was 1500 million. By the 1950s this had doubled to 3000 million and today it is 5300 million. By about 2030 it is expected to be 9 billion.

things to think about •

Human development can also create habitats. Find out or think about how motorways and their verges, canal redevelopment for tourism, green corridors in towns, and gardens provide habitats.

Acid rain

Acid rain is produced when acid gases in the air dissolve in water vapour, which then falls as rain.

Some acidic gases, for example carbon dioxide and sulphur dioxide, are present in the atmosphere naturally.

Natural events like volcanic eruptions increase the levels of carbon dioxide and sulphur dioxide.

Human activity, such as burning fossil fuels, increases their levels further.

Fossil fuels contain carbon. Burning carbon in air produces carbon dioxide.

$$\text{carbon} + \text{oxygen} \longrightarrow \text{carbon dioxide}$$
$$C + O_2 \longrightarrow CO_2$$

These fuels also usually have sulphur impurities. Burning sulphur in air produces sulphur dioxide.

$$\text{sulphur} + \text{oxygen} \longrightarrow \text{sulphur dioxide}$$
$$S + O_2 \longrightarrow SO_2$$

High temperatures can make nitrogen and oxygen in the air react together to make acidic nitrogen oxides. These dissolve in water to produce nitric acid. Thunderstorms and the ignition spark in petrol engines can both convert nitrogen and oxygen in the air into nitrogen oxides.

Acid rain damages the environment. It causes chemical weathering of rocks and buildings. For example:

nitric acid + calcium carbonate (limestone) $\longrightarrow$ calcium nitrate + water + carbon dioxide

Acid rain corrodes metals. For example:

$$\text{sulphuric acid} + \text{copper} \longrightarrow \text{copper sulphate} + \text{water}$$
$$H_2SO_4 + Cu \longrightarrow CuSO_4 + H_2O$$

Acid rain can also:

- harm water organisms and affect food webs
- lower the pH of soil and affect plant growth.

Rain as acidic as lemon juice (pH 2.5) has fallen in Japan.

rain water becomes acid

nitrogen oxides formed in thunderstorms

acid rain can damage plants and water organisms

lake

low soil pH affects crop growth

some power stations and factories burn fossil fuels

acid rain can damage buildings

domestic users of electricity

cars burn fossil fuels and emit
sulphur dioxide
carbon dioxide
nitrogen oxide

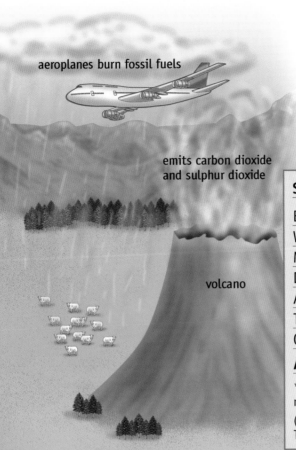

aeroplanes burn fossil fuels

emits carbon dioxide
and sulphur dioxide

volcano

cargo ships burn fossil fuels

Here is some information about UK emissions of chemicals that produce acid rain from 1991 to 2005. The emissions include sulphur dioxide, nitrogen oxides and ammonia, expressed in thousand tonnes of sulphur dioxide equivalent.

Clear patterns can be seen.

Source	1991	1998	2005*
Electricity, gas and water supply	3020	1330	639
Wholesale and retail trade	90	50	54
Manufacturing and construction	980	630	487
Domestic	640	440	271
Agriculture, mining and quarrying	770	680	643
Transport and communication	570	520	1004
Other industries	240	160	114
All sources	**6310**	**3810**	**3212**

*Some categories have changed since 1998, so comparisons may not be accurate.

(Adapted from statistics provided by the National Environmental Technology Centre: Office for National Statistics.)

things to think about •

What trends can you see in the data table? How reliable do you think your conclusions are?

There are several ways to reduce acid rain pollution.

- Removing sulphur from fuels – low-sulphur petrol means less sulphur dioxide is emitted in exhaust gases.
- Reducing the amount of acidic gases emitted by car exhausts – catalytic converters decrease the amount of acidic gases emitted by car exhausts.
- Reducing the quantity of acid gases emitted from burning fossil fuels – power stations neutralise sulphur dioxide in flue gases by reacting it with an alkali.

We can also reduce the amount of gases emitted from burning fossil fuels by:

- reducing the amount of electricity we use
- producing electricity without using fossil fuels
- reducing personal use of fossil fuels, such as for transport
- finding new ways of powering vehicles.

Changes to the global environment

Global warming and damage to the ozone layer affect the Earth and everything living on it.

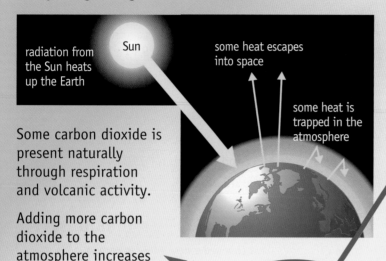

radiation from the Sun heats up the Earth

Sun

some heat escapes into space

some heat is trapped in the atmosphere

The Earth as a whole is getting warmer. Global warming is partly caused by carbon dioxide in the atmosphere, which traps heat in the atmosphere and warms up the Earth. This is called the greenhouse effect.

Some carbon dioxide is present naturally through respiration and volcanic activity.

Adding more carbon dioxide to the atmosphere increases the greenhouse effect.

We have added to the greenhouse effect by:

- burning more fossil fuels
- cutting down trees.

The greenhouse effect and global warming

Global warming can cause:

- higher temperatures – warmer winters
- more extreme weather events like hurricanes
- sea level rise flooding many coastal areas – particularly if it gets warm enough for ice caps to melt
- drier climate and drought in some areas
- changes to habitats, affecting species living there
- long-term changes to food webs

We cannot say that global warming causes any single event. We can only predict that it will cause these events to increase.

Deforestation in Brazil, seen from space

Flooding caused by hurricane

There is evidence from ice cores and tree rings that the Earth's temperature has always varied. These measurements have a lot of uncertainty in them.

Data from the last 100–200 years shows the Earth's average temperature is increasing, but different sources give slightly different figures. Most scientists believe our increased use of fossil fuels is the main cause of current global warming. Evidence is sometimes conflicting, so some scientists are less certain. There may be other causes – such as changes in the Earth's orbit and geological activity.

Scientists examining an ice core in Antarctica

Venus is not as close to the Sun as Mercury, but it is the hottest planet – because of the huge amount of carbon dioxide in its atmosphere. The surface temperature averages about 464°C, which could melt lead.

things to think about

Why is global warming data from the past 50 years more reliable than measurements from ice cores and tree rings? What data could you look for to try to prove that global warming is linked to our use of fossil fuels?

We are already:

- reducing use of fossil fuels by looking for alternative energy sources
- looking for ways to reduce our overall use of energy
- researching technologies to capture and store carbon dioxide.

You could personally:

Reduce your energy use
Reuse
Recycle

Plants remove carbon dioxide from the atmosphere by photosynthesis.

- Burning forests to clear land removes trees that could have removed carbon dioxide and adds further carbon dioxide to the atmosphere.
- Replanting forests would remove more carbon dioxide from the atmosphere.

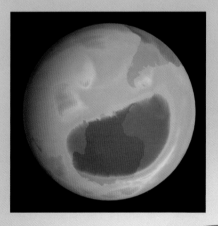

The atmosphere has an ozone layer. It absorbs much of the Sun's ultraviolet radiation.

Some chemicals, especially CFC gases (formerly used in aerosols and refrigerants), react with ozone. In the 1990s, scientists detected a huge ozone hole over the southern hemisphere.

Damage to the ozone layer

Without the ozone layer more ultraviolet radiation reaches Earth. This can cause skin cancer. There may be serious consequences for marine life around Antarctica.

Damage to the ozone layer has been reduced by:

- changing the gases used in aerosols and in cooling equipment
- disposing of old fridges more carefully.

We must look and act globally – what happens in any one part of the Earth affects the whole atmosphere. Everyone must act together to solve these problems.

Sustainable development

Population growth and increased industrialisation mean a greater demand for resources such as food and fuels. Our generation must consider how best to use the resources we have to make sure there will be enough in the future too. This is what using resources sustainably means.

Using land to build houses, factories and transport systems, to mine metals or grow food causes habitat loss.

Waste products can cause pollution too – including the impact of global warming on ecosystems.

So sustainable development also means protecting the air, water and the food chain. At a local, national and global level, society should ask:

- What energy resources should we use?
- How can we reduce energy use?
- What types of transport and housing are best?
- What is the best way to use land?
- How should we grow and distribute food?

At the present growth rate of 1.1% per year, the population of the US will double to about 560 million in the next 60 years.

More food needs to be grown. This means:

- more fertilisers and pesticides needed – using up resources and possibly damaging the environment
- more land cleared to grow crops
- more transport needed.

Extracting raw materials:

- uses a lot of energy
- causes pollution – including acid rain and greenhouse gases
- can make the landscape look ugly
- takes away finite resources we cannot replace.

More people and goods will be transported. This means:

- more land cleared to build roads, railways, ports and airports
- more energy needed to run vehicles
- increased pollution – including acid rain and greenhouse gases.

We need more energy to supply to more people and to operate more transport and machinery, so more electricity has to be generated.

Using more fossils fuels to generate electricity means:

- more pollution is caused
- these finite resources will run out very quickly.

more housing means:

- more land cleared
- more raw materials extracted
- more energy used to run machines
- more transport of materials.

New technology and industrial growth have made technology available to more people. This means:

- more raw materials extracted
- more energy used to run machines
- more transport of goods.

things to think about •

In some parts of the world, land that was used to grow food now grows plants for biofuels. Biofuels can be used in cars instead of petrol and diesel. This conserves fossil fuels and produces less carbon dioxide. Is using biofuels sustainable?

Scientists from many specialisms have developed technologies to help reduce waste and overall use of energy. Now there is a much better understanding of the environment from local to global scales, and how living things are interdependent.

We **can** act to use resources sustainably and minimise pollution.

- Managing fishing and forestry means these resources can be used sustainably.
- More efficient devices and industrial processes conserve energy and raw materials.
- Improved extraction processes have less environmental impact in mines and quarries.
- Renewable energy resources conserve finite resources and produce smaller amounts of greenhouse gases.
- Recycling uses less energy and conserves resources.

Particle model

Scientists believe that everything is made from very tiny particles. They use this idea, called particle theory, to explain what happens to solids, liquids and gases when they are heated and cooled. The particle model uses diagrams to help explain what happens.

Solids

- Solids have a fixed shape and a fixed size.
- Their particles are very close together and held in place by strong forces (bonds).
- Their particles cannot move around but they do vibrate.
- Because the particles cannot move around, a solid has a fixed shape.

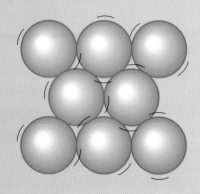

expansion

As the solid is heated, its particles gain more energy. This makes the particles vibrate faster and they move further apart. The solid expands.

The particles themselves don't expand – their size stays the same. Their mass stays the same too.

Gases and liquids also expand when they are heated, because their particles gain more energy and move around more.

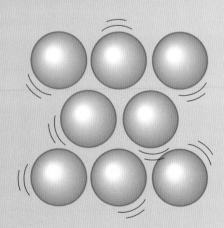

Expansion can be a problem – for example railway lines can expand and buckle in hot weather.

Expansion can be useful too – thermometers work because the liquid inside expands when it is heated and contracts when it is cooled.

things to think about

What do you think would happen to a bimetallic strip if it was cooled to well below room temperature? Can you explain why you think this would happen?

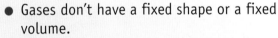

Liquids

● Liquids do not have a fixed shape but they do have a fixed volume.
● Their particles are very close together. Most of the particles touch each other.
● The particles can move around.
● Because the particles can move around, a liquid can:
  – flow
  – take the shape of its container.

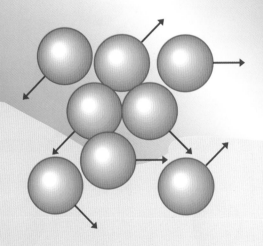

All the air in your classroom can be compressed into a volume smaller than the eye of a needle!

Gases

● Gases don't have a fixed shape or a fixed volume.
● Their particles move around all the time and spread out. This is why a gas fills its container.
● A gas can be compressed into a very small space – this pushes the particles closer together.

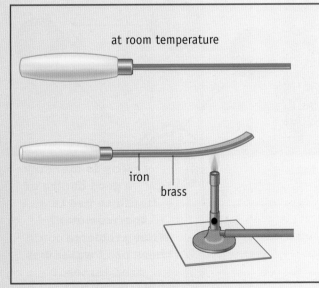

at room temperature

iron

brass

A bimetallic strip is made from two metals joined together. These metals expand at different rates when they are heated. This makes the strip bend.

The metal on the outside of the curve has expanded more than the metal inside the curve.

Bimetallic strips are often used in thermostats like the ones that control your central heating at home. The strip could touch a contact in an electric circuit when it is cool and then bend away from the contact when it gets hot – breaking the circuit.

Changing state

A material changes its state because (thermal) energy is either added or taken away from it.

Adding energy to a solid makes its particles move further and faster until the bonds between particles weaken enough for the particles to move past each other – the solid has now melted into a liquid.

Adding energy to a liquid makes its particles move around further and faster until they have enough energy to break their bonds and become free to move anywhere. When this happens the liquid has become a gas.

A liquid can become a gas in two ways.

Evaporation
- Only the particles at the surface of the liquid are involved – they are the only particles with enough energy to break free.
- The liquid doesn't bubble.
- Evaporation happens at all temperatures.

Boiling
- All the particles in the liquid are involved – they all have enough energy to break free.
- The liquid bubbles.
- Boiling happens at a fixed temperature.

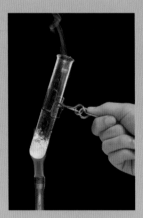

M E L T I N G

B O I L I N G AND E V A P O R A T I O N

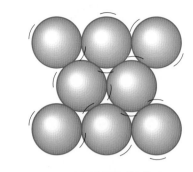

ADD ENERGY

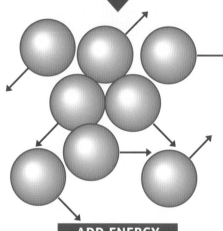

ADD ENERGY

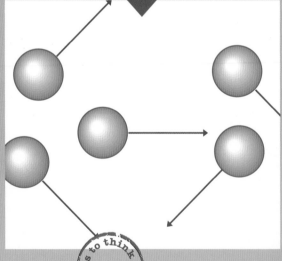

Boiling and melting happen at fixed temperatures for a given liquid. These temperatures are different for different liquids.

Liquid	Melting point	Boiling point
Pure water	0 °C	100 °C
Mercury	−39 °C	360 °C

things to think about • **Why is mercury a good choice of liquid to use in a thermometer? What problems could there be if water was used instead?**

Changing state can be useful when working with materials.

- Glass blowing – the glass is heated until it starts to melt, blown into shape and cooled to keep the new shape.
- Casting metal – the molten (melted) metal is poured into a mould and cooled.

F
R
E
E
Z
I
N
G

REMOVE ENERGY

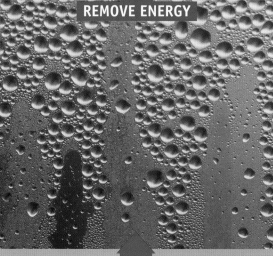

C
O
N
D
E
N
S
A
T
I
O
N

REMOVE ENERGY

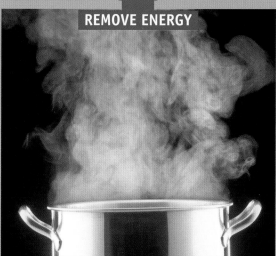

Change of state is a physical change – it can be reversed.

Cooling a gas takes energy from its particles so they slow down and move closer together. The gas condenses into a liquid.

Cooling a liquid takes energy from its particles so they can't move around and can only vibrate. The liquid freezes into a solid.

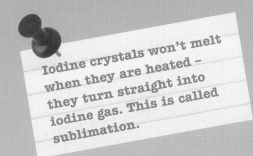

Iodine crystals won't melt when they are heated – they turn straight into iodine gas. This is called sublimation.

When they change state, particles do not change size or mass – they just arrange themselves differently.

If you melt 1 kg of solid iron you will get 1 kg of liquid iron!

Solidity and density

things to think about •

Do you think these substances
are solid, liquid or gas?
● ice cream ● foam ● toothpaste

SOLIDS

● have a fixed volume and a fixed shape.

Solids can be elastic.

This means they return exactly to their
original shape after bending or stretching.

Solids can be hard.

This is because their particles are close
together and held in place by strong bonds.
It can take a lot of force to break these
bonds.

LIQUIDS

● have a fixed volume but
no fixed shape.

Liquids take the shape of their container.

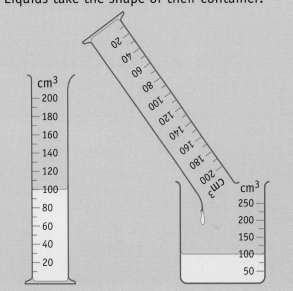

GASES

● have no fixed volume and
no fixed shape.

Gases expand to fill the space available and
can also be compressed into a very small
space.

Solids can be dense.

This is because their particles are packed closely together.

This means that there can be quite a large mass in a small volume of material.

Density measures how concentrated the mass of an object is.

- If an object has its mass spread over a large volume then its density will be low.
- If all the mass is concentrated into a small space then its density will be high.

To measure the density of an object we have to:

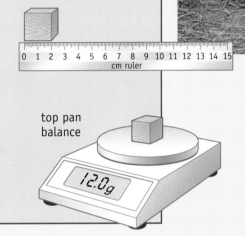

top pan balance

- measure its volume (for example by measuring its length, width and height with a ruler)
- measure its mass (for example using a top pan balance).

The density of a black hole is more than a million tonnes per cubic centimetre. This means that just 1 cm³ of a black hole would have a mass of over 1 million tonnes and one teaspoonful of black hole material would have a mass of over 2.5 million tonnes!

An object will float if its density is less than the density of the liquid it is in. Some types of wood are less dense than water so they will float on water. Most metals are denser than water so they won't float on water.

Materials that float easily are described as buoyant.

As a general rule, solids are denser than liquids and liquids are denser than gases.

SOLIDS – highest density, because their particles are closest together

LIQUIDS

GASES – lowest density, because their particles are furthest apart

But there are some exceptions.

Liquids with a low density can float on liquids with higher density – oil floats on water! Gases with lower densities float on higher density gases too – warm air will rise and float on colder air.

Dissolving

When a solid dissolves in a liquid, its particles slip into the gaps between the particles of the liquid. This means that the two different types of particles become completely mixed up.

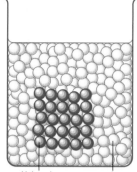

solid solute particle   solvent particle

Solute – the solid that is being dissolved.
Solvent – the liquid the solute is being dissolved in.
Solution – the liquid that is formed when the solute has dissolved in the solvent.

Solids which dissolve are soluble. Solids which do not dissolve are insoluble.

Mass doesn't change when a solid is dissolved in a solvent.

This is because you have the same number of particles at the end as you had to start with – they just get mixed up.

mass of solute

Water isn't the only liquid we can dissolve things in.

Many different liquids are used as solvents. Some solids are insoluble in water but soluble in certain other liquids.

- Gloss paint won't dissolve in water so you need to clean the paint brush in a solvent like turpentine.
- Nail varnish won't dissolve in water so you need to use nail varnish remover. This usually contains a solvent called acetone.

Dissolving is a physical change so it can be reversed.

For example, if you leave salt water solution (brine) to evaporate, the water particles gradually leave the solution and the salt particles will be left behind.

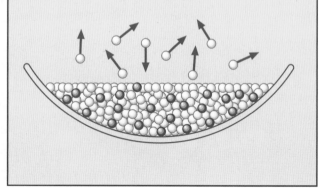

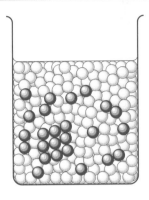
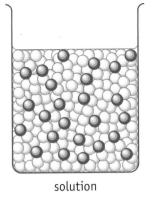

solution

A solution is described as saturated when it contains as much solute as it can hold.

If you keep adding solute to a saturated solution it will not dissolve.

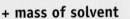

+ mass of solvent

= mass of solution

In a clear salt solution, you can't tell if there is any solute present. How could you prove the liquid you have is salt solution and not pure water?

You could investigate what materials dissolve best, or what factors affect how easily dissolving takes place.

Remember that to carry out a fair test or valid comparison you must make sure that you change only one variable. All the other variables need to be kept the same every time. The factor that you change is the independent variable. The factor that you measure is the dependent variable.

You should record all of your results in a table. Don't forget to include the units in the top row of the table.

To make sure your results are reliable you should repeat your readings. You can then check that you are getting similar results.

To reach a conclusion, you could plot a graph of the dependent variable (*y* axis) against the independent variable (*x* axis).

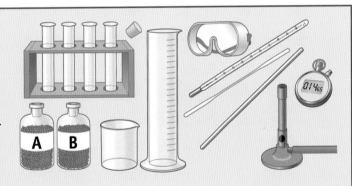

temperature of water (°C)	time taken to dissolve 1 cm³ of sugar (s)	
	1st attempt	2nd attempt
40	32	34
50	26	27
60	23	22
70	18	18
80	15	14

Diffusion

Moving particles will spread out if they have space to move into. This is called diffusion. Diffusion happens even if there is no breeze or current.

During diffusion, particles move from areas where they are strongly concentrated to areas where there are fewer of them. This means that the particles are spread out more evenly after diffusion than before.

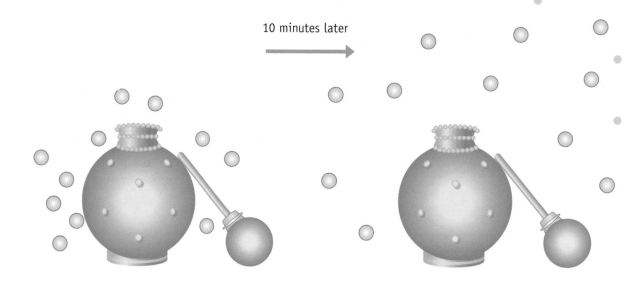

10 minutes later

Gases diffuse easily because their particles can move freely.

Liquids can also diffuse. Diffusion in a liquid usually happens slowly.

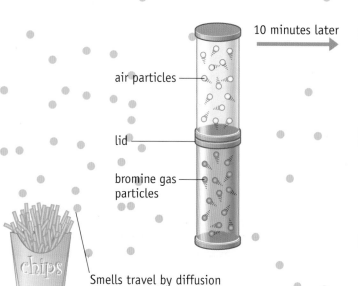

air particles

lid

bromine gas particles

10 minutes later

Smells travel by diffusion

How quickly particles diffuse depends on a number of factors.
For example:

- the size of the particles – the smaller and lighter the particles are, the faster they diffuse.
- the temperature – the higher the temperature of the gas or liquid, the more energy the particles will have and the faster they will diffuse.
- the difference in concentration between where the particles were when they started and where they are moving into – the greater the difference, the faster they will diffuse.
- any other particles that are in the way – they could bump into other particles which would slow the diffusing particles down.

You could investigate the variables that affect how quickly a gas or liquid diffuses.

You would need some way of telling that the particles have spread out.

You could use a coloured gas – but as most coloured gases are hazardous, this would need to be done in a fume cupboard.

Another way would be to see how quickly a dye diffuses through water.

Potassium manganate(VII) crystals will dissolve in water to produce a purple dye. The dyed water will then diffuse through the rest of the water.

You need to make sure you carry out a fair test – so you only change the one variable you have decided to investigate.

For example, make sure the volume of water is the same each time.

To measure the volume of water precisely, use a measuring cylinder – not a beaker. A measuring cylinder can read to the nearest cm^3 but a beaker usually measures only to the nearest $50\,cm^3$.

Why do you think most gases diffuse quite slowly through air? What stops diffusion being fast?

Applying the particle model

Models help us understand new ideas by relating them to things we already know about. We use the particle model of solids, liquids and gases to explain their behaviour.

If scientists find that their model cannot explain what is happening, they try to develop a better model that can explain things more accurately.

things to think about · As an aircraft flies higher the pressure inside the cabin has to be reduced. Why is this? What could happen if it wasn't reduced?

DENSITY	Materials have different densities because: • the particles may be closer together in one material than another • each particle in one material may be heavier than each particle in the other material.	
HARDNESS	Solids can be hard because their particles are held together by strong bonds. The stronger the bond between the particles in a material, the harder the material is.	
ELASTICITY	Solids can be elastic because the forces (bonds) between their particles resist the stretching force trying to pull the particles apart. Some solids are more elastic than others – because the forces holding the particles together are different.	particles held together with stretchy bonds when you pull on the material, the bonds stretch the bonds spring the particles back to their original positions

The particle model of solids can explain the regular shapes of crystals.

The particle model explains how heat is conducted and why solids are the best conductors of heat – particles must be close together to pass the heat energy on.

Air pressure is huge! In 1650 in the city of Magdeburg in Germany, it took two teams of eight horses to separate two hollow brass hemispheres with a vacuum inside because the air pressure pushing them together was so strong.

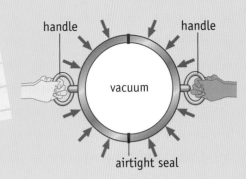

handle   handle

vacuum

airtight seal

BROWNIAN MOTION	Brownian motion is the movement of particles being pushed by other, smaller, particles. We can see the particles that are being pushed but the particles that are pushing them are too small to see. Because air is a gas, its particles move around randomly all the time. This causes specks of dust in the air to move.	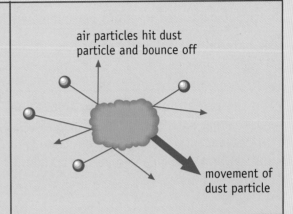 air particles hit dust particle and bounce off movement of dust particle
GAS PRESSURE	As gas particles move around they hit objects. This causes gas pressure. The faster the gas particles move, the more force they exert so the greater the pressure is. The hotter the gas, the more energy its particles have and the harder they hit the container.	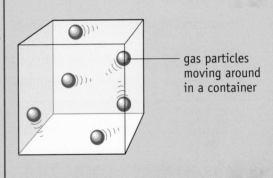 gas particles moving around in a container

Air particles moving around cause air pressure (atmospheric pressure). Air pressure acts in all directions.

If air pressure is greater on one side of a surface, the unbalanced forces can make the object collapse. Remove the air from inside the can shown here and the can collapses.

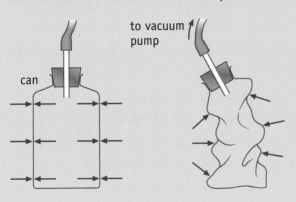

can

to vacuum pump

Aerosols, steam turbines, straws and pneumatic drills all use air or gas pressure to work.

Two thousand years ago, the Egyptian scientist, Hero of Alexandria, designed machines that used air pressure to move objects.

Density

Density measures how much mass there is in a fixed volume of a material.

The higher the density of material, the more mass there is in each cubic centimetre (cm^3).

Density is measured in grams per cubic centimetre (g/cm^3).

If a material has a density of $2\,g/cm^3$ it means that each cm^3 has a mass of $2\,g$.

You can use a top pan balance to measure mass. Some balances are more accurate than others, because they have been made well and calibrated (compared with a standard mass).

- Choose the best quality instrument available.
- Set the balance at zero before you put the mass on.

mass
(g)

density
(g/cm^3)

volume
(cm^3)

$$\text{density} \atop (g/cm^3) \quad = \quad \frac{\text{mass (g)}}{\text{volume } (cm^3)}$$

Because the density of a material depends on how far apart its particles are, solids are usually the most dense and gases the least dense types of materials.

solid

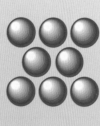

liquid

gas

When something is heated it expands because its particles move further apart. This makes it less dense.

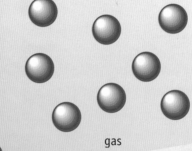

Salt water is denser than fresh water so some objects that sink in fresh water will float in salt water. Ships float higher in salt water than in fresh water. The Plimsoll Line on a ship tells you how much cargo you can safely load when the ship is in different types of water without it being in danger of sinking when it travels into a different type of water.

To find the volume of a solid that has a cuboid shape, measure its length, width and height with a ruler.

volume = length × width × height

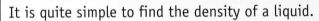

You can use a measuring cylinder to measure the volume of any small solid.

- Put a known amount of water into the measuring cylinder.
- Gently place the object into the water. Make sure it is completely under water.
- Measure the rise in volume.

volume of object = (volume of water + object) − (volume of water alone)

For bigger objects, use a displacement can to measure volume.

- Completely fill the displacement can with water. Add the object gently.
- Catch the water displaced in a measuring cylinder.
- Read its volume.

volume of water displaced = volume of the object

It is quite simple to find the density of a liquid.

- Find its mass – first find the mass of the empty measuring cylinder, then find the mass of the cylinder plus the liquid.

mass of liquid = (mass of liquid + cylinder) − (mass of cylinder alone)

- Find its volume − just pour it into a measuring cylinder!

Make sure the cylinder has an appropriate range and scale for your measurement. A cylinder with cubic centimetre scale divisions will give greater precision than a cylinder with divisions only every 2 or 10 cm^3.

To get reliable results, be consistent – make sure you always measure to the bottom of the meniscus. Your eyes should be level with the meniscus.

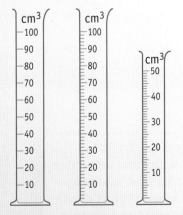

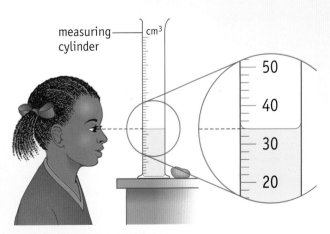

Separating mixtures

FILTERING

Filtering is used to separate insoluble solids from liquids.

Sand can be separated from a mixture of sand and salt water by filtering.

Filtering works because the small liquid particles pass through the filter paper into the container below but the insoluble solid can't get through. The insoluble solid stays on the filter paper.

For example, if a mixture of salt solution and sand is filtered, the salt solution passes through the filter paper but the sand does not.

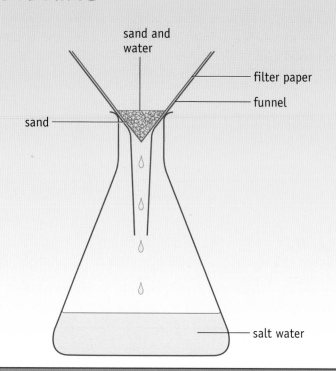

sand and water

filter paper

funnel

sand

salt water

CHROMATOGRAPHY

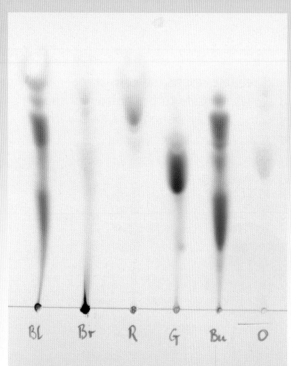

Chromatography is used to separate a mixture of different coloured dyes.

An example is separating out the different coloured dyes that are mixed together to make the ink in different coloured pens.

Chromatography works because the different dye particles dissolve and travel along the damp chromatography paper at different rates.

For example, in this chromatograph the red dye has travelled faster than all the others. The black, brown and red inks all contain red dye.

things to think about

Forensic scientists sometimes use chromatography to investigate inks and make-up found at a crime scene. What could this tell them? Why is it helpful?

EVAPORATION

Evaporation is used to separate a soluble solid from the liquid it is dissolved in.

For example, evaporation can be used to separate salt from water in a salt water solution.

Evaporation works because the solvent particles in the solution evaporate and leave the solid (solute) behind.

In simple evaporation only the solid can be collected because the liquid has evaporated away into the air.

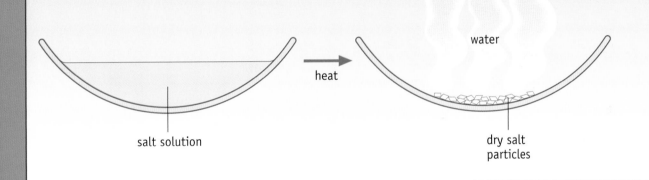

salt solution → heat → water / dry salt particles

DISTILLATION

Distillation is used when you want to separate and collect the liquid part of a solution (the solvent). For example, pure water can be distilled from a salt water solution.

In distillation, the solution is heated until it boils and the solvent particles turn into a gas. The gas is then cooled by the cold water running around the condenser. Cooling makes the gas condense back into a liquid. The liquid (pure solvent) is then collected. The solid is left behind in the original container so it can be collected too.

If salt solution is distilled both the salt and pure water can be collected separately.

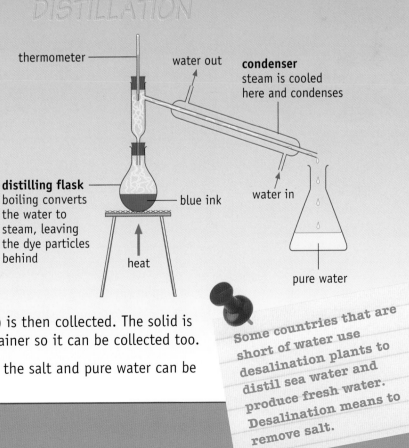

thermometer

water out

condenser
steam is cooled here and condenses

distilling flask
boiling converts the water to steam, leaving the dye particles behind

blue ink

water in

heat

pure water

Some countries that are short of water use desalination plants to distil sea water and produce fresh water. Desalination means to remove salt.

Atoms and elements

An element is a pure substance that cannot be split up into simpler substances.

There are 92 elements found naturally on Earth. These elements are listed in the Periodic Table. Every element has different properties such as hardness or melting point.

You cannot make elements out of other materials.

Each element contains only one type of particle, called an atom.

Every element has a chemical symbol. Scientists use these symbols as a shorthand version of an element's name. Here are some examples of elements and their chemical symbols:

Element	Chemical symbol
Copper	Cu
Sulphur	S
Mercury	Hg
Carbon	C
Iodine	I
Bromine	Br
Gold	Au
Lead	Pb
Fluorine	F
Chlorine	Cl
Silver	Ag
Oxygen	O
Hydrogen	H

When you use a chemical symbol, it is important to write it correctly. If the symbol is just one letter, that letter must be a capital. If the symbol is two letters, then the first must be a capital and the second must be lower case.

I ✓   i ✗   Ag ✓   AG ✗   ag ✗

The Ancient Greeks had ideas about elements and atoms 2000 years ago.
Some thinkers believed that everything was made up from four elements – Earth, Air, Fire and Water.
Others thought that everything contained small particles called atoms. The word atom actually comes from a Greek word which means indivisible ... so they had the idea that an atom couldn't be divided into anything smaller.

An atom is the smallest part of an element that has the properties of that element. It is the basic particle from which all elements are built up.

Atoms are far too small to see, even with a microscope.

The atoms that make up different elements are different from each other. For example:

- hydrogen gas contains only hydrogen atoms

- oxygen gas contains only oxygen atoms
- hydrogen atoms are different from oxygen atoms

- gold atoms are different from both of these. This is why gold is a heavy metallic solid and hydrogen is a light gas.

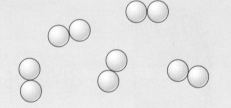
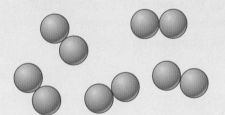
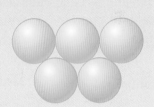

Scientists have believed for over 200 years that different elements are made out of different atoms, because the model works well. This theory explains, for example:

- why some new materials can be made by combining other materials
- how some chemical compounds can be split into other simpler substances
- why different elements are different from each other.

During recent years scientists have also been able to produce images of individual atoms using high-technology equipment like electron microscopes.

cobalt atoms individually placed using a scanning tunnelling microscope

Sodium and lead are both metals. Sodium is very light. Lead is very heavy. What might be different between the atoms of sodium and the atoms of lead?

Combining elements – compounds

Compounds are made from more than one element chemically joined together. This happens when two or more substances react together. A new substance is formed – this is a chemical change.

A particular compound always contains the same set of elements combined in the same way.

Some examples of compounds include:

- sodium chloride
- copper sulphate
- carbon dioxide
- hydrochloric acid
- sodium hydroxide
- water.

The name of a compound usually tells you about some of the elements it contains. Every compound has a chemical formula. This tells you exactly what elements it is made out of, using the symbols for elements.

- sodium chloride $NaCl$
- copper sulphate $CuSO_4$
- carbon dioxide CO_2
- carbon monoxide CO
- hydrochloric acid HCl
- water H_2O

Though both carbon dioxide and carbon monoxide are made from carbon and oxygen only, they are different compounds because their molecules contain different proportions of oxygen.

salt   SODIUM   CHLORINE

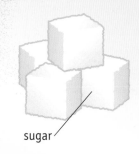
sugar   CARBON   HYDROGEN   OXYGEN

PETROL   HYDROGEN   CARBON

Sulphuric acid   corrosive   HYDROGEN   SULPHUR   OXYGEN

> **things to think about**
> The gems spinel and ruby are often mistaken for each other – the 'ruby' in the centre of one of the British Crown Jewels is actually a spinel. Spinel is magnesium aluminium oxide ($MgAl_2O_4$) and ruby is aluminium oxide (Al_2O_3). The eleventh-century scientist Al-Biruni worked out a method to tell ruby and spinel apart.
> **How do you think he did this?**

If the name of a compound ends in 'ide' then it normally contains only two elements. If it ends in 'ate' it contains three or more different elements, one of which is oxygen.

The chemical formula for hydroxide is OH, sulphate is SO_4 and carbonate is CO_3.

A molecule is the smallest part of a compound that has the properties of that compound.

Molecules are made from atoms joined together by chemical bonds. All the molecules of a particular compound contain the same combination of atoms. Different compounds have different molecules, with different combinations of atoms.

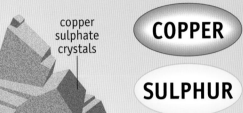
copper sulphate crystals

COPPER

SULPHUR

OXYGEN

The chemical formula of a compound tells you about the number and type of atoms in its molecule.

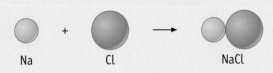
Na + Cl → NaCl

- A sodium chloride molecule is made up of one sodium atom and one chlorine atom bonded together.

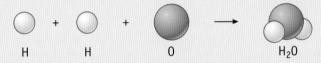
H + H + O → H₂O

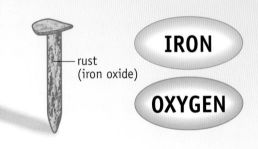
rust (iron oxide)

IRON

OXYGEN

- A water molecule is made up of two hydrogen atoms (H_2) and one oxygen atom bonded together.

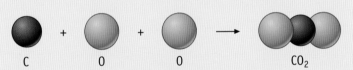
C + O + O → CO₂

- A carbon dioxide molecule is made up of one carbon atom and two oxygen atoms (O_2) bonded together.

water

HYDROGEN

OXYGEN

Any chemical reaction can be written as a word equation. The substances that react together are called reactants. The substances formed during a chemical reaction are called products.

Compounds are made when elements react together.

- Combustion – when materials burn they react with oxygen to form a new compound.

  magnesium + oxygen → magnesium oxide

- When materials react with water they form a new compound.

  calcium + water → calcium hydroxide + hydrogen

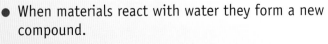

105

Mixtures and compounds

You have a mixture when two or more substances are mixed together without any chemical reaction taking place. These substances could be elements or compounds. The substances in a mixture are not chemically bonded together.

iron filings

Air is a mixture. Air contains several different gases, for example:

- nitrogen
- oxygen
- carbon dioxide
- water vapour.

But these gases stay separate from each other. They do not react to form new compounds.

Salt water is a mixture. Though the salt is dissolved in the water, the salt molecules do not chemically combine with the water molecules. They just fill up the spaces between water molecules.

mix

mixture

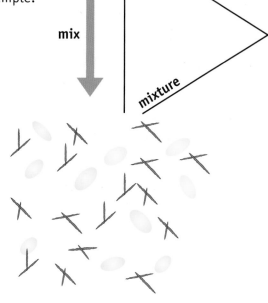

Mixtures can be separated easily by physical methods (no chemical reaction is needed). Some of the methods used to separate the substances in mixtures are:

- filtering
- chromatography
- evaporation
- distillation.

iron and sulphur mixture

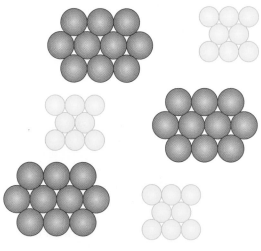

the iron and sulphur particles stay separate from each other

The nitrogen and oxygen in air do not normally react together. However, these elements can be combined to form the compound nitrous oxide. Nitrous oxide is sometimes called 'laughing gas'. 'Laughing gas' has been used by doctors and dentists for many years to relax patients.

sulphur powder

heat

compound

In a compound, the different substances it contains have been chemically reacted together. New molecules have been formed. The atoms of different elements in the compound are chemically bonded together.

A compound has different physical and chemical properties from the elements it contains. For example, copper sulphate contains atoms of copper, sulphur and oxygen.

- Copper sulphate is a bright blue crystalline substance.
- Copper is an orangey/brown metal.
- Sulphur is a yellow non-metallic solid.
- Oxygen is a colourless gas.

copper + sulphur + oxygen ⟶ copper sulphate

(Remember, compounds that end in 'ate' contain three or more elements, one of which must be oxygen.)

Compounds can only be separated into their different elements by using chemical reactions. This is because the atoms of the elements have been chemically bonded together. It is harder to separate compounds than mixtures. Different types of chemical reactions have to be used, depending on the elements that the compound contains.

For example, a compound may break down when it is heated. This is called a thermal decomposition reaction.

iron sulphide

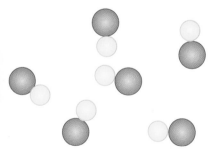

the iron and sulphur particles combine chemically to form iron sulphide molecules

Air is a mixture of compounds and elements.

The compounds air contains include carbon dioxide and water vapour.

The elements air contains include nitrogen and oxygen.

things to think about

How could you investigate whether an unknown substance was a mixture or a compound?

107

Mixtures and pure substances

Mixtures contain two or more substances that are not chemically joined together. These substances can be separated by physical means.

Separation methods aim to separate and collect a pure substance from a mixture.

A material is chemically pure when it contains only one substance (element or compound).

Separation methods include:

- filtering – to separate insoluble solids from liquids
- chromatography – to separate a mixture of different dyes
- evaporation – to separate a solute from a solvent
- distillation – to separate and collect the solvent
- magnetism
- freezing
- melting
- fractional distillation.

If only one of the substances in a mixture is magnetic, then it will be attracted towards a magnet but the rest of the mixture will not.

A mixture of two or more different liquids can be separated by freezing. The different liquids freeze at different temperatures. The liquid with the highest melting point freezes first. The liquid with the lowest melting point freezes last.

In the example shown, the water freezes before the ethanol (alcohol).

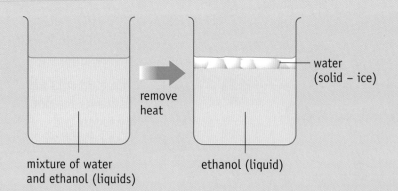

mixture of water and ethanol (liquids)

remove heat

water (solid – ice)

ethanol (liquid)

A mixture of two or more different solids can be separated by melting. The solid with the lowest melting point melts first.

Alloys are mixtures of two or more different metals. Alloys are melted to separate out the different metals. As each metal melts it is poured off into a separate container.

The freezing and melting methods work because:

- every material has a set melting point
- different materials have different melting points.

A simple physical test for purity and to help identify a substance is to find its boiling point. For example, pure water is the only clear liquid that boils at 100 °C.

Adding salt to cooking water raises its boiling point – because the water is no longer pure. This means the water gets hotter than 100 °C before it boils. Because the water is hotter, the food can cook more quickly.

Fractional distillation separates out the different substances in a mixture of two or more liquids.

It works because the different liquid 'fractions' have different boiling points.

- The mixture is heated.
- The fraction with the lowest boiling point boils first.
- As it boils it becomes a gas and travels down through the condenser.
- It cools and condenses into a liquid in the condenser.
- The liquid is collected.

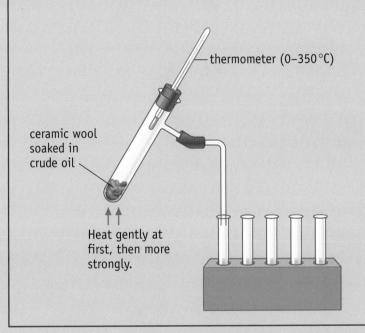

thermometer (0–350 °C)

ceramic wool soaked in crude oil

Heat gently at first, then more strongly.

As the temperature rises, the fraction with the next lowest boiling point boils, condenses, and is collected.

As each fraction boils it is collected in a different container.

Crude oil is a liquid. It is a mixture of many different compounds. These compounds are separated using fractional distillation.

Fractional distillation works because:

- every material has a set boiling point
- different materials have different boiling points.

Adding impurities to pure substances changes their melting and boiling points.

Adding impurities:

- raises the boiling point, and
- lowers the melting point.

things to think about ·

In the UK we get most of our salt from salt mines. Rock salt is a mixture of dirt and sand. To use this salt it has to be separated from its impurities. How could we do this? How could you separate the mixture of gases that make up air?

109

Periodic Table

All the elements with their symbols are listed in the Periodic Table.

The table is arranged so that elements with similar physical and chemical properties are grouped together in the same column. These columns are called groups.

Metals are found on the left of the thick red line and non-metals on the right.

Hydrogen is a gas. It is the lightest element.

In chemical reactions hydrogen can behave like a metal, even though it isn't one.

The first two columns (groups) are the reactive metals. They quickly form a dull coating (a metal oxide) when the metal reacts with oxygen in the air.

The most reactive metals are at the bottom of each column with reactivity getting less as you move up.

These metals are not hard like typical metals.

These are the other metals. They all have metallic properties (such as hardness, good electrical conduction, high melting point) but are not chemically reactive like the reactive metals.

Any element whose name ends in 'ium' is a metal.

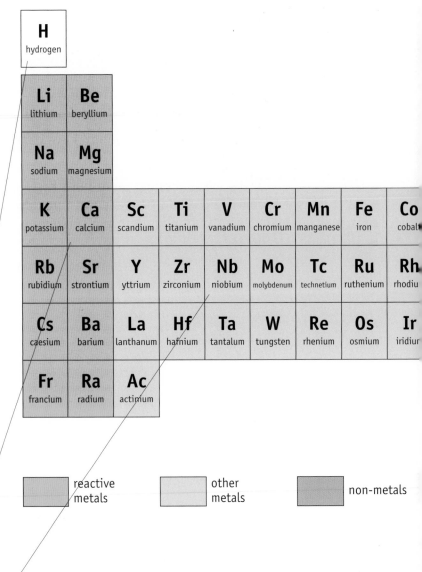

reactive metals   other metals   non-metals

Many scientists helped to find the patterns to organise the Periodic Table. The most famous is Mendeleev.

The scientists started by organising the elements in order of their mass. Then they looked for patterns in their properties, placing elements with similar properties into columns. Mendeleev thought there might be some undiscovered elements. He decided to leave 'gaps' to predict the properties of these elements. When these elements were discovered, their properties matched his predictions.

He
helium

B	C	N	O	F	Ne
boron	carbon	nitrogen	oxygen	fluorine	neon

Al	Si	P	S	Cl	Ar
aluminium	silicon	phosphorous	sulphur	chlorine	argon

Ni	Cu	Zn	Ga	Ge	As	Se	Br	Kr
ckel	copper	zinc	gallium	germanium	arsenic	selenium	bromine	krypton

Pd	Ag	Cd	In	Sn	Sb	Te	I	Xe
adium	silver	cadmium	indium	tin	antimony	tellurium	iodine	xenon

Pt	Au	Hg	Tl	Pb	Bi	Po	At	Rn
tinum	gold	mercury	thallium	lead	bismuth	polonium	astatine	radon

The chemical symbols for many of the elements in the Periodic Table come from their Latin names.

NAME	LATIN NAME	CHEMICAL SYMBOL
Lead	Plumbum	Pb
Mercury	Hydrogyrum	Hg
Gold	Aurum	Au

These are the inert gases or noble gases. They are all gases and are very unreactive.

It is very difficult to get any of these gases to react with anything.

This group is the halogens – very reactive non-metals.

The most reactive is fluorine. Reactivity decreases as you move down the column.

All the halogens have names that end in 'ine'.

These are non-metal elements. All the elements to the right of the thick red line are non-metals.

☐ halogens   ☐ inert gases

Similar elements are close to each other in the Periodic Table. For example gold (Au), silver (Ag) and platinum (Pt) are all unreactive and shiny, so are used for jewellery and decoration.

Germanium (Ge) and silicon (Si) are next to each other vertically. Though germanium is a metal and silicon is a non-metal, they have similar properties. Both are used as semiconductors in electronic circuits.

things to think about

How might scientists have decided where an element belongs in the Periodic Table? What do you think these elements might be like: indium, barium, bismuth, boron, radon?

Chemical changes

Chemical reactions make a new substance. This is called a chemical change. The change cannot be reversed without another chemical reaction.

Melting and boiling are physical changes. For example, changing ice to water or water to steam can be reversed – and no new substance is formed.

Here are some everyday changes that are chemical reactions.

What happens to copper or to zinc when they react with water?

Iron reacts with oxygen in the air or in water to form iron oxide (rust). Other metals have similar reactions with oxygen, but could react faster or slower.

When you bake a cake using flour, baking powder, eggs, sugar and margarine, new substances are formed. You can't get the original ingredients back again.

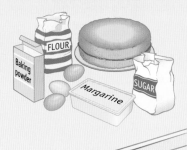

After burning, a match is black. Soot is one product of the burning reaction.

The chemicals in fireworks explode and produce coloured light.

When you add baking powder or bath salts to water you get bubbles.

Many useful new products are made using chemical reactions.

Most plastics and many modern clothing fibres have been made from reactions using oil.

Toilet cleaners are powerful chemicals. Never mix different toilet cleaners as they could react and produce toxic gases – or even an explosion.

The chemicals that react together are called reactants. The substance or substances formed are called products. Chemists write word equations to show what happens in a chemical reaction.

iron + oxygen → **iron oxide**
REACTANTS   PRODUCT

Some signs that a chemical reaction has occurred:

● colour change – the reactants look different from the products

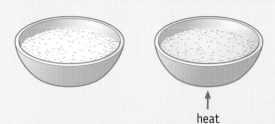

heat

● there is a change in temperature, or light is emitted

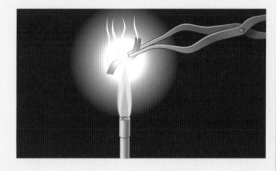

● bubbles of gas are produced, such as when acid is poured on a metal.

Chemical reactions are often started by heating, so you need to know these safety points for using a Bunsen burner.

● Use the blue flame when heating.
● Use the yellow flame when the Bunsen is not being used.
● Ensure hair is tied back and no loose clothing is near the Bunsen.
● Keep the Bunsen well away from the edges of the desk, from people and from anything flammable.
● Use a heatproof mat.
● Wear eye protection.
● Always watch the Bunsen.

The yellow flame is easier to see. This why it is called the safety flame. It is not quite as hot as the blue flame.

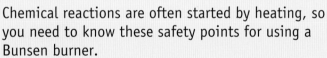

The blue flame is very hot and doesn't move about much.

Combustion

Burning – or combustion – is a chemical reaction. When oxygen reacts with a substance energy is transferred, mainly as heat. This is called combustion.

Combustion is an example of an irreversible reaction – you can't get a piece of paper back after you have burned it!

 This symbol tells us that the material burns easily in air.

Inputs

heat – to get the reaction going

fuel – contains carbon and hydrogen

oxygen – from the air

A Bunsen burner uses methane as a fuel.

The air hole controls the amount of air (oxygen) that mixes with the methane. When the air hole is open, more oxygen reaches the fuel and the flame is at its hottest (the blue flame).

Carbon dioxide and water vapour are produced when a Bunsen burner is used.

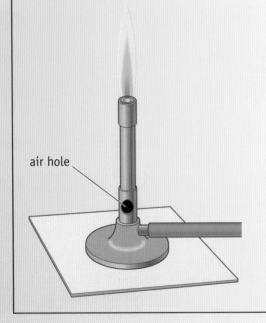

air hole

OXYGEN

FUEL

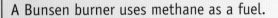

fuel + oxygen –

All three parts of the fire triangle need to be there for combustion. If any is removed then the fire will go out.

- No fuel – no combustion
- No oxygen – no combustion
- No heat input – no combustion

The temperature of a flame can be many thousands of degrees Celsius (°C). The temperature of a Bunsen flame can be as high as 2000°C. When acetylene is burned in oxygen, the flame temperature is over 3000°C!

The colour of a flame changes depending on its temperature. Red is the coolest, then orange, yellow and finally, the hottest flames are white.

Products

heat

carbon dioxide

water

HEAT

This is a test for carbon dioxide.

Limewater is a clear, colourless liquid.

When you add carbon dioxide to limewater, the limewater turns 'milky'.

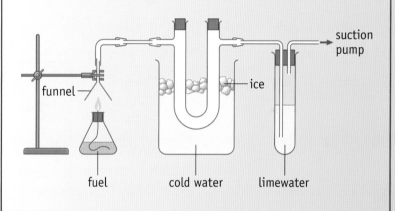

funnel

fuel

cold water

ice

limewater

suction pump

carbon dioxide + water

Carbon dioxide is made when fuels burn. Carbon dioxide is an oxide. Carbon in the fuel reacts with oxygen in the air. Oxides are also produced when other elements react with oxygen.

If too little oxygen reacts with the carbon in the fuel then carbon monoxide will be produced instead of carbon dioxide. This is very dangerous, as carbon monoxide is poisonous. This is why it is very important to have good ventilation whenever fuels are being burned.

things to think about

Can you explain how fire extinguishers work? What do they do that helps put out a fire?

Acids and alkalis

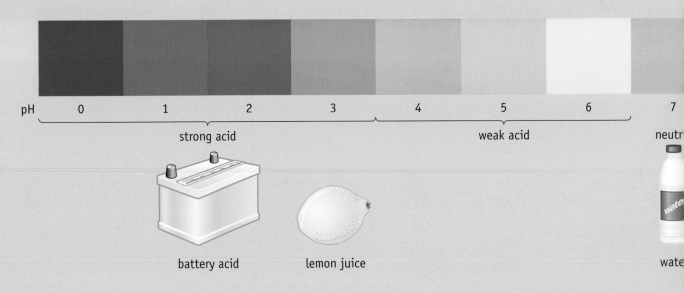

pH	0	1	2	3	4	5	6	7

strong acid   weak acid   neutr

battery acid   lemon juice   water

Acids

- have a low pH – less than 7
- can be corrosive
- are neutralised by alkalis.

The strongest acids have the lowest pH.

These are some of the acids you will use in the laboratory:

- hydrochloric acid
- nitric acid
- sulphuric acid.

Concentrated acids and alkalis are corrosive – they can destroy living tissue.

corrosive

Acids and alkalis can be made less concentrated by diluting them with water. Dilute acids are not corrosive but they may be labelled with the warning sign for 'irritant'. This means that they will make your skin red or blistered and damage your eyes.

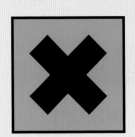

irritant

You must wash off any splashed on your skin, using plenty of water.

You must wear eye protection when you work with acids and alkalis.

Your skin is slightly acid – about pH 4.5 to 6. Soaps and detergents have a pH of 9 to 10. Shampoos and shower gels that are 'pH balanced' have the same pH as skin.

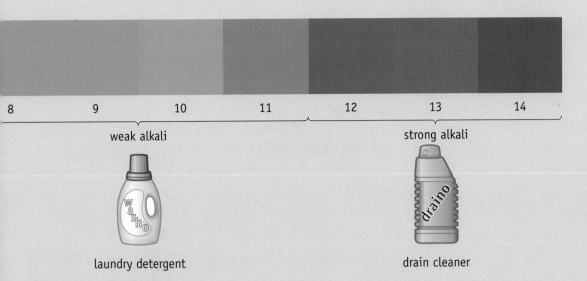

| 8 | 9 | 10 | 11 | 12 | 13 | 14 |

weak alkali   strong alkali

laundry detergent   drain cleaner

Alkalis you may come across in the lab include:

- sodium bicarbonate
- sodium hydroxide
- ammonia.

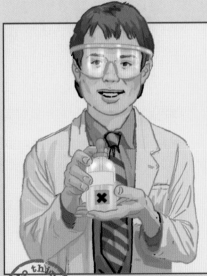

To avoid spills always carry bottles of acids or alkalis correctly. Use **two** hands. **Never** carry the bottle by its neck.

things to think about •

The acidity or alkalinity of soil affects how plants grow. Different plants grow best in soils with different pH values – how do gardeners find out how acid or alkaline their soil is? Some plants change colour depending on the type of soil they are grown in – do you know an example?

Alkalis

- have a high pH – more than 7
- can be corrosive
- are neutralised by acids.

The strongest alkalis have the highest pH.

A strong acid can be made safer by adding an alkali. This makes the pH closer to 7, which is neutral (neither acid nor alkali).

Lime (an alkali) is used to change the pH of acidic soil.

The extracts of some plants can be used as 'indicators' – they change colour in acids or alkalis. In the laboratory we use two main indicators, litmus and universal indicator.

- Acids always turn litmus red.
- Alkalis always turn litmus blue.

Universal indicator is a different colour at each point on the pH scale. It gives the same range of colours as shown in the top diagram.

You can also test for acidity or alkalinity with an electronic pH meter.

Neutralisation

Acids and alkalis react together to form a neutral substance (pH 7). This reaction is called neutralisation.

The neutral substances formed are called salts.

acid + alkali ➡ salt + water

Common salt (sodium chloride) is just one example of a salt. All salts have two-part names like this:

- sodium chloride
- silver bromide
- magnesium sulphate.

Try to guess the names of five more salts.

Examples of using neutralisation include:

- Antacid tablets – these contain carbonates which are alkalis. This neutralises some of the stomach acid.
- Farmers and gardeners add alkalis to acid soil to make the soil slightly alkaline and encourage plant growth.

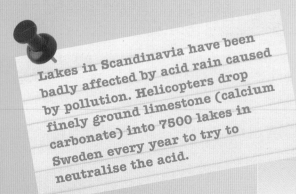

Lakes in Scandinavia have been badly affected by acid rain caused by pollution. Helicopters drop finely ground limestone (calcium carbonate) into 7500 lakes in Sweden every year to try to neutralise the acid.

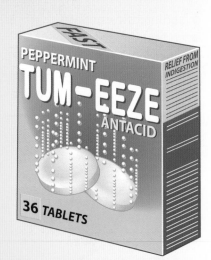

PEPPERMINT
TUM-EEZE
ANTACID
36 TABLETS
FAST
RELIEF FROM INDIGESTION

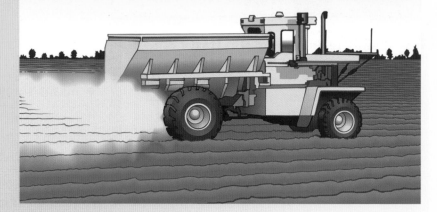

The acid and alkali have to be added in just the right amounts. If you add a dilute alkali to a concentrated acid you will only neutralise some of the acid. You then have to add more alkali to get a neutral solution.

You could use the idea of neutralisation to compare how effective different antacid tablets are.

- When all the 'stomach' acid has been neutralised the pH will be 7.
- An indicator can show when this happens.
- A pH meter will give continuous readings.

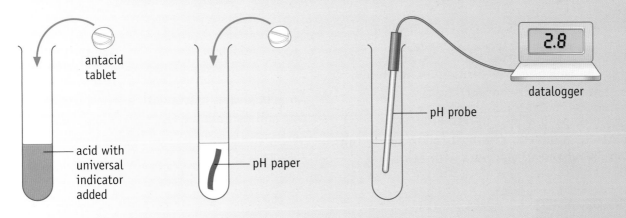

pH is a continuous scale so a pH meter can give more precise measurements as well as taking measurements very often.

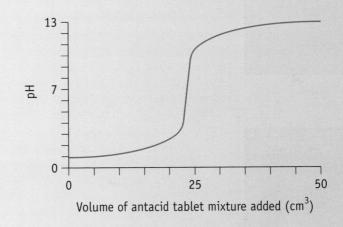

Variables that could have an effect are:

- type of antacid
- amount of antacid
- form the antacid comes in – powder or tablets?
- pH of 'stomach' acid
- amount of 'stomach' acid.

You could test your ideas by measuring, for example:

- how much antacid it takes to neutralise the 'stomach' acid
- how much 'stomach' acid is neutralised by a set mount of antacid
- the change in pH when a set amount of antacid is added to the 'stomach' acid.

Remember that to carry out a fair test you must make sure that you change only one variable. All the other variables need to be kept the same every time.

Reactions of acids

There are patterns to the way acids react with different chemicals.

The reactions on this page are all chemical reactions. New substances are made.

Acids can be 'corrosive', 'irritant' or 'harmful' depending on their concentration.

Reactions using acids can also produce dangerous products. You must follow safety rules carefully whenever you work with acids.

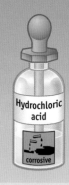

corrosive

harmful or irritant

use eye protection

An acid always reacts with a metal to produce a salt and hydrogen gas.

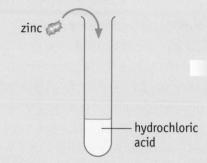

zinc

hydrochloric acid

An acid always reacts with a carbonate to produce a salt, water and carbon dioxide gas.

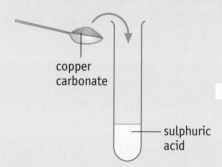

copper carbonate

sulphuric acid

An acid always reacts with an alkali to produce a salt and water. This is a neutralisation reaction. A solution of the product has a pH of 7.

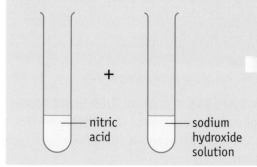

+

nitric acid

sodium hydroxide solution

Salts always have the same type of name. Their name is in two parts and the first part is the name of a metal.

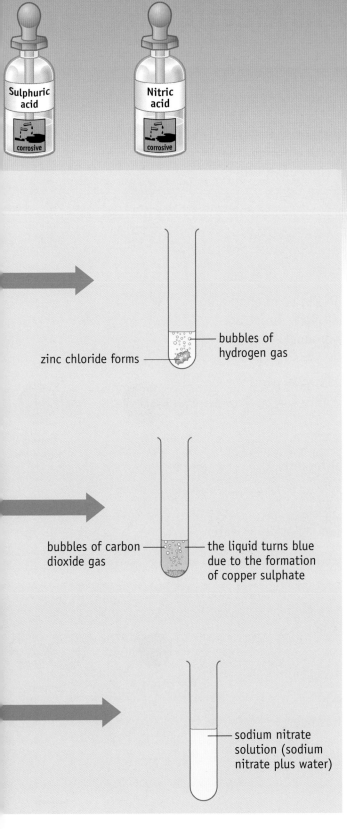

zinc chloride forms — bubbles of hydrogen gas

bubbles of carbon dioxide gas — the liquid turns blue due to the formation of copper sulphate

sodium nitrate solution (sodium nitrate plus water)

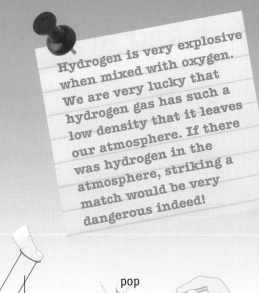

Hydrogen is very explosive when mixed with oxygen. We are very lucky that hydrogen gas has such a low density that it leaves our atmosphere. If there was hydrogen in the atmosphere, striking a match would be very dangerous indeed!

gas collects in test tube

pop

splint

Test the gas produced. A lighted spill makes hydrogen explode with a 'pop'.

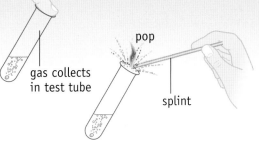

limewater

Test the gas produced. Carbon dioxide makes limewater turn milky.

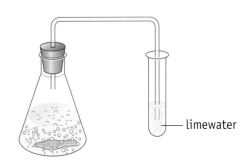

things to think about •

How would you collect the hydrogen produced in the reaction between an acid and a metal? How could you tell how much hydrogen was produced?

You can predict the name of the salt made in a neutralisation reaction if you know the names of the acid and alkali reactants:

nitric acid + **sodium** hydroxide ⟶ **sodium** nitrate + water

sulphuric acid + **calcium** hydroxide ⟶ **calcium** sulphate + water

121

Atoms and molecules in reactions

When chemical reactions take place, the atoms in the reactants become arranged differently to form the products.

When two elements react together to form a compound, atoms of the elements combine. For example when sodium reacts with chlorine, the sodium and chlorine atoms bond together to make a compound called sodium chloride.

sodium atom   chlorine atom

    sodium + chlorine ➞ sodium chloride

The mass has stayed the same.

In compounds, the atoms of the different elements in the compound are bonded together. During a reaction these bonds break. New bonds are formed to produce the compounds that make up the product.

A reaction takes place when hydrochloric acid is mixed with sodium hydroxide.

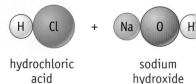

hydrochloric acid   sodium hydroxide

- The hydrochloric acid splits up into atoms.
- The sodium hydroxide splits up into atoms.
- The atoms in both compounds become arranged differently and form new bonds.
- Sodium chloride and water are formed as products.

    hydrochloric acid + sodium hydroxide ➞ sodium chloride + water

When a substance burns, it reacts with oxygen.

When carbon is burned the carbon and oxygen atoms bond together to make a carbon dioxide molecule.

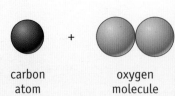

carbon atom   oxygen molecule

    carbon + oxygen ➞ carbon dioxide

The carbon dioxide molecule has the same mass as the carbon and oxygen atoms added together. Nothing has been gained or lost.

When copper is burned the copper and oxygen atoms bond together to make the compound copper oxide.

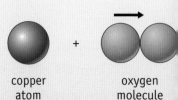

copper atom   oxygen molecule

    copper + oxygen ➞ copper oxide

The copper oxide produced has the same mass as the copper and oxygen atoms added together.

Fuels contain carbon and hydrogen.

- When fuels burn, carbon dioxide and water are formed.
- Carbon and oxygen atoms bond together to make carbon dioxide molecules.
- Hydrogen and oxygen atoms bond together to make water molecules.
- The atoms are just rearranged to form new substances.

sodium
chloride

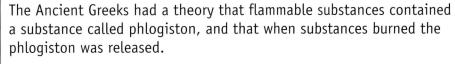

sodium
chloride

water

The Ancient Greeks had a theory that flammable substances contained a substance called phlogiston, and that when substances burned the phlogiston was released.

According to this theory, all substances should lose mass when they burn because they lose their phlogiston.

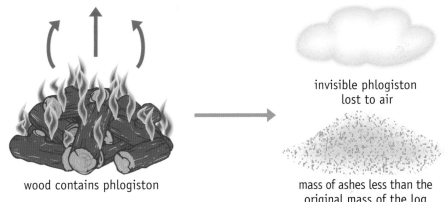

wood contains phlogiston

invisible phlogiston
lost to air

mass of ashes less than the
original mass of the log

Once scientists were able to weigh materials accurately they found that this theory didn't fit their results because most substances gain mass when they burn. This is due to the oxygen they react with when they burn.

So mass is conserved in combustion, you just have to weigh all the reactants and all the products.

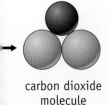

carbon dioxide
molecule

things to think about

Though oxygen is an element, it usually exists as a molecule with two oxygen atoms bonded together – O_2. When carbon reacts with oxygen, carbon dioxide is usually produced, but it is also possible to produce carbon monoxide. What is the formula for carbon monoxide? How many carbon atoms would have to react with an oxygen molecule to form carbon monoxide as the product?

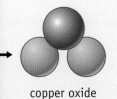

copper oxide

Energy transfer in chemical reactions

Some chemical reactions produce heat. This energy is transferred from the chemicals to the surroundings. This is an exothermic reaction.

The temperature in the reaction mixture usually rises.

Examples of exothermic reactions include:

- combustion
- explosions.

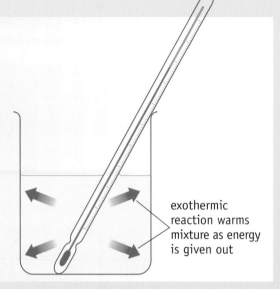

exothermic reaction warms mixture as energy is given out

Burning a fuel (combustion) is an exothermic reaction – heat is produced.

methane + oxygen ⟶ carbon dioxide + water + heat

Other exothermic reactions can be used as sources of energy. Self-heating coffee cans use the reaction between water and another chemical in a sealed pouch.

Advantages: There is no fuel, electricity or flame.

Disadvantage: The pack can only be used once.

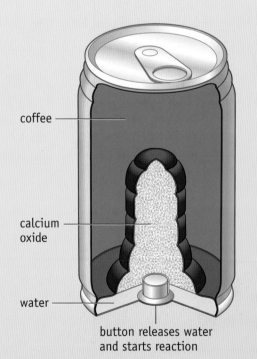

coffee

calcium oxide

water

button releases water and starts reaction

Energy is needed to break bonds between atoms in the reactants and to make new bonds between atoms in the products.

For example, when potassium reacts with water:

- the bonds between the hydrogen and oxygen atoms in the water molecule have to be broken
- new bonds have to be formed between the potassium, oxygen and hydrogen atoms.

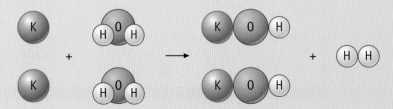

Some chemical reactions need energy for the reaction to take place. Energy – usually heat – is taken in from the surroundings. This is an endothermic reaction.

The temperature in the reaction mixture usually falls.

Examples of endothermic reactions include getting metals from their oxides.

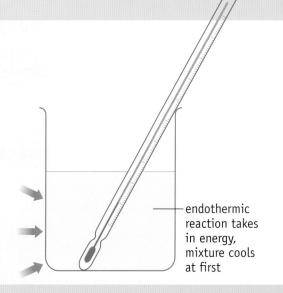

endothermic reaction takes in energy, mixture cools at first

When an energy transfer takes place, this is evidence that a chemical reaction has happened even if the reactants do not appear to change.

The energy transfer in or out is not always heat. Sound or light energy can be transferred in chemical reactions.

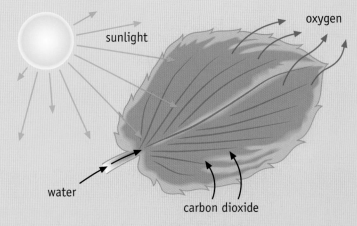

sunlight

oxygen

water

carbon dioxide

- Photosynthesis is a type of endothermic reaction that needs light energy, not heat, to be transferred to the reacting chemicals.
- Glow sticks produce light when the chemicals inside react together.

Fireworks exploding are an example of an exothermic reaction. The temperature of most fireworks is at least 1500 °C. Even sparklers have a temperature of about 2000 °C!

things to think about

Why are some reactions exothermic and some reactions endothermic, if they both involve breaking bonds and then making bonds?

Writing chemical equations

Reactions can be represented as word equations or equations with chemical symbols.

Both types of equations are useful because they let you see what is happening in a reaction.

Word equations are simpler to write than chemical equations, but scientists prefer equations using symbols.

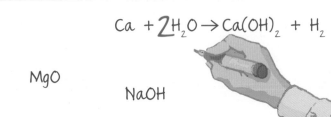

NaOH

H_2

MgO

O_2

Adding calcium to water

calcium + water $\longrightarrow$ calcium hydroxide + hydrogen

calcium hydroxide's formula is $Ca(OH)_2$ so...

$$Ca + 2H_2O \rightarrow Ca(OH)_2 + H_2$$

Here are some examples of word and chemical symbol equations for some common reactions.

MgO

NaOH

H_2

O_2

- Adding zinc to copper sulphate solution (displacement reaction):

  zinc + copper sulphate $\longrightarrow$ zinc sulphate + copper

  Zn + $CuSO_4$ $\longrightarrow$ $ZnSO_4$ + Cu

- Burning carbon in air (oxidation)

  carbon + oxygen $\longrightarrow$ carbon dioxide

  C + O_2 $\longrightarrow$ CO_2

- Adding hydrochloric acid to sodium hydroxide (neutralisaton)

  hydrochloric acid + sodium hydroxide $\longrightarrow$ sodium chloride + water

  HCl + $NaOH$ $\longrightarrow$ $NaCl$ + H_2O

When you use chemical symbols, the first letter of each symbol must be a capital – any others must be lower case (C, Ca, H, He).

Any numbers – like the '2' in CO_2 – must be written slightly below the letters. They are not written above, like in a 'squared' sign.

CO_2 ✓ CO^2 ✗

A bracket in a formula means that everything inside the bracket is multiplied by the number to the right of the bracket.

For example, the formula for calcium hydroxide is $Ca(OH)_2$. This shows that for every calcium atom in the compound there are two oxygen atoms and two hydrogen atoms.

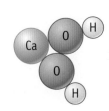

Scientists prefer to use chemical symbol equations because:

● they show you which types of atoms are in the reactants and products – using the symbols for elements
● they show you how many atoms of each element are in the reactants and the products – using the formula for compounds
● they let you predict exactly what products you will get from a reaction – by balancing the amounts of each atom
● they are the same in any language.

If you are given a chemical symbol equation you should be able to write the word equation.

Remember that all the atoms in the reactants must also appear in the products.

Balancing an equation means making sure you have the same number of each type of atom before and after the reaction has taken place. To make equations balance, numbers may have to be added in front of one or more formulae for the reactants and products.

In the reaction:

magnesium + oxygen ⟶ magnesium oxide

the formula for magnesium oxide is MgO and the formula for oxygen is O_2 so you could try replacing the words in the equation with symbols:

Mg + O_2 ⟶ MgO

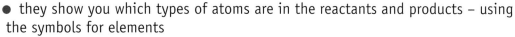

This equation is not balanced. There are two oxygen atoms on the left-hand side, but only one oxygen atom on the right-hand side.

The equation is balanced by adding a 2 in front of the MgO to balance the oxygen atoms, and a 2 in front of the Mg to balance the Mg atoms as there are now 2 atoms of Mg in the product:

2Mg + O_2 ⟶ 2MgO

Here is another example, adding sodium to water:

2Na + $2H_2O$ ⟶ 2NaOH + H_2

Some of the longest words in the English language are names of chemical compounds. For example the name of the compound which has the chemical formula $C_{1289}H_{2051}N_{343}O_{375}S_8$ is 1913 letters long!

Which would you rather put into a chemical equation – the word or the symbol?

Can you balance the equation for making iron oxide Fe_2O_3, from iron (Fe) and oxygen (O_2)? What would the particle diagram look like?

Reactivity series

Very reactive substances combine with others easily to form compounds – and can be difficult to extract from compounds.

By comparing how easily they react, scientists have produced an order of reactivity for metals. This is called the reactivity series.

Carbon and hydrogen are not metals. We include them in the reactivity series because they often behave like metals in chemical reactions.

most reactive

Potassium
Sodium
Calcium
Magnesium
Aluminium
(Carbon)
Zinc
Iron
Lead
(Hydrogen)
Copper
Silver
Gold

least reactive

- Silver and gold are not very reactive so they are good metals to make jewellery from. They doesn't react easily with sweat on your skin.

- Magnesium is reactive. It burns easily in air with a bright white light. This makes it good to use in distress flares.

- Very unreactive metals, like gold, can be dug out of the Earth as pure metals (elements). They do not form compounds easily.

- More reactive metals like calcium and aluminium are only found naturally as compounds in minerals.

Observing what happens when metals react with water helps place them in the reactivity series.

- Potassium reacts violently and bursts into flames as the hydrogen produced catches fire. You have to use a safety screen to view this reaction even when only a tiny piece of potassium is used.

- Magnesium produces bubbles of hydrogen very slowly – much more quickly if it is heated in steam.

- Copper does not react noticeably with water or steam.

When metals react with water, a metal hydroxide and hydrogen are formed. For example:

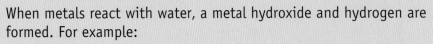

potassium + water $\rightarrow$ potassium hydroxide + hydrogen

$$2K + 2H_2O \rightarrow 2KOH + H_2$$

Observing what happens when metals react with oxygen in the air helps place them in the reactivity series.

- Sodium and potassium are shiny when freshly cut but immediately tarnish on exposure to air.

- Magnesium burns in air with a bright white flame – to protect your eyes it is sensible to look away after initially observing the flame. A dark glass filter may also be used.

- When copper is heated in air a dull grey coating of copper oxide forms on the surface.

When metals react with oxygen a metal oxide is formed. For example:

$$magnesium + oxygen \longrightarrow magnesium\ oxide$$

$$copper + oxygen \longrightarrow copper\ oxide$$

A reactive metal can displace a less reactive metal from a solution of a salt of that metal. So, if you add zinc to copper sulphate solution:

$$zinc + copper\ sulphate \longrightarrow zinc\ sulphate + copper$$

$$Zn + CuSO_4 \longrightarrow ZnSO_4 + Cu$$

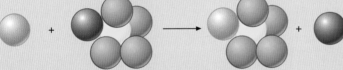

This type of reaction is called a displacement reaction. Zinc is more reactive than copper so it can displace copper from a solution of a copper salt.

A copper coin in silver nitrate solution displaces the silver

A metal cannot displace another metal that is more reactive. For example:

$$copper + zinc\ sulphate \longrightarrow copper + zinc\ sulphate\ \text{no reaction happens!}$$

Nothing happens because the copper is not reactive enough to displace the zinc from a solution of zinc sulphate.

You should be able to make predictions about whether a displacement reaction will occur, based on each metal's position in the reactivity series.

Even though aluminium is quite reactive it is often used in metal window frames. When aluminium is in contact with the air, a coating of white aluminium oxide quickly forms. This oxide creates a protective layer over the aluminium and prevents any further reactions from taking place ... so the window frame doesn't corrode away.

things to think about •
You have been asked to find out whether an unknown metal is silver or magnesium.
You have some iron sulphate solution available. How could you use the iron sulphate to identify the unknown metal?

Patterns in reactions with acids

Reactions follow patterns. If we understand these patterns we can predict what will happen when we react substances together.

This helps chemists decide which reactants are needed to make a chosen product.

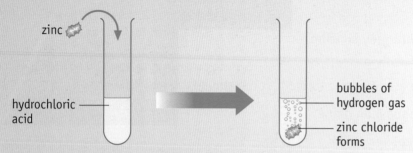

● When a **metal** reacts with an **acid**:

metal + acid ➝ salt + hydrogen

For example:

magnesium + hydrochloric acid ➝ magnesium chloride + hydrogen

$$Mg \quad + \quad 2HCl \quad ➝ \quad MgCl_2 \quad + \quad H_2$$

magnesium + sulphuric acid ➝ magnesium sulphate + hydrogen

$$Mg \quad + \quad H_2SO_4 \quad ➝ \quad MgSO_4 \quad + \quad H_2$$

You can test the gas is hydrogen by using a lighted splint.

Based on this pattern you should be able to write a word equation to predict the products of the reaction between other metals and acids.

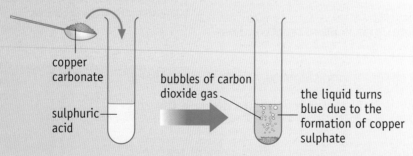

● When a **carbonate** reacts with an **acid**:

carbonate + acid ➝ salt + water + carbon dioxide

For example:

copper carbonate + sulphuric acid ➝ copper sulphate + water + carbon dioxide

$$CuCO_3 \quad + \quad H_2SO_4 \quad ➝ \quad CuSO_4 \quad + \quad H_2O \quad + \quad CO_2$$

You can test whether the gas is carbon dioxide using limewater.

Based on this pattern you should be able to write a word equation to predict the products of the reaction between acids and other carbonate compounds.

Caesium is the most reactive metal scientists have worked with. It explodes when it reacts with water due to the heat produced and rapid generation of hydrogen gas. Francium would be even more reactive than caesium, but it's so rare that no one has ever got enough together to try reacting it with water or acid. There is less than 30 g of francium present in the Earth's crust at any one time.

things to think about

What are the products when magnesium carbonate reacts with hydrochloric acid? Can you think of two chemicals which could be reacted together to produce magnesium sulphate?

We can use the fact that hydrogen gas is produced when a metal reacts with an acid to compare the reactivity of different metals. You could:

● measure the amount of hydrogen produced in a given time
● time how long it takes to produce a given amount of hydrogen.

Also, because the reaction is exothermic, you could compare reactivity by comparing the temperature rise in different reactions.

These methods will only produce a valid comparison if the only variable that is changed is the metal used.

The reactivity series found when metals react with acids is the same as the order of reactivity when metals react with water.

things to think about

Why might it be difficult to make sure your experiment was valid if you used a zinc-coated (galvanised) nail, compared with a piece of magnesium ribbon?

Properties of materials

A material is a substance out of which things are made. We can use their properties to classify materials into different groups. For example:

- solids, liquids and gases
- elements, compounds or mixtures
- metals and non-metals.

We can also classify materials depending on whether they are natural or synthetic (manufactured).

Examples:

Name	Solid, liquid or gas	Element, compound or mixture	Metal or non-metal	Natural or synthetic
iron	solid	element	metal	natural
crude oil	liquid	mixture	non-metal	natural
helium	gas	element	non-metal	natural
steel	solid	mixture (alloy)	metal	synthetic
wood	solid	mixture (composite)	non-metal	natural
glass	solid	compound	non-metal	synthetic
quartz	solid	compound	non-metal	natural

Properties that can make materials useful include:

- elasticity
- absorbency
- flammability
- reactivity with water and other chemicals.

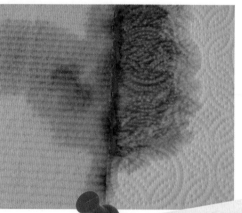

jewellry

cookware

electric wiring

We choose materials for particular uses because of their properties. There would be no point making a frying pan out of something with a low melting point – the pan would melt when you put it on the hob!

Databases of materials can hold a large amount of information, and can be searched to find materials matching certain properties.

Spider silk (silk thread made by spiders) is incredibly strong yet very light. It can be made into bullet-proof clothing, seat belts, vehicle panels and artificial tendons or ligaments.
Spider silk has the advantages compared with metals and kevlar of being a renewable and biodegradable product which is produced in a non-polluting way.

Most metals have similar properties:

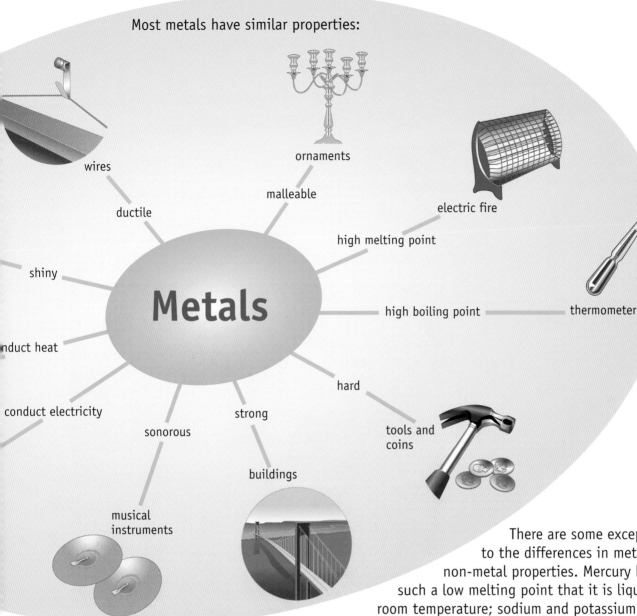

wires
ductile
ornaments
malleable
electric fire
shiny
high melting point
Metals
high boiling point
thermometer
conduct heat
hard
conduct electricity
strong
tools and coins
sonorous
buildings
musical instruments

Many of the properties of metals are special ones that most non-metals do not have. Only metals:

- are easy to shape (malleable), such as when hit with a hammer. Non-metals often break or shatter when hammered.
- can be pulled into thin strands like wires (ductile)
- are sonorous (make a ringing sound when you hit them)
- conduct electricity and heat well.

The only magnetic materials are the metals iron (and steel), cobalt and nickel.

All these properties make metals useful.

There are some exceptions to the differences in metal and non-metal properties. Mercury has such a low melting point that it is liquid at room temperature; sodium and potassium are soft enough to cut with a knife; and lead is not very shiny.

Carbon isn't a metal but in the form of graphite it is quite a good electrical conductor (called a semiconductor). Other semiconductors include silicon (a non-metal) and germanium (a metal).

Many non-metals have some of the same properties as metals. For example, diamond, another form of carbon, is very hard.

things to think about

Which other metals don't have all the usual metal properties? Are there any non-metals that have several of the usual metal properties?

133

Making new materials

Scientists use their knowledge of chemistry to make new materials. They can produce materials with particular properties suitable for a specific job – with a specific technical purpose.

Specialists – such as metallurgists, polymer scientists or chemical engineers – work closely with designers, physicists, engineers or doctors to develop a new material.

New materials are made by:

- chemical reactions – making new compounds
- mixing two or more materials – making composite materials.

Examples of materials made from chemical reactions include:

- plastics (made from crude oil)
- synthetic fibres such as Lycra® and nylon
- medicines (pharmaceuticals)
- pesticides and fertilisers
- detergents.

Mixing two or more materials can produce composite materials (such as concrete and this carbon fibre-reinforced ceramic) and alloys (such as steel and solder).

Alloys are mixtures of metals. The aerospace and car industries need alloys that are very strong yet lightweight – for example, aluminium alloys.

Tiles used on the Space Shuttle had to be strong, smooth, light and able to resist very high temperatures. A new type of ceramic compound was designed and produced.

When space travel was first developed scientists had to develop materials that could withstand the stresses, strains and high temperatures involved. This led to the development of many new materials. One of these was Teflon® – now used as a non-stick coating for cookware.

Thermochromic pigments change colour depending on their temperature and photochromic pigments are sensitive to ultraviolet light – clothing coloured with these can have interesting effects! Kettles that change colour as the water inside gets hotter are made from compounds containing thermochromic pigments.

Sometimes the new material does the same job as the material it replaces, but has an advantage such as:

● being less toxic to the environment
● using less energy in manufacture
● using a renewable resource.

Many new materials are made from crude oil. The world's supply of crude oil is limited and will run out before long. The more oil we use to make new materials the faster it will run out and the less we will have for other uses.

Instead of using crude oil, renewable biological sources can be used to make bioplastics. Polylactide is made from sugar cane and can be used in packaging and disposable nappies. It is biodegradable – polymers made from crude oil are not.

Making any new material is likely to use large amounts of energy. This energy will probably be provided by power stations that burn fossil fuels. This will add to the greenhouse effect.

The adhesive used in Post-it® notes was created in 1970 when chemists were trying to make a new, strong adhesive. Instead they made a very weak adhesive that had no use. Four years later, one of the scientists involved needed a marker to keep his place in a hymnbook. He tried putting a little of the new adhesive on a piece of paper – and the Post-it note idea was formed!

things to think about

Can you think of one other use for each of the new materials mentioned on this page and explain why they are suitable for that use?

Manufacturing with chemicals

To manufacture new chemical compounds or to separate compounds we need to carry out chemical reactions. If the chemical we are manufacturing is to be used for pharmaceuticals or food, then it must be pure.

The main types of chemical reactions and examples of their uses are:

- oxidation – burning fuels to release energy
- reduction – extracting metals from their ores
- decomposition – getting calcium oxide (used in cement) from limestone
- neutralisation – to produce soluble aspirin (aspirin is derived from salicylic acid)
- displacement – getting metals from salts.

Oxidation

Oxygen is gained when a substance is reacted with oxygen to form a new product – an oxide.

Combustion is an example of oxidation.

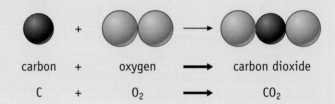

$$C \quad + \quad O_2 \quad \longrightarrow \quad CO_2$$

Reduction

Oxygen is lost in reduction. This is usually because it has been taken away by another chemical.

In this example, magnesium oxide has been reduced.

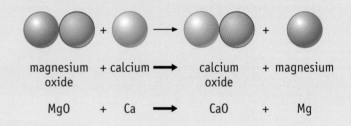

$$MgO \quad + \quad Ca \quad \longrightarrow \quad CaO \quad + \quad Mg$$

Decomposition

This is when a compound is split into two or more simpler substances. There are two main types of decomposition reactions.

- Thermal decomposition uses heat to separate the compound.
- Electrolysis uses electricity to separate the compound.

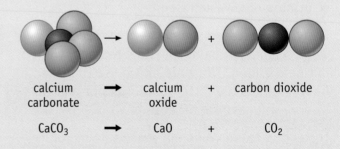

$$CaCO_3 \quad \longrightarrow \quad CaO \quad + \quad CO_2$$

Electrolysis is only used for separating salts or decomposing water into hydrogen and oxygen. It works because salts and water are made up of ions which are positively or negatively charged. The material you are decomposing must be in the liquid state so the particles can move.

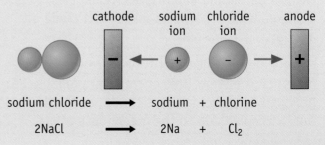

$$2NaCl \quad \longrightarrow \quad 2Na \quad + \quad Cl_2$$

Neutralisation

An acid and an alkali neutralise each other.

acid + alkali ⟶ salt + water

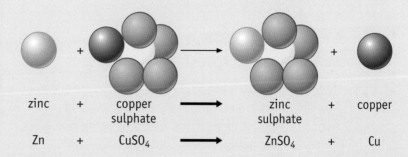

hydrochloric + sodium ⟶ sodium + water
acid   hydroxide   chloride

HCl + NaOH ⟶ NaCl + H$_2$O

Displacement

This is where the metal part of a compound takes the place of the metal part of a different compound. Metals will only displace less reactive metals.

zinc + copper ⟶ zinc + copper
       sulphate   sulphate

Zn + CuSO$_4$ ⟶ ZnSO$_4$ + Cu

Remember, in any type of reaction the total mass of the products will be the same as the total mass of the reactants. In a chemical reaction atoms are not created or destroyed – just rearranged.

Other types of reactions include 'redox' and polymerisation.

Redox is short for reduction–oxidation. In many reactions both reduction and oxidation take place at the same time. One substance loses oxygen and the other one gains it. A good example of a redox reaction is when iron ore (iron oxide) is heated with carbon in a blast furnace to make iron.

iron oxide + carbon ⟶ carbon dioxide + iron

The iron is reduced (loses oxygen) and the carbon is oxidised (gains oxygen).

Polymerisation reactions are used to make most plastics. Molecules in the shape of long chains are joined together to make even longer chain molecules to make a polymer such as PVC – poly(vinyl chloride).

Light sticks that glow in the dark have a small glass container, holding one chemical solution, placed inside a bigger plastic container, holding a different solution. When you bend the tube, the glass container breaks, the two solutions meet and react together. The product of the reaction emits light.

things to think about •

If two materials are reacted together in a redox reaction, how could you tell which one has gained oxygen and which one has lost oxygen?

In some polymers, the molecule chains are cross-linked. How could this affect their properties?

137

Earth science

Earth science is concerned with the processes involved in forming the Earth as it is now.

Studying rocks tells us how the Earth was formed, how the Earth has changed over millions of years and how and where volcanoes erupted.

We can use our knowledge of rocks to predict events such as earthquakes.

Studying fossils helps us learn about plants and animals that lived at different times, and how the climate has changed over millions of years. This helps us work out how and why living things evolved and changed over time.

Rocks are made from particles (grains) held together. Different types of rocks are formed from different particles or from particles held together in different ways. The grains can be interlocking (crystals that fill all the space) as in the top picture or non-interlocking (rounded grains that leave gaps) shown in the lower picture. This gives the rocks different properties.

Properties of rocks include:

- hardness
- porosity
- reaction with acids and other chemicals
- colour
- density.

Porous rocks absorb water. Non-porous (impervious) rocks do not.

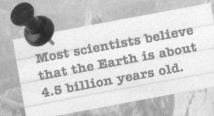

Most scientists believe that the Earth is about 4.5 billion years old.

What affects the properties of a rock?

Property	What it depends on
Hardness	<ul><li>the type of particles</li><li>how closely they are packed or stuck together</li><li>how the rock was formed</li></ul>
Porosity	<ul><li>how closely the particles are packed</li><li>whether the grains are held together (cemented) or are interlocking crystals</li></ul>
Reaction with acids and other chemicals	<ul><li>the elements and compounds (minerals) the rock is made from</li></ul>
Colour	<ul><li>mainly on the type of minerals the rock contains</li></ul>
Density	<ul><li>the types of particles</li><li>how closely they are packed</li></ul>

Rocks are resources. The main uses of rocks are:

- building materials
- sculptures and ornaments.

Porous rocks collect rainwater underground. This can be extracted and used for drinking water.

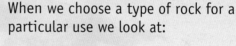

When we choose a type of rock for a particular use we look at:

- its properties
- how easily available it is
- its cost.

Marble and granite are useful rocks because they are hard, strong, non-porous and very attractive to look at.

Minerals are also resources. Minerals are extracted from rocks.

- Quartz (silicon dioxide) is found in granite and used both in industry and for decoration.
- Metal ores (rocks or minerals from which a metal can be extracted) are processed to obtain important materials. For example, aluminium and iron are used for construction and copper is used for electrical wiring.

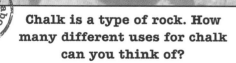

things to think about

Chalk is a type of rock. How many different uses for chalk can you think of?

Weathering of rocks

Weathering is when rocks are broken down due to physical, chemical or biological processes. This can slowly change the appearance of the landscape, or of buildings made from rock or brick.

PHYSICAL

Physical weathering is caused by forces that break rocks to smaller pieces. Most physical weathering is caused by changes of temperature.

Freeze–thaw weathering happens when water gets into cracks in rocks. When water freezes it expands. The large forces caused by expansion push the rock apart, making the crack widen and causing bits of rock to break off.

CHEMICAL

Chemical weathering happens when chemicals in the rain or in the soil react with the rock and change its chemical composition.

Rain is naturally acidic because of carbon dioxide in the air. Pollution can cause rain to be even more acidic. When rain falls on rocks, this acid can react with the rocks. Rocks that are made from carbonates (such as limestone, chalk or marble) react with even dilute acid.

In desert areas, heating by the sun in the daytime causes the rock surface to expand. At night, when it is colder, the rock contracts. Expansion and contraction of the rock's surface weakens it and causes it to flake off.

calcium   +   carbonic acid   ➡   calcium
carbonate   hydrogencarbonate

   (solid)   (rainwater)   (solution)

   $CaCO_3$ H_2CO_3 $Ca(HCO_3)_2$

The rock slowly reacts and the products of the reaction are carried away as a solution.

Chemicals secreted by bacteria can also affect rocks chemically. These bacteria live in soil or in pore spaces in the rock.

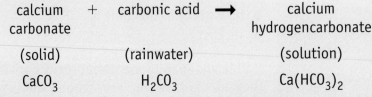
Microbes living inside rocks are called endoliths. Until recently scientists thought these microbes only lived near the Earth's surface. New discoveries show endoliths can exist several kilometres deep. Here, they might reproduce only once every 100 years.

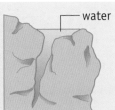

(a) Water can fill cracks in the rock.

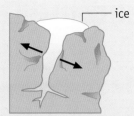

(b) The water expands when it freezes.

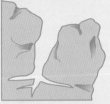

(c) The force of the ice expanding makes the crack bigger.

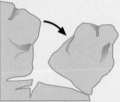

(d) Eventually the crack gets so big that part of the rock breaks off.

BIOLOGICAL

Biological weathering is weathering caused by living things. The processes can be either chemical or physical. Examples include:

- Rocks being worn away by people walking on them.
- Tree roots growing in fractures in rocks and breaking them apart
- Animals burrowing under rocks and weakening them so they break up easily.
- Lichen growing on rock or bacteria in soil.

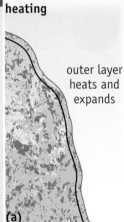

heating

outer layer heats and expands

(a)

cooling

cracks form as rock cools

(b)

heating

gradually the repeated heating and cooling turns the outer surface into flakes

(c)

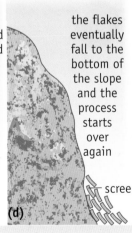

the flakes eventually fall to the bottom of the slope and the process starts over again

scree

(d)

How might looking at rock samples brought back from Mars give us information about the possibility of life on Mars?

Earth science

141

Erosion and sedimentation

Erosion is the removal and transportation of rocks. Transportation means moving the pieces of rock from their original site to somewhere else. Rock pieces are usually transported by:

● gravity
● wind
● water
● moving glaciers.

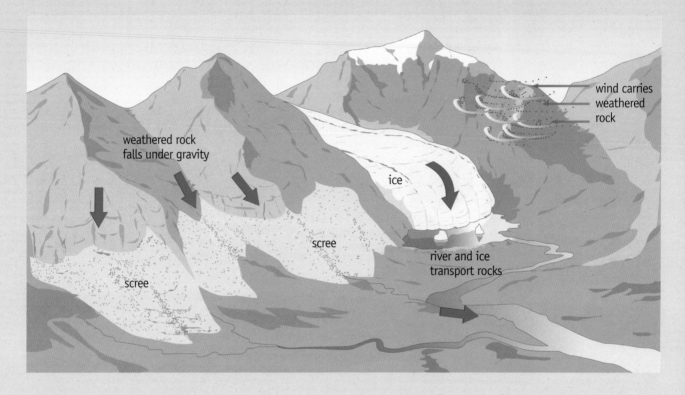

As the rock pieces are moved they become smoother – because of friction with other pieces of rock. This is how sand and mud particles form. The further the rock fragments are transported, the more rounded the pebbles or grains become.

angular rock pieces → rock fragments rub together as they are transported → sharp edges are rubbed off and the fragments become smaller

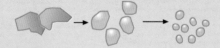

The size of the grains (texture) in sedimentary rocks provides evidence for the environment at the time the sediment was deposited. The larger the grains, the more energetic the environment – for example fast-moving water (waves and currents) or wind moving sand dunes. Smaller grains settled out in low-energy conditions – slower-moving or still water.

Soil forms when the broken down remains of rocks interact with plant and animal life. Tiny animals keep soil aerated. Bacteria and fungi turn dead plants into organic matter.

Sedimentation happens when the eroded rock is deposited in its final position.

Later, a second layer is deposited on top of the first. Even later a third layer is deposited ... and so on. The build-up of thick layers takes place slowly over millions of years.

As each new layer of sand, mud or carbonate is formed, it presses down on the layers below it, compressing them. Compression makes the layers denser and less porous – the particles also become cemented. The sediment is now a sedimentary rock.

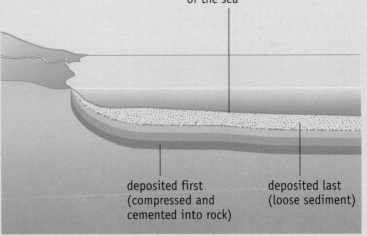

rock fragments or biological remains settle at the bottom of the sea

deposited first (compressed and cemented into rock)

deposited last (loose sediment)

Fossils are found in sedimentary rocks. The types of plant and animal fossils found in a rock tell us about conditions such as climate at the time when the rock was formed.

The composition (minerals present) of sedimentary rocks tells you about the source material.

● Carbonate sediments and their fossils are evidence for a warm shallow sea environment at the time and place the rock formed.
● Non-carbonate sediments must have been eroded from source rocks such as granite or sedimentary rock.

Limestone, chalk and other carbonate rocks are formed by biological processes over millions of years.

● Animals, plankton and plants live in warm shallow seas.
● When they die, the animal skeletons, plankton and plants fall to the sea floor.
● These remains form sediments.

Evaporite rocks such as gypsum are formed as dissolved solids left behind when the solvent evaporated. Most are formed in areas which were once sea bed. The solids dissolved in sea water remained behind when it evaporated. This is evidence for evaporation of part of the ocean over a long period of hot conditions.

things to think about

It is common to find rocks containing fossilised large ferns. What do you think the climate was like at the time that these fossils were formed? How can fossils found in different layers of sedimentary rock tell us about how living things have evolved over time?

The fossilised remains of dinosaurs can be found in rocks in some parts of Britain. The first ever dinosaur fossil was found in England in 1674. It was probably a thigh bone from a Megalosaurus – but its discoverer identified it as the thigh bone of a human giant.

Volcanoes and igneous rocks

Molten rock beneath the Earth's surface is called magma. Magma forms in areas where the Earth's crust is so hot that the rock is given enough energy for it to partially melt. When magma rises upwards through a crack or volcano to reach the surface it is called lava. When magma or lava cools it forms igneous rocks.

When underground gases in magma have built up a high pressure, volcanic eruptions can be explosive.

- Tonnes of ash are thrown out into the air. In time, layers of ash can form new sedimentary rock.
- Sometimes lava can contain trapped gas bubbles. This is how pumice stone is made.

Pumice stone has such a low density that it can usually float on water. Huge 'pumice rafts' like this one are occasionally found floating on the ocean surface after volcanic island eruptions.

The igneous rock formed when magma or lava cools is crystalline. The rock texture (size of the crystals) depends on how quickly the lava cooled down.

- slow cooling $\longrightarrow$ large crystals
- fast cooling $\longrightarrow$ small crystals

Magma trapped below the surface is insulated by the rocks above it so loses heat slowly. Lava at the surface cools quickly. Studying the crystals in igneous rock tells us about the environment in which the rock was formed.

ash and particles of solidified lava

cooled lava (igneous rock)

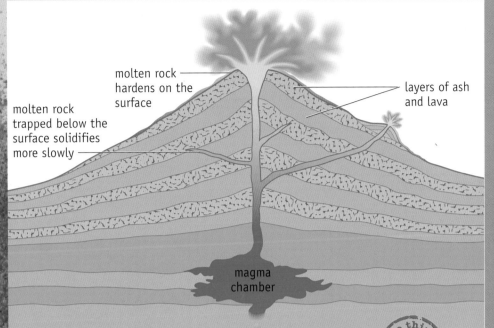

molten rock hardens on the surface

molten rock trapped below the surface solidifies more slowly

layers of ash and lava

magma chamber

rising magma

lava

Every time a volcano erupts, another layer of igneous rock is formed on top of earlier layers. Layers of solidified volcanic ash can also build up – these are sedimentary rock. These layers could be formed hundreds or thousands of years apart – depending on how frequently the volcano erupts.

things to think about

Lava is sometimes thixotropic – it flows more easily when it is agitated (stirred or shaken). Do you know any other thixotropic materials?

Volcanoes affect people's lives. When volcanic eruptions happen very quickly, they can be hazardous as people are not prepared.

- Lava kills living things and can destroy buildings in its path.
- Ash produced can pollute the atmosphere for hundreds of miles and make it very difficult for people nearby to breathe.

Also, in the longer term:

- Volcanic ash can help make soil more fertile.
- Sulphur dioxide emitted produces acid rain.
- Carbon dioxide emitted adds to the greenhouse effect.

As geologists learn more about volcanoes they can provide risk maps, alert people and help more effectively when a volcano erupts.

When Vesuvius erupted in 79AD the towns of Pompeii and Herculaneum were devastated and thousands of people died. There were warning signs that an eruption was going to happen but no one understood what the signs meant or knew what they needed to do when the eruption happened.

The rock cycle

The rock cycle explains how rocks are produced and change over time.

Some parts can happen very fast – such as when a volcano erupts.

Rocks can take millions of years to form and reform.

Melting, metamorphism and extreme heat and pressure do not happen all the time – only at certain times and in certain places. The rock cycle is not continuous.

The melting that produces igneous rocks and the heat and pressure that produce metamorphic rocks are caused by:

- radioactive decay (which is the source of the heat in the Earth)
- slow movement of a number of very large plates on the Earth's surface.

The erosion that causes sediment to move is mainly driven by the Sun through winds and rain. Gravity also makes rock pieces move downwards and creates the pressure that compresses sediments into new rock.

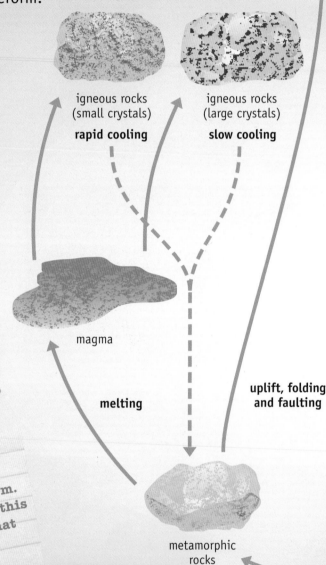

uplift, folding and faulting

rocks at the Earth's surface

igneous rocks (small crystals)

rapid cooling

igneous rocks (large crystals)

slow cooling

magma

melting

uplift, folding and faulting

metamorphic rocks

metamorphism

In 1963, an Icelandic fisherman saw smoke rising from the sea. Within a day, a new volcanic island, Surtsey, had started to form. Islands like Surtsey, seen from the air in this picture, are formed from recycled crust that has melted to form magma. The whole of Iceland formed like this!

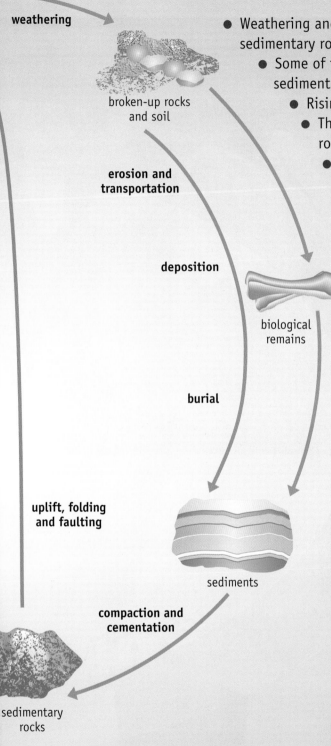

weathering

broken-up rocks
and soil

**erosion and
transportation**

deposition

biological
remains

burial

**uplift, folding
and faulting**

**compaction and
cementation**

sediments

sedimentary
rocks

- Weathering and erosion of rocks produces sediments that form sedimentary rocks.
  - Some of these are gradually eroded to form new sedimentary rocks.
    - Rising magma causes igneous rocks to form.
      - These are eroded over time to form new sedimentary rocks.
        - Sedimentary or igneous rocks can be changed into metamorphic rocks by very high heat or pressure.
          - These are eroded over time to form new sedimentary rocks.

things to think about •

**Why is the rock cycle called
a cycle?**

When sedimentary rocks are changed into metamorphic rocks they:

- become less porous
- become harder – the particles recrystallise.

Very high heat or pressure turns limestone into marble.

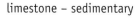
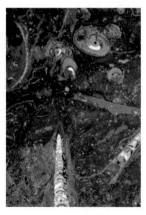

limestone – sedimentary   marble – metamorphic

Metamorphism and melting happen when rocks are heated to very high temperatures and/or when they are under very high pressures. The temperatures and pressures needed to melt rocks are greater than those needed for metamorphism.

Travelling sound

These musicians are all producing sound. To produce sound you need to make something vibrate. There are many ways you can do this – these musicians are using their hands or sticks to hit the drums and the xylophone. The people behind them can hear the music because the sound travels through the air to their ears.

The object that produces the sound is called a sound source. An object that detects the sound (such as a microphone) is called a receiver. A microphone converts sound vibrations into an electrical signal. You can then study the sound by displaying the electrical signals on an oscilloscope.

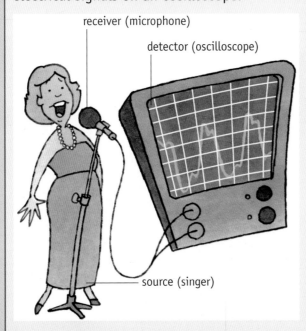

receiver (microphone)

detector (oscilloscope)

source (singer)

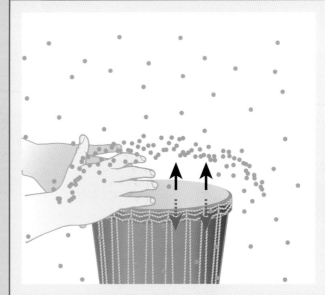

When an object vibrates it collides with the particles in the medium surrounding it. In this case the particles are air molecules. Sound can travel through solids, liquids and gases.

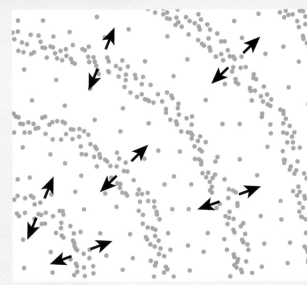

You can think of sound as a transfer of energy. A vibrating sound source transfers energy to the air as sound. The vibrating air transfers energy to your eardrum. Since the sound energy spreads out, the sound is quieter the further away you are from the source.

For a sound to be heard a long way away, the source must be very loud. Howler monkeys are so loud that they can be heard up to a distance of 5 km. Some whales do even better. They can be heard up to 1800 km away! These whales are extremely loud and also sound travels much better in water than it does in air.

The loudest shout ever recorded was by Annalisa Wray – nearly 122 dB. This is as loud as if you were standing near to a jet engine…

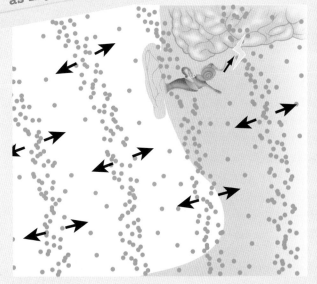

The particles in the medium then collide with each other. So the vibrations (not the particles themselves) travel outwards from the sound source.

We can hear the sound because the vibrating particles collide with our eardrums. This makes our eardrums vibrate. Our ears convert these vibrations into electrical signals which can be interpreted by the brain.

Travelling light

Lasers are sources of very bright light. Since light travels in straight lines, a narrow laser beam can travel vast distances without spreading out very much. This is very useful in creating spectacular laser light displays. If somebody stood inside the laser display the laser light wouldn't bend round them. They would block out the light and form a shadow.

Light travels about a million times faster than sound. It would take a light beam about 0.003 s to travel the length of the UK.

When you look at the night sky you can see objects that are sources of light and also objects that aren't. The planets and the Moon are not sources of light. They reflect light from the Sun. However stars are sources of light. They shine just like the Sun (which is also a star) although they are much further away than the Sun. Other common sources of light are light bulbs and television screens.

When light travels from a source to a receiver it transfers energy. The receiver transforms the light energy into other forms. Examples of receivers are your eyes, photographic film and solar cells used to make electricity.

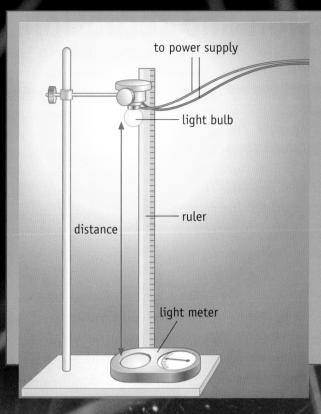

to power supply

light bulb

distance

ruler

light meter

Here is an experiment to investigate whether the intensity (brightness) of the light varies with distance. You can change the distance by moving the light bulb up and down. A light meter measures the intensity.

To make it a fair test you need to make sure that no other variable affects the intensity apart from the distance. You should carry out the experiment in a dark room so that there are no other light sources.

A graph of the results shows that as the distance increases, the light intensity decreases.

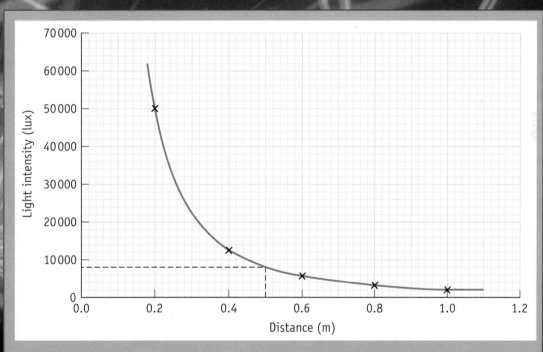

The reason that you plot a line graph is that distance is a continuous variable. Continuous variables can, in theory, have any value within the range.

Line graphs are useful because you can interpolate from them. This means you can find values even if you haven't measured them. For example, the graph shows you that the light intensity is 8000 lux at a distance of 0.5 m, although this is not at one of the data points.

Sound transmission and reception

There are many things going on when you are talking to someone on the telephone. First of all you need to produce the sound of your voice. You do this by making your vocal cords vibrate. The telephone needs to produce sound as well. The part of the phone that vibrates is the loudspeaker. The loudspeaker responds to electrical signals from the telephone line and vibrates to produce the sound that you hear.

When you hear sound, your ear converts the vibrations of the air particles into electrical signals. The telephone needs to convert sound into electrical signals as well. This happens inside the microphone. Electrical signals from the microphone pass down the telephone line.

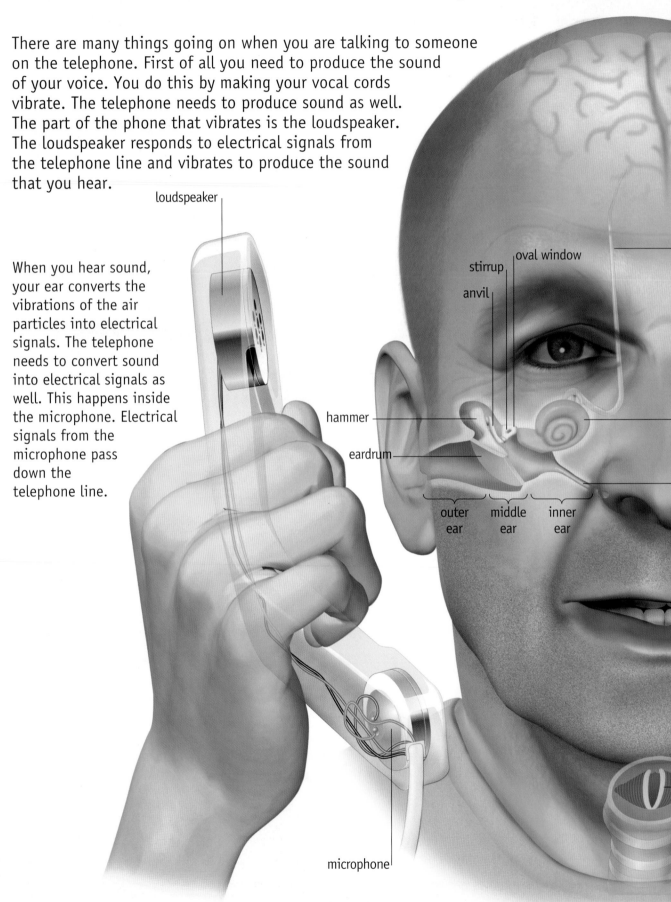

loudspeaker

stirrup
oval window
anvil

hammer

eardrum

outer ear
middle ear
inner ear

microphone

Your outer ear channels sound energy towards your eardrum. Sound energy is transmitted by vibrations in the air. The vibrating particles of air collide with your eardrum and they make it vibrate as well.

Your eardrum is connected to three little bones called the hammer, anvil and stirrup. These bones act like levers and they make the vibrations bigger. The vibrating stirrup is connected to another membrane (like the eardrum) called the oval window.

The vibrations then pass into a fluid which fills an organ called the cochlea. Nerves in the cochlea convert the vibrations into electrical signals. These signals travel to the brain along the auditory nerve. The brain processes the signals and we hear the sound.

y nerve

— cochlea

— eustachian tube

— vocal cords

Sound needs a substance to travel through (a medium). From the loudspeaker to your ear, sound travels through the air. It also travels through the air from your vocal cords to the microphone. Particles in the air vibrate and pass these vibrations on to other particles. If there is a vacuum then you can't hear any sound. There aren't any particles in a vacuum.

You can show this by pumping the air out of a bell jar which has a ringing alarm clock inside. Light can travel through a vacuum, so you can see the clock ringing when you can no longer hear it.

things to think about •

What would life be like if you could hear the Sun instead of just seeing it?

Astronauts on the Moon need to use radios to talk to each other – even if they are close together. There is no air to transmit sound.

Sound waves

Sound travels through a medium due to the vibrations of the medium's particles. The particles move backwards and forwards as the sound energy travels from the source to the receiver. This motion produces a sound wave.

Sound waves are a series of compressions (where the particles are closer together than usual) moving through the medium. You can see a similar wave moving through a slinky spring if you hold one end of the spring and shake it backwards and forwards.

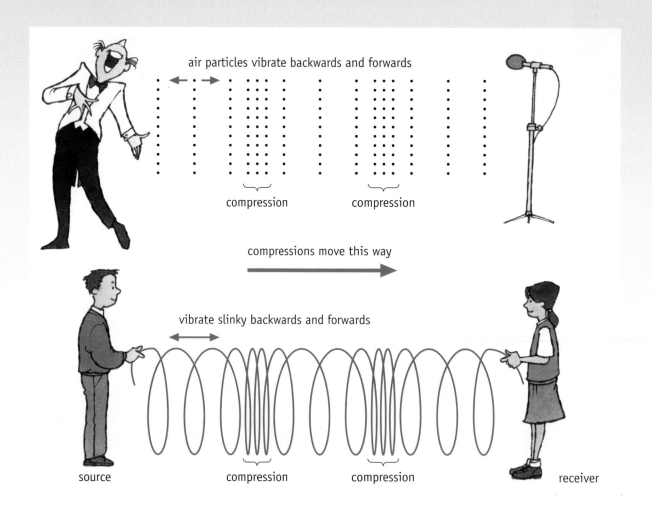

air particles vibrate backwards and forwards

compression compression

compressions move this way

vibrate slinky backwards and forwards

source compression compression receiver

The frequency of sound is equal to the number of sound waves (or vibrations) per second. Frequency is measured in hertz (Hz). So if you sing a note at 200 Hz, you are producing sound waves (and your vocal cords are vibrating) 200 times every second. The frequency of the sound determines its pitch. As you pluck the strings of a harp, from the long strings up to the short strings, the musical notes sound at a higher and higher pitch. The frequency increases from about 50 Hz to 3000 Hz.

Another property of a sound wave is its amplitude. This is related to the size of the vibrations. If you hit a drum very hard more energy is transferred and the amplitude of the sound waves is bigger than if you hit a drum softly. The greater the amplitude, the louder the sound.

If the sound is very loud, the amplitude of the vibrations becomes so large that it can damage your ears. This can cause permanent hearing loss at certain frequencies and other problems such as tinnitus (permanent ringing in the ears).

People who work in noisy environments need to wear ear protectors to reduce the risk of these problems.

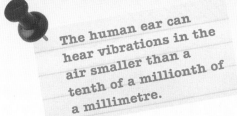

The human ear can hear vibrations in the air smaller than a tenth of a millionth of a millimetre.

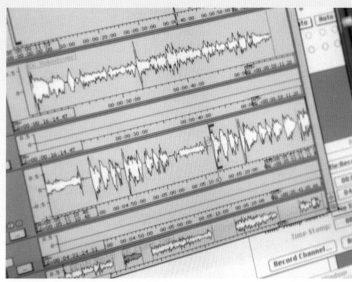

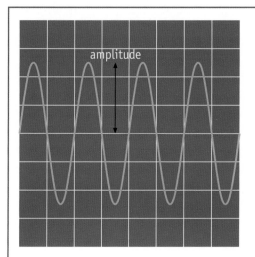

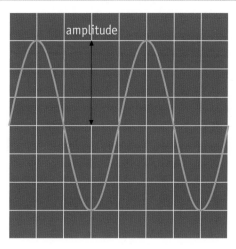

You can study sound waves on an oscilloscope or by using a computer. The screen displays the electrical signals from a microphone that receives the sound. The trace on the screen can show both the frequency and the amplitude of the sound.

The screen on the left shows the oscilloscope trace for a high note. There are four waves produced in the time shown on the screen. The second screen is for a low note. There are only two sound waves produced in the same time, so it is a lower frequency. This is also a louder note – it has a bigger amplitude.

Light reflection and refraction

Light travels in straight lines away from the source. It is often useful to think of a light ray as a very narrow beam of light. A ray diagram with arrows shows the path of light rays from a source to an object, and what happens after they touch the object.

When a light ray hits the surface of a mirror it bounces off again at the same angle. We call this reflection.

We measure the angle between each ray of light and a normal line. This is a line at right angles to the mirror's surface. The ray approaching the mirror is called the incident ray and the ray leaving the mirror is called the reflected ray. The angle of incidence is always equal to the angle of reflection.

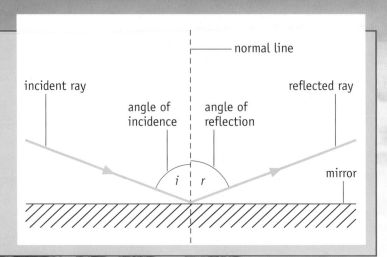

Shiny surfaces and white surfaces reflect nearly all the light that falls on them. So why do you see an image in the pond but not in the snow?

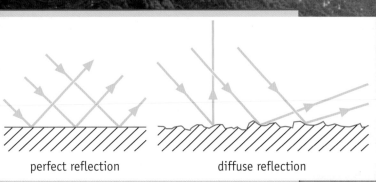

The reason is that shiny surfaces are very smooth. They reflect the rays in a regular way. Some of these rays enter your eye and form a clear image. The snow's surface is very irregular and reflects the light rays in lots of different directions. You can't see an image because the rays entering your eye have become jumbled up.

- Some objects allow light rays to pass through them in a regular way. These objects are transparent. You can see through them easily.
- Translucent objects still let most of the light rays through but they scatter the rays in lots of different directions. So you can't see through them clearly.
- Opaque objects don't let any light through at all.

Light rays travel at different speeds in different mediums. For example light travels more slowly in water or glass than in air. When a light ray passes at an angle into a medium where it changes speed, it also changes direction. We call this refraction. The straw in the photograph appears to bend at the air–water boundary due to refraction.

bends towards normal line

rectangular glass prism

bends away from normal line

When a light ray passes from air to glass (or water) it bends towards the normal line. When it passes from glass (or water) into air it bends away from the normal line. You can see both of these effects when a ray of light passes through a rectangular glass block.

things to think about • If you churned up the water in the pond, why would it look as white as the snow?

157

When you pass white light through a triangular prism you can see that it splits into lots of different colours. We call this the dispersion of white light. The range of colours that you can see is called the visible light spectrum. The full spectrum extends beyond these colours. This includes infrared light beyond the red end of the spectrum and ultraviolet light beyond the violet end.

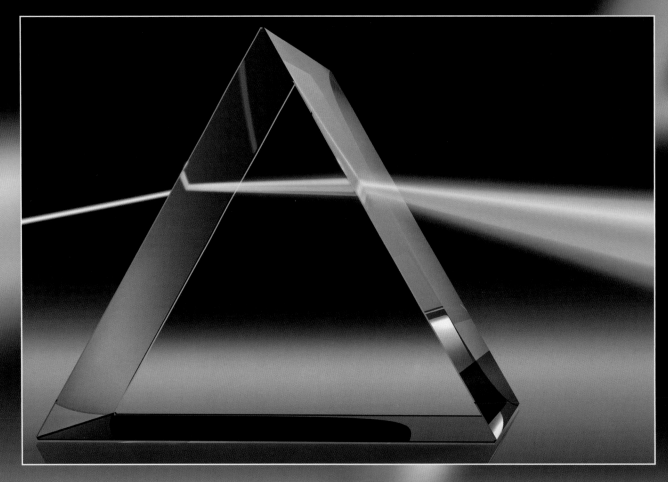

There are three sets of specialised cells at the back of your eye called cones. Each set detects one of the primary colours. The cells send signals to your brain, which interprets the actual colour of the object you are looking at. If the cells or nerves in this process do not work properly you can be colour blind.

These sets of dots test for colour blindness. People with the most common form of colour blindness will easily read a number on each card.

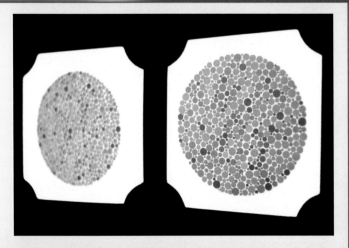

The dispersion of white light through a prism tells us that white light isn't a pure colour. It is made up from lots of different colours superimposed together. In fact, our eyes can only really see three pure colours – red, green and blue. That's why we call red, green and blue the primary colours. If you look very closely at a TV screen, you can see that the picture such as this white number '2', is just made up from red, green and blue pixels.

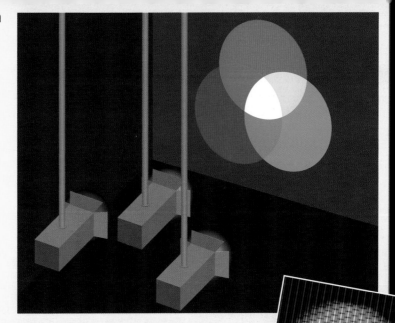

All of the other colours that we think we see are just a combination of these three primary colours at different brightnesses.

If you shine red, green and blue lights of equal brightness and make them overlap then you get white light. You get secondary colours when two of the primary colours overlap. Red and green light of equal brightness produce yellow light, red and blue light produce magenta and blue and green light produce cyan. So yellow, magenta and cyan are the secondary colours.

A blue shirt in white light...

looks black in red light...

and blue in magenta light.

A yellow shirt in white light...

looks red in red light...

and red in magenta light.

Objects appear a certain colour in white light because they absorb some of the colours in the light but they reflect others. You can picture this by thinking about what happens to the primary colours. For example, what happens when white light shines onto a blue T-shirt?

The shirt absorbs the red and the green light but it reflects the blue light. Only the blue light enters your eyes so the shirt looks blue. If you shone red light onto the shirt, it would look black because it would absorb the red light and no other light would be reflected.

When there isn't much light the cone cells don't function well, so you see in black and white.

What colour would a cyan carpet appear to be in yellow light?

Sound and music

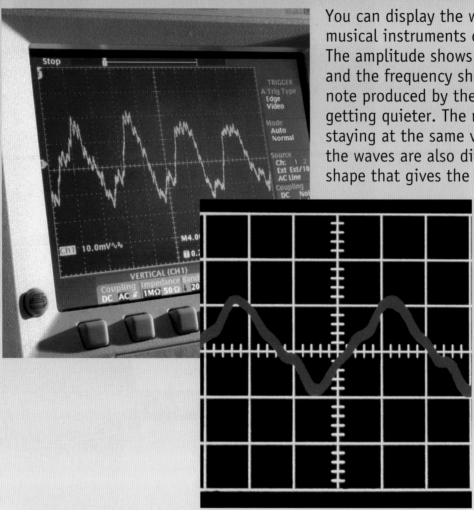

You can display the waveforms from musical instruments on an oscilloscope. The amplitude shows how loud the sound is and the frequency shows the pitch. The note produced by the guitar (on the left) is getting quieter. The recorder (below) is staying at the same volume. The shapes of the waves are also different. It is the shape that gives the tone quality of the sound. A recorder sounds different from a guitar so their waveforms are different shapes.

Mixing desks help sound engineers to change the volume of sounds. These devices also can change the shape of the waveform, or vary the overtones (see box on opposite page) that make up the sounds. Some electronic systems actually change the frequency of the notes. This helps pop stars to sound as though they're singing in tune.

Instruments produce their sounds in different ways. First something needs to vibrate. This could be a string on a guitar or a column of air in a saxophone. You usually change the pitch of the note by varying the length of the thing that is vibrating.

- Placing your fingers on different frets on a guitar changes the length of the vibrating string.
- The keys on a saxophone make the vibrating column of air longer or shorter.
- Organs use different pipes – their different lengths produce different pitches.

This waveform produced by a human voice is very complicated. The frequency, amplitude and shape of the waves are varying all the time. Voice recognition software analyses the waveform and uses the theory behind sound to convert the waveform into text. It would convert this particular waveform into the word 'baby'.

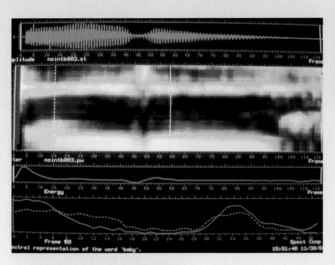

Spectral representation of the word 'baby'.

things to think about

What happens when you rest your finger lightly at the middle of a guitar string and then play the note? Can you explain what is happening?

The sound of a guitar comes from the vibration of the string. The lowest (fundamental) frequency that the string can vibrate (shown at the top of this picture) gives the note's pitch. The picture shows some other ways the string can vibrate, each producing a note of a different, higher pitch. When you pluck a guitar string it actually vibrates in lots of different ways all at the same time, and the sound you hear is a combination of all of these notes together – although it sounds like a single note. The higher notes are called overtones.

It is the overtones that give the guitar waveform its characteristic shape. The fundamental and the overtones are also called harmonics. The fundamental is the 1st harmonic; the overtone with twice the fundamental frequency is the 2nd harmonic, and so on.

161

Effects of forces on shape

Forces can have many different effects on objects. They can stretch or squash (compress) them, bend or twist them or even permanently change their shape. Studying how the shape changes can tell you about the forces involved.

A spring stretches when you apply a force. The distance the spring stretches is called the extension. The girl is using a newton meter to measure the force of the load (weight) pulling down on the spring. Forces are measured in newtons (N).

things to think about

What safety precautions should you take when carrying out this investigation?

When these cars crashed they exerted a force on each other. These forces changed the shape of the cars. They have been compressed and crumpled. You can see that the size of the force on each of the cars was about the same since there was an equal amount of damage. As well as having a size, a force has a direction. The forces acting on the cars must have had equal sizes but opposite directions.

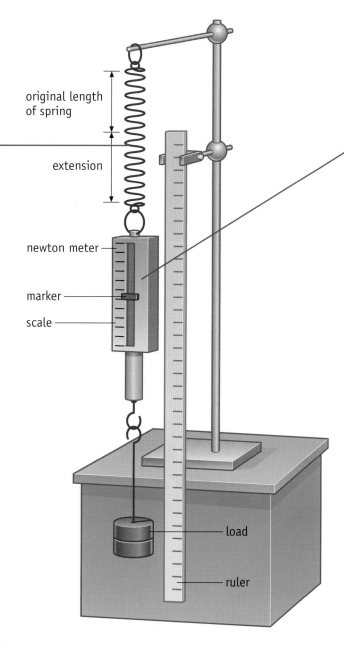

original length of spring

extension

newton meter

marker

scale

load

ruler

Inside the newton meter is another type of spring. Larger forces stretch both springs by greater amounts and the marker moves further down the scale. Reading where the marker is on the scale tells you the size of the force.

You can investigate how forces change the shape of a spring using this apparatus. The extension depends on the force, so we call the extension the dependent variable and the force the independent variable. The independent variable is the one that you change – in this case by adding more masses to the load. You must keep all of the other variables (such as the type of spring) the same in order to make it a fair test.

You should record all of your results in a table. It is a good idea to repeat your readings. You can check that your repeat readings are similar. If they aren't then you should take your measurements again. Don't forget to include the units in the top row of the table.

force (N)	extension 1 (cm)	extension 2 (cm)	average extension (cm)
0.0	0.0	0.0	0.0
1.0	4.1	4.0	4.1
1.9	7.9	8.1	8.0

A graph to show extension against force for a spring

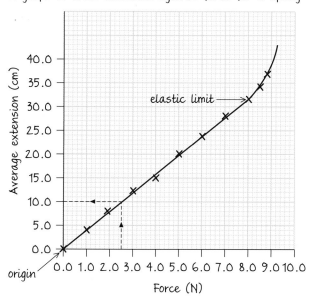

elastic limit

origin

Line graphs are useful because you can interpolate (read between the points). For example the graph shows that a force of 2.5 N would produce an extension of 10 cm.

The graph starts as a straight line through the origin. So for this spring the force is proportional to the extension. Doubling the force doubles the extension. However, once you apply a force larger than the elastic limit, the spring no longer stretches in proportion to the force. Forces of this size will permanently change the shape of the spring.

163

Balanced and unbalanced forces

This brother and sister are having a tug of war. They are both pulling on the rope and exerting a force on it.

Forces have a size and a direction. We can draw arrows to represent the size of a force. The longer the arrow, the bigger the force. The direction of the arrow shows the direction of the force.

Because they are pulling with equal forces, the forces acting on the rope balance each other out. The rope is not moving. If the girl gave a sudden extra pull, then the forces would be unbalanced and the rope (and her brother) would begin to move towards her.

The forces are balanced on the sumo wrestlers as well, but here they are pushing rather than pulling.

This square magnet is levitating above a special material called a superconductor. Superconductors apply a magnetic force that repels any magnets that are near to them. The magnet also feels the force of gravity pulling it downwards (this pull is the weight of the magnet). Here the magnetic force from the superconductor has the same size as the force of gravity on the magnet, so the forces are balanced. This makes the magnet hover just above the surface.

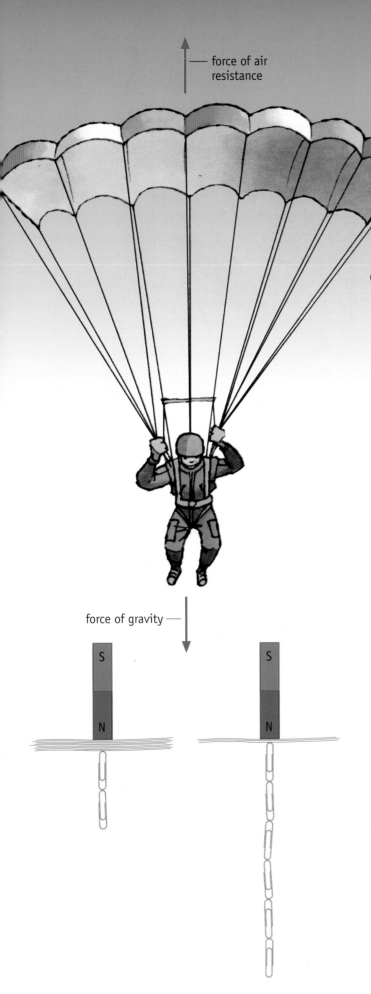

— force of air
resistance

force of gravity —

S

N

S

N

Balanced forces don't just keep things still. If an object is already moving, balanced forces keep it moving at a steady speed. This parachutist is not hanging in mid air. He is falling to the ground at a steady speed since the force of air resistance is balancing out the force of gravity. If the forces become unbalanced, then objects can change their speed, direction or shape.

In both these experiments the forces on the paper clips are balanced. The magnetic force attracting the paper clips upwards to the magnet has the same size as the force of gravity acting downwards.

Since the weight of the paper clips in the left-hand diagram is less, then the magnetic force, acting through more sheets of paper, must also be less.

The magnetic force exerted by each atom in a magnet is about 1000 million million million million times larger than the gravitational force exerted by each atom in the Earth.

Friction forces

Friction is a force that acts when two surfaces move against each other. This force either stops objects from sliding or, once they're moving, acts to slow them down.

Max wants to push his new washing machine into the right place in his kitchen.

When he tries to push it with a small force the washing machine stays still. The force of friction balances Max's pushing force.

Max has to push really hard to make the washing machine slide along. His force is larger than the maximum friction force. The forces are unbalanced and the washing machine starts to move.

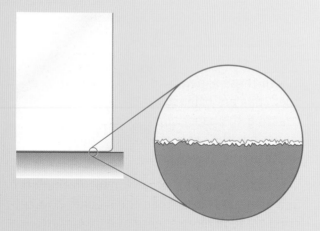

If you look closely at surfaces you can see that they are quite rough. In order for surfaces to slide past each other they need to lift up and down a little to get past all of the bumps. Therefore Max needs to apply a force so that his washing machine can slide along the floor.

There are several things that Max could do to reduce the friction. He could make the surfaces as smooth as possible or use a lubricant. This gets between the gaps and holds the surfaces slightly apart.

Friction can be a very useful force. High-tech climbing shoes have special rubber soles that increase friction between feet and rock. Brake pads use friction to oppose the motion of a bicycle. Applying the brakes unbalances the forces and makes the bicycle slow down. Air resistance works in the same way when a skydiver opens a parachute.

Would you be able to walk if there wasn't any friction at all?

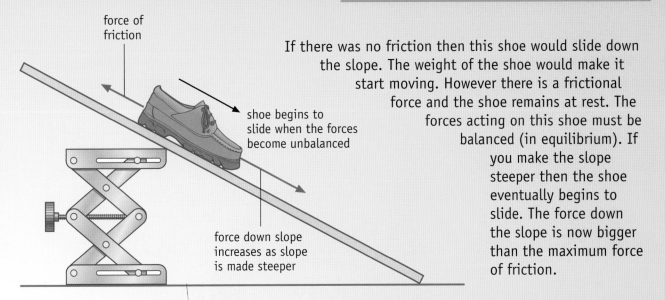

force of friction

shoe begins to slide when the forces become unbalanced

force down slope increases as slope is made steeper

If there was no friction then this shoe would slide down the slope. The weight of the shoe would make it start moving. However there is a frictional force and the shoe remains at rest. The forces acting on this shoe must be balanced (in equilibrium). If you make the slope steeper then the shoe eventually begins to slide. The force down the slope is now bigger than the maximum force of friction.

type of surface	height 1 (cm)	height 2 (cm)	average height (cm)
shoe	56	52	54
lubricated shoe	42	40	41
sandpaper block	50	52	51

You can investigate friction between different surfaces by measuring the height of the slope when the objects begin to slide. To make sure your results are reliable you need to repeat your readings. You can then check that you are getting similar results.

You also need to decide which variable you want to investigate. All of the other variables that affect friction need to be kept the same to make it a fair test. We call these control variables. In this example we need to keep the weight and the surface area of the objects the same.

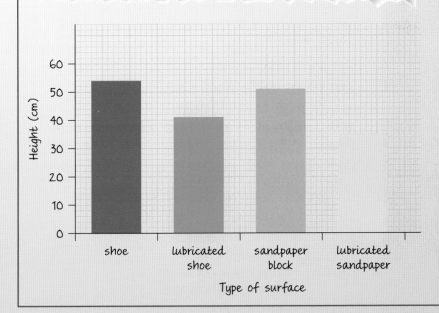

167

Turning forces

These two men are about to push some rocks with the same weight along the path using wheelbarrows. One of the men is finding it a lot easier. He has made the handles of his wheelbarrow much longer so that he doesn't need to lift up with as much force. You can understand what is happening by thinking about the turning forces.

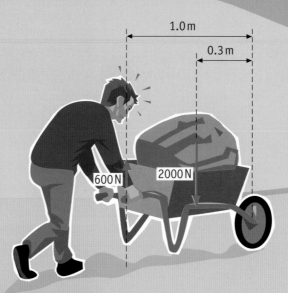

The technical term for the turning effect of a force is the moment of a force. You work out the moment by multiplying the size (or magnitude) of the force by the distance of the force from the pivot. The unit for the moment of a force is the newton metre (N m).

The centre of the rock is 0.3 m away from the pivot (the wheel of the wheelbarrow). So the moment produced by the rock's weight is $2000 \times 0.3 = 600\,\text{N m}$. You can see that each of the men also produces a moment of 600 N m. This is how levers work. A longer lever has a larger moment and so can be used to lift larger weights.

What do these acrobats have to do to stay balanced?

things to think about

3.0 m

0.3 m

200 N

2000 N

For an object to be balanced (in equilibrium), all of the forces **and** all of the moments must balance each other out. Each man turns the wheelbarrow with a moment of 600 N m, which balances the turning effect due to the weight of the rocks.

On the see-saw, the girl has to sit nearer the pivot than her younger brother. To balance the turning effects, the larger force needs to be nearer to the pivot than the smaller force.

things to think about • The forces on each wheelbarrow must be balanced too. What would the upward force on the wheel of each wheelbarrow be?

169

Force interactions

This girl is leaning against a wall. If she had nothing to lean against she would fall over. She doesn't fall over because the wall exerts a force back on her.

When two objects interact, there is always a pair of forces. The force the wall exerts on the girl is a reaction to the force the girl exerts on the wall, so we call it a reaction force. We call the girl's push on the wall the action force.

The action and reaction forces always act on different objects – one force on each object involved in the interaction.

The reaction force always has the same magnitude as the action force, but it always acts in the opposite direction. This gives us the well-known phrase 'every action has an equal and opposite reaction'.

force of girl pushing on wall

force of wall pushing back on girl

Rockets work by exerting an action force on exhaust gases. The gases are pushed behind the rocket. The reaction force from the gas pushes the rocket in the opposite direction.

Colliding footballers exert action and reaction forces on each other. The reaction force may bring each footballer to a sudden stop.

This man is hoping that the net will exert a reaction force on him when he lands in it, or he will fall through.

The Indonesian Jesus lizard can actually walk on water. The lizard's legs push down on the water so there is a reaction force from the water on the lizard. This reaction force is large enough to support the lizard's weight.

When you paddle a canoe, you push on the water and the water pushes back on you. This reaction force propels you forwards.

If everyone went to the equator and walked in the same direction that the Earth is spinning, what would happen?

When you jump out of a tree you start moving towards the ground because the Earth exerts a gravitational force on you downwards. If every action has an equal and opposite reaction, then what must your body be doing to the Earth?

Pressure

When you concentrate a jet of water into a very small area you can use it to cut through materials like glass. The actual force of the water jet is not very large. However, since the force acts on a really small area it becomes much more effective at cutting the glass. We say that the water is at a high pressure.

Pressure is really a measure of how effective a force is. We work out the pressure by dividing the magnitude of the force by the area that it acts on.

$$\text{pressure (in Pa)} = \frac{\text{force (in N)}}{\text{area (in m}^2)}$$

There are lots of different units for pressure. If the force is in newtons (N) and the area is in cm^2 then the unit is N/cm^2. If the area is in m^2 then the unit is N/m^2 or pascals (Pa). Remember that there are $10\,000\,cm^2$ in $1\,m^2$.

force = 628 N
area of both feet = 312.5 cm²
pressure = force / area
= 628 / 312.5
= 2.01 N/cm²
= 20 100 Pa

You can measure the pressure you exert on the floor by dividing your weight (the force of gravity on you) by the area of your feet. Measure the area of your feet by drawing around them on some graph paper.

scales calibrated in newtons

Try to find the area as precisely as you can by using the small squares as well as the bigger ones. Precision is related to the smallest scale division you can read when you make a measurement.

We use high pressure in many devices. Gases can be put under pressure. High pressure steam turns turbines to drive electrical generators in most power stations. Aerosol cans use gas at a high pressure to propel fine droplets of liquid towards your armpits.

Sometimes you need to reduce the pressure. Tractors and tanks use wheels with a large tread (large surface area). The smaller pressure means that they don't sink into the mud.

The pressure within fluids (gases and liquids) acts in all directions. The size of the pressure depends on the weight of the gas or liquid above and so pressure in a fluid increases with depth. Atmospheric pressure at the Earth's surface (due to the weight of the air above) is around 100 000 Pa. The pressure at the bottom of the oceans is huge. Deep sea divers have to wear thick protective suits to stop them from being squashed to death.

The pressure at the centre of the Earth is about the same as if the whole weight of a Space Shuttle was on each cm² of your body.

Hydraulic machines use liquids in pipes to transmit pressure and control the force that is applied. By changing the area you can convert the effect of a small force into a large force. Power steering and the brakes in a car use hydraulics. You can also use a hydraulic jack to lift a car up when you need to change the tyre.

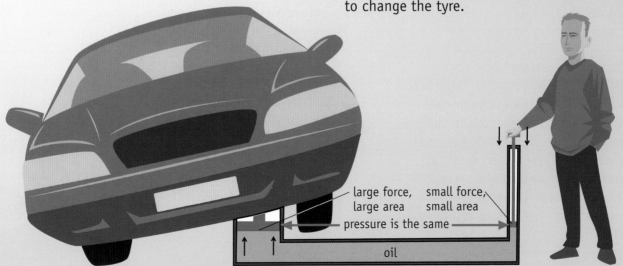

large force, large area

small force, small area

pressure is the same

oil

Effect of force on speed

When an object is at rest it remains at rest if the forces on it are balanced. Balanced forces also keep an object moving at a constant speed in a straight line, if the object was moving to start with. If the forces are unbalanced then the object changes its speed or changes its direction.

To make a car accelerate (increase speed) the forces must be unbalanced in the direction of its motion. Here the force from the engine creates an unbalanced force. The car starts to move and gets faster and faster.

Friction forces produced by the car's moving parts or by air resistance resist the car's motion when it is moving. If the driving force in one direction matches the friction forces in the other direction, the forces are balanced. The car travels at a steady speed.

You can investigate how forces affect speed by rolling a ball down a slope. There is an unbalanced force down the slope due to the ball's weight. This makes the ball start to move and then speed up. You can get an idea of how much the ball speeds up by timing how long it takes the ball to roll down the slope.

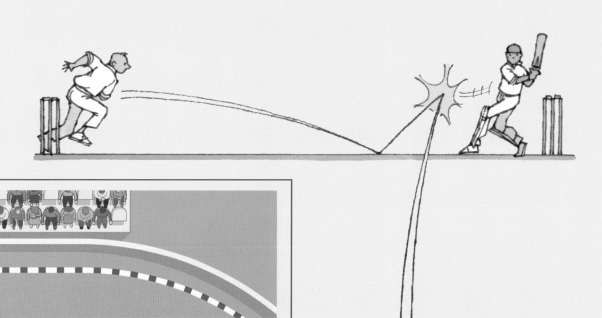

To slow a car down (decelerate) the forces must be unbalanced in the opposite direction to its motion. Here the force of the brakes (plus air resistance) provides this unbalanced force. The car slows down.

When you carry out an investigation you could make a prediction about what would happen if you change some of the variables. Making predictions based on theory and then testing them by experiment is an important process in science. If the results agree with your prediction then it suggests that your theory is correct. How would the results change if you made the slope steeper?

An unbalanced force can also make a moving object change direction. You can see this happening when a cricketer hits a cricket ball. The racing cars would also need an unbalanced force to change the direction of their motion so they could get round the corner.

Unbalanced forces acting on a moving object cause it to:

- change shape
- speed up
- slow down
- or change direction.

things to think about

Once the ball reaches the horizontal bench it begins to slow down. This is due to the effect of friction forces. If there was no friction at all, what would be the motion of the ball?

Studying motion

The police use speed cameras to produce evidence that a car is speeding. To do this, the camera takes two photographs of the car. The marks in the road act like a ruler. The police use the marks to measure the distance that the car travels in between the two photos. The police also know the time interval between the two photos. Once you know the distance and the time, you can work out the average speed.

For example, if a car travels 25 m during 0.5 s then its average speed = 25/0.5 = 50 m/s. That's 180 km/h (112 mph)!

$$average\ speed = \frac{distance}{time}$$

The units for speed come from the units for the distance and the time. If the distance is in metres (m) and the time is in seconds (s), then the speed is in metres per second (m/s). Other common units for speed are kilometres per hour (km/h) and miles per hour (mph).

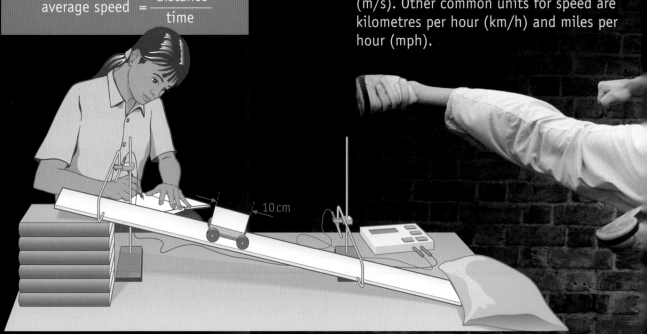

10 cm

You can measure average speed in a laboratory using light gates. The light gate measures how long it takes for a piece of card to pass through it. It does this by timing how long the light beam was interrupted by the card. The distance the object travels in that time is equal to the length of the card. If the object goes fast the time is very short, so the timers have to be quite precise. They need to measure to the nearest 100th (0.01) or even 1000th (0.001) of a second. Repeat readings can improve the reliability of the data.

You can measure the change in speed of a trolley going down a ramp by using two light gates. These show how much the speed increases between these two points. How would the results change if you made the ramp

light gate 1		light gate 2	
time (s)	speed (cm/s)	time (s)	speed (cm/s)

Distance divided by time only gives the average speed. If a long car journey had an average speed of 60 km/h you wouldn't be going at that speed all the time. You will be speeding up (accelerating) and slowing down (decelerating) and your actual speed could vary a great deal. We can draw speed–time graphs to study motion more thoroughly. This speed–time graph shows an object accelerating from rest and then travelling at a constant speed of 10 m/s.

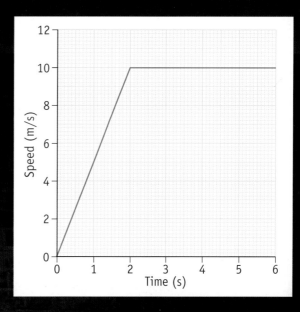

Motion can also be studied by using strobe photography. Lots of photos are taken at very short time intervals. When the photos are superimposed one on top of each other, you can see how the speed changes. The images are close together when the speed is slow and far apart when the speed is fast. Athletes can use strobe photography to check their technique.

What would the speed–time graph look like for an object that reached the same speed of 10 m/s but had a smaller acceleration?

177

Falling objects

These rocks look quite startling. This is because we think that, any second, they will fall to the ground. Objects fall to the ground because there is a force on them. This is the force of gravity.

In science there is an important difference between mass and weight.

- The mass of an object is a measure of how much matter there is. Mass is measured in kilograms (kg).
- An object's weight is the force of gravity on it. Weight is measured in newtons (N) since it is a force.

For example, consider an astronaut with a mass of 72 kg. On the Earth his weight would be about 720 N. If the astronaut goes to the Moon, his mass will still be 72 kg (since he hasn't lost any matter) but his weight will only be about 120 N. The Moon exerts a gravitational force about a sixth as much as the Earth's.

- Your mass is a measure of the amount of matter in you (in kg)
- Your weight is the force of gravity that is acting on you (in N)

Rockets need huge thrust forces to escape the Earth's gravitational pull. However, gravity isn't just a force exerted on objects by large masses like the Earth. It is exerted between all objects that have mass. All objects attract each other due to the force of gravity. This force is very large when one of the objects is very massive like the Earth (and even greater for more massive planets like Jupiter), but even you exert a very small gravitational force on all objects.

Gravity also depends on distance – the greater the distance, the smaller the force. If you left Earth in a rocket, your weight would gradually get less the further away from Earth you went.

Your gravity is attracting the person next to you with a force of about 0.000 000 3 N.

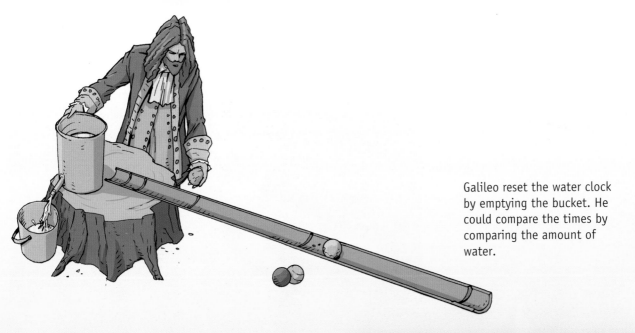

Galileo reset the water clock by emptying the bucket. He could compare the times by comparing the amount of water.

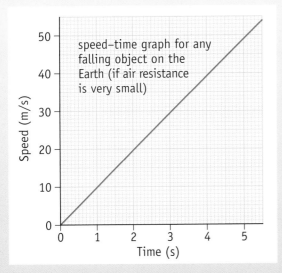

speed–time graph for any falling object on the Earth (if air resistance is very small)

Speed (m/s) axis: 0, 10, 20, 30, 40, 50

Time (s) axis: 0, 1, 2, 3, 4, 5

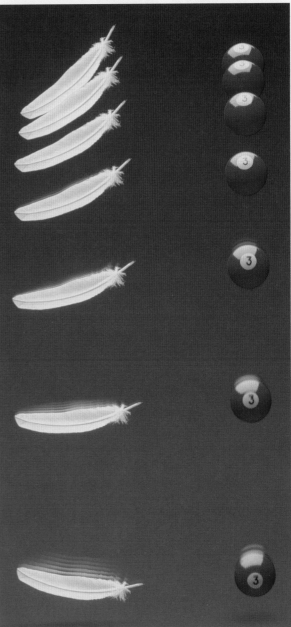

Gravity produces a force downwards. If this force is unbalanced then objects accelerate towards the ground. Galileo was the first person to realise that this acceleration was the same for any falling object if there is no air resistance. He rolled balls with different masses down a slope and timed them with a water clock. They all took about the same time. The balls also hit the little dimples in the track at regular intervals. Since the dimples got further apart this showed the balls were accelerating.

When there is no air (a vacuum) a feather falls to the ground with the same acceleration as a pool ball.

things to think about

How would the speed–time graph and photograph of the feather and ball differ if the experiments were done on the Moon?

Streamlining

The kingfisher's body is shaped to make the frictional force (resistance) of air and water very small. This helps it dive into the water as quickly as possible. Streamlining reduces friction forces or drag by creating a smooth surface and an aerodynamic shape.

The lady isn't diving very fast. Her body is positioned to make the resistance as large as possible. She just wants to make a big splash.

As you try to move faster through the air, its resistance increases. It is easy to pass through the air at walking pace, but you begin to feel the effect of air resistance if you cycle very quickly.

At 150 mph, this speed-skier's posture and clothes needs to be very streamlined. The air flows very smoothly around him. Without streamlining the air wouldn't flow smoothly. This is called turbulent flow. Turbulent flow makes the force of air resistance much bigger. Air resistance acts in the opposite direction to motion, so the skier wouldn't be able to ski as fast.

You can investigate what shapes are streamlined by timing how long it takes different pieces of Plasticine® to reach the bottom of the container. How can you make the comparison reliable and valid?

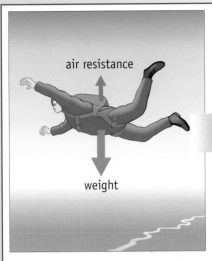
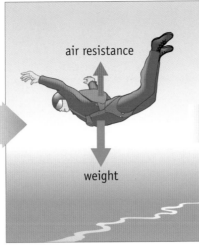

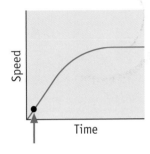
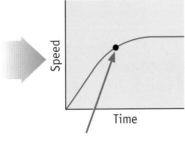
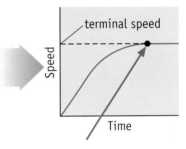

At first, this skydiver isn't falling very fast. The air resistance is small. The force of gravity (the skydiver's weight) provides an unbalanced force. The skydiver accelerates.

The skydiver is now falling faster. Air resistance has got larger. There is still an unbalanced force downwards, but not as large. The skydiver continues to accelerate but not as quickly.

The skydiver is falling so fast that the air resistance is as large as the force of gravity. The forces are balanced and the skydiver falls at constant speed. This speed is called the terminal speed.

What factors affect an object's terminal speed?

Underwater animals tend to be much more streamlined than land animals. That's because water resistance is much larger than air resistance. You experience this if you try running in a swimming pool. Engineers copy the shapes of underwater animals when they design fast trains or cars.

Using electricity

There are hundreds of different electrical devices. All these devices transform electrical energy into forms of energy that we can use. Heaters, lights, MP3 players, motors that turn washing machines or the wheels of an electric car, televisions and robots are all examples of electrical devices.

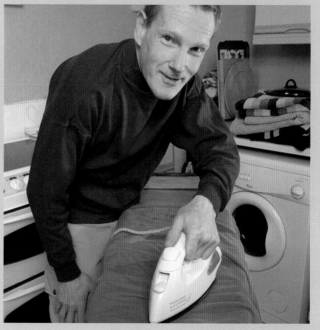

Low-energy light bulbs are better because, for the same amount of light, they give out much less heat. This house is using about five times as much energy as it would do using low-energy light bulbs. LEDs are another way of transforming electrical energy into light. They use even less energy because they don't get hot. The battery in an LED torch lasts for ages.

The light bulbs used to decorate this house are quite wasteful because they transform electrical energy into a lot of heat as well as light.

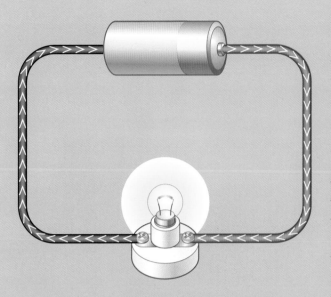

Electrical devices transfer energy from cells, batteries or the mains supply when a current flows through them. The electric current only flows when the energy source, the device and all the connecting wires and switches make a complete circuit.

A cell stores a fixed amount of energy using chemicals. Once all of this energy has been transferred to the circuit the cell runs out. If the cell is rechargeable, energy transferred from the mains supply can charge the cell up, ready to be used again. The energy transferred from the mains supply comes from power stations where electricity is generated.

This 3 tonne sculpture is made from different devices that people use every day. They have all been thrown away. An average person throws away this amount of waste electrical and electronic products in a lifetime.

We can also be quite wasteful in the way we use electrical equipment. TVs, computers and mobile phones all use energy for their display lights, even if they're not producing pictures and sound any more. Do you make sure you turn these off completely once you've finished using them?

At a typical pop concert there are about 10 km of electric cables. The concert uses about the same amount of electricity as it takes to power one hundred houses.

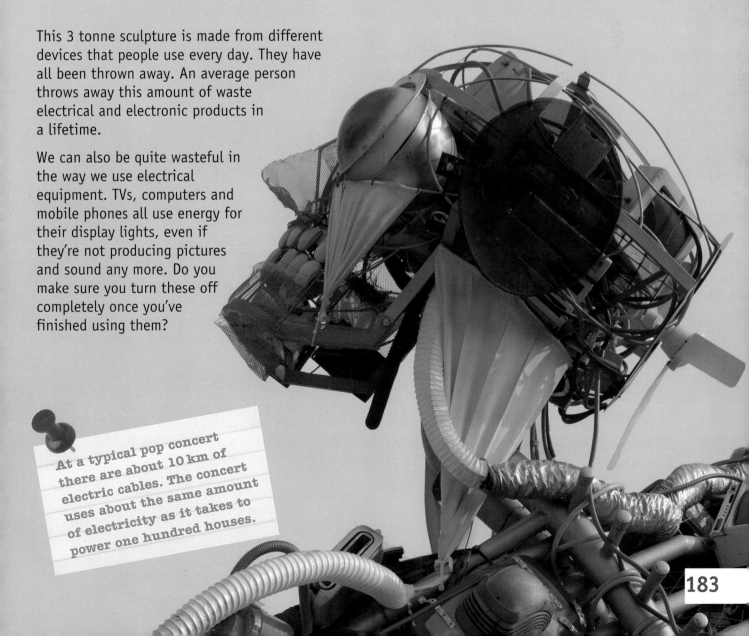

Electrical circuits

Even a simple electrical device needs several components. A kettle contains an electrical heater as well as a switch and a light to show when it is on. A circuit diagram uses standard symbols to represent the different components in electrical circuits.

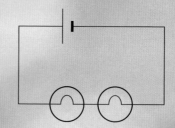

You can connect up components in series or parallel. Components in series form a single loop (as in the top circuit diagram). The bottom diagram shows two light bulbs connected in parallel. The photographs show what the series and parallel circuits would look like.

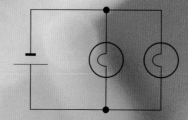

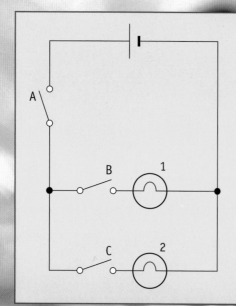

If you put a switch anywhere in a series circuit then it can switch the whole circuit off. This happens in a set of Christmas tree lights that are connected in series. If a bulb breaks there is a gap like an open switch and the rest of the lights go off too.

Switches in parallel work differently. Each light can be switched on and off separately. If switch A is open no current can flow, so both light bulbs are off. If switch A is closed, switch B can turn light bulb 1 on and off. Similarly switch C controls light bulb 2.

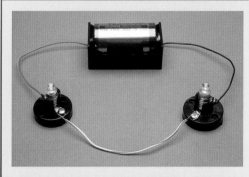

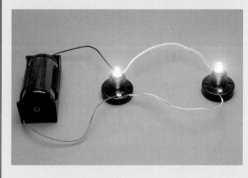

These two circuits use identical light bulbs and an identical battery. However, the light bulbs in the series circuit are much dimmer than in the parallel circuit. If you added a third bulb in series then all of the bulbs would be even dimmer. But a third bulb in the parallel circuit would be just as bright as the other two. The brighter light bulbs are transferring energy much faster than the dimmer ones. The battery in the parallel circuit will run down much more quickly.

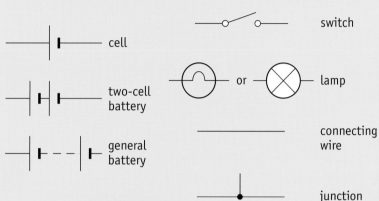

————		————	cell
————| || |————	two-cell battery
————| |– –	|————	general battery
——o o——	switch
lamp
———————	connecting wire
———•———	junction

A microprocessor in a computer uses hundreds of millions of components. If you wanted to draw the circuit diagrams you would need a piece of paper that covers about four football pitches.

When you connect up a circuit you need to make sure that you don't have a short circuit. This happens when the current flows all the way around a circuit without meeting any components (other than the power source). If there is a short circuit you get a very large current. Current flowing through a wire heats the wire, so a very large current produces a lot of heat which could cause a fire. A short circuit in the mains supply can be very dangerous indeed.

We use fuses to switch the circuit off very quickly if a short circuit develops in an electrical device. You should be very careful when you deal with mains electricity. A very small current passing through you is enough to kill you.

Magnetism

You can write messages by placing magnetic letters on a fridge door. This works because the door is made out of a magnetic material. Magnetic materials aren't magnets themselves but they do feel a force of attraction when you place a magnet near them. The two most common magnetic materials are iron and steel. You couldn't use magnetic letters on an aluminium fridge – aluminium isn't a magnetic material so there wouldn't be a magnetic force.

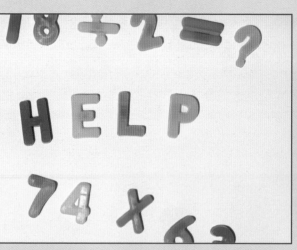

As well as attracting magnetic materials, magnets can exert forces on each other. These can be forces of both attraction and repulsion. Each end of a bar magnet is called a pole. One end is a north pole and the other a south pole. A north pole attracts a south pole but it repels another north pole. Similarly two south poles repel each other but a south pole attracts a north pole.

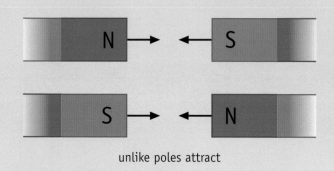

unlike poles attract

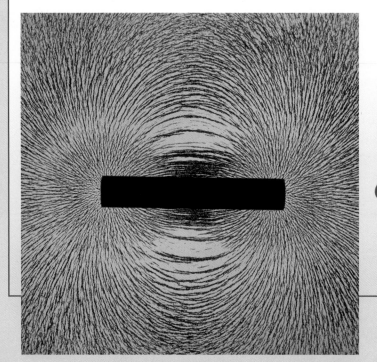

Magnetic fields have a particular shape. You can see this easily by using iron filings. Place the magnet under some paper and sprinkle the filings on the top. When you tap the paper, the filings fall back down in lines – called field lines.

You couldn't go on an expedition to Earth's North magnetic pole and place a flag on it. The pole moves erratically around the surface – too fast for you to catch it up.

Magnets can attract paper clips towards them without touching them. This is because there is a magnetic field surrounding the magnet. A magnetic field is a region where the magnetic force acts. The Earth is like a giant magnet. Its magnetic field stretches over the whole of its surface and into space. Magnetic compasses feel the force of the Earth's magnetic field and this makes them point due North.

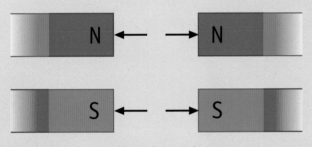

like poles repel

The ends of a bar magnet are called poles because the magnet will always line up with one end pointing towards the Earth's North Pole and the other end towards the South Pole if you allow it to move freely. This is due to the magnetic forces from the Earth's magnetic field. A magnetic compass works in exactly the same way.

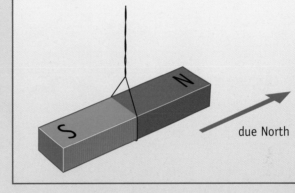

due North

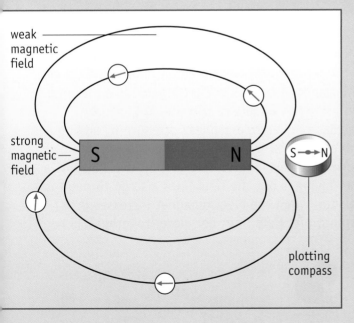

weak magnetic field

strong magnetic field

plotting compass

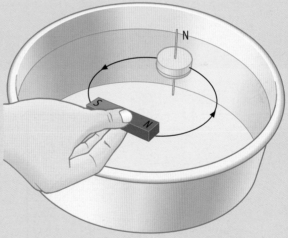

You can see the field shape by using a compass. Field lines show the direction that the magnet would push another magnetic north pole. You can see this happening by making a magnetised steel rod float in some water near to the magnet. The rod floats in the direction of the field lines. As well as showing the direction of the magnetic force, field lines also show the magnitude. The magnetic force is strongest where the field lines are closest together.

Electromagnetism

It would be no good using a bar magnet in a scrap metal yard. The magnet would be able to pick up the iron and steel but it wouldn't be able to release it again. Instead we use electromagnets. Electromagnets consist of a coil of lots of turns of wire wrapped around an iron core. When you pass an electric current through the coil, the electromagnet is magnetised.

Electromagnets lose their magnetism once the electric current is switched off. This means that you can pick up the scrap metal and put it down again where you want it to go.

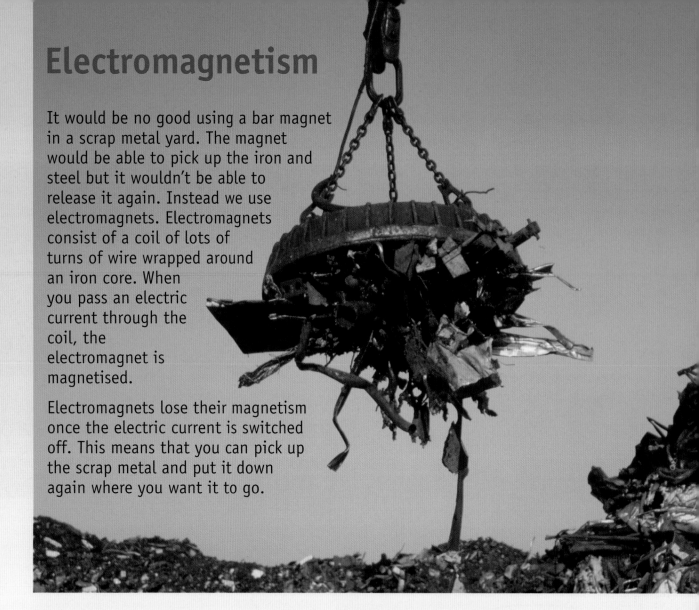

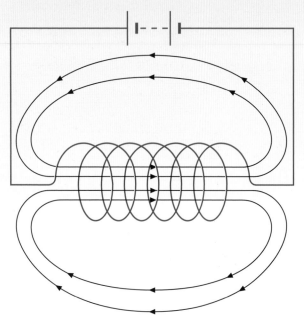

An electromagnet works because an electric current produces a very weak magnetic field. This field gets thousands of times stronger if you add a piece of iron into the middle of the coil. You can also increase the electromagnet's strength by adding more coils and by increasing the size of the current. The magnetic field is the same shape as a bar magnet's but the field lines also go through the middle. When the electromagnet increases in strength its field lines get closer together.

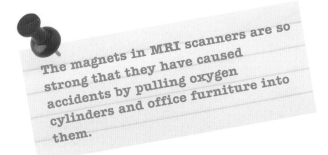
The magnets in MRI scanners are so strong that they have caused accidents by pulling oxygen cylinders and office furniture into them.

You can investigate what factors affect the strength of an electromagnet by seeing how many iron nails it can pick up. You could investigate the number of turns of wire and the size of the current. Remember to change only one factor at a time and to control the other variables. How would you make your results as reliable as possible?

current

things to think about •

What would happen to an electromagnet if you wound half of the turns one way and half of them the opposite way?

The invention of the electromagnet has had an enormous impact on our lives. Motors have electromagnets inside them. Washing machines, drills, hair dryers, DVD players, robots and vacuum cleaners all use motors to work.

Several countries are working on Maglev trains that use electromagnets to repel the train from the track. These trains could travel at very high speeds because friction is reduced.

Electromagnets are also used inside microphones and loudspeakers. If there were no electromagnets then you wouldn't be able to talk on the phone.

MRI scanners use very strong electromagnets to create detailed images of organs inside the body. Doctors can use these images to work out if anything is wrong with you without having to use harmful X-rays.

189

Current and voltage

Electric charge is moving onto this girl from the metal dome of a Van de Graaff generator. The charges on every part of her body repel each other so her hair stands on end.

A flow of electric charge is called an electric current, just like a river current is a flow of water.

It is harder for electric charge to flow through some objects than to flow through others. These objects have a higher electrical resistance. The greater the resistance, the smaller the flow of current.

Charge passes easily through metals – they have a low electrical resistance. Underground electricity cables need to carry large currents. They are made from very thick metals to make it as easy as possible for the charge to flow. The metal filaments in light bulbs are very long and thin. They have a higher resistance than the cables so a smaller current flows.

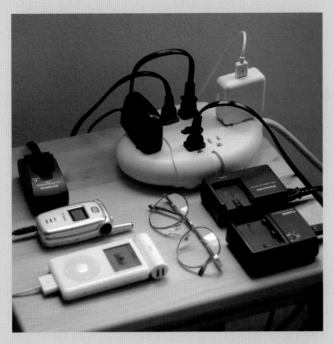

Sometimes an electric current passing through a material can cause chemical changes. This happens in rechargeable batteries. When you charge up a battery, the electrical current reverses the chemical reactions that occur when the battery is in use. Once all the reactions have been reversed, the battery is fully charged ready to be used again.

Thunderclouds can produce voltages of 100 million volts. This makes charge travel through the air as lightning. During the lightning strike, there is enough energy to run all of the TVs in the world 1000 times over.

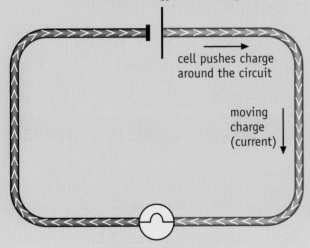

cell transfers energy to the charge

cell pushes charge around the circuit

moving charge (current)

light bulb transfers energy from the charge (as light and heat)

The size of the current also depends on how strongly the charge is pushed. Cells push electric charge around a complete circuit. You can think of the voltage (potential difference) of a cell as the size of this push. Increasing the number of cells in a circuit increases the voltage.

Another way to think about voltage is in terms of the difference in electrical energy between two parts of a circuit. There is a voltage across the light bulb because it is transforming electrical energy into light and heat energy. You would measure the same voltage across the cell. This is because the cell is transforming the same amount of its chemical energy into electrical energy.

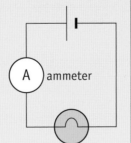

Electric current (the flow of charge) is measured in amperes (A). If a current changed from 1 A to 2 A it would mean that the charge was flowing twice as quickly.

A ammeter

You measure the current in a circuit using an ammeter. The ammeter needs to be connected in series.

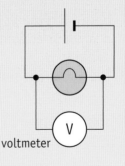

The voltage (potential difference) is the energy transferred to or from the charge. It is measured in volts (V). If the potential difference changed from 1V to 2V it would mean that the same amount of charge would be transferring twice the energy.

voltmeter V

You measure the voltage across a component using a voltmeter. The voltmeter needs to be connected in parallel, across a component.

A model for current and voltage

In parallel circuits, the current can split into two or more parts at a junction. Currents can also join together. Since no charge can appear or disappear, the total current entering a junction must be the same as the total current leaving it.

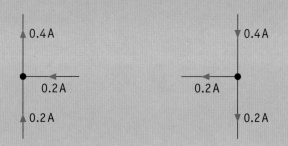

In a series circuit the electrical energy from the cell is shared between the other components. If the two light bulbs are identical, then they will each transfer half of the total energy. Therefore the potential difference across each light bulb will be half of the cell's potential difference.

Adding more light bulbs in series makes them dimmer since they have a smaller share of the energy.

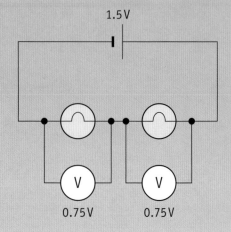

We can use a model to compare current in a circuit with something else. Modelling is a tool scientists use to help understand a process. An electric circuit is a bit like a hot water system.

- Both are complete circuits.
- The electric current is like the flow of the water.
- The cell delivers electrical energy to the charge and pushes it around the circuit through the light bulb. This is similar to the boiler and the pump heating the water and pushing it around the pipes through the radiators.
- The voltage is similar to the temperature change of the water.

things to think about...

How does the hot water system model explain the voltage readings in the series and parallel circuits?

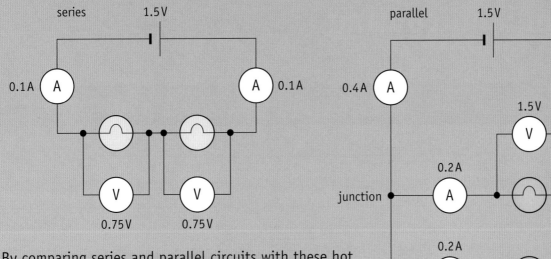

By comparing series and parallel circuits with these hot water systems you can make sense of the voltmeter and the ammeter readings above. The current is similar to the rate that the water flows and the potential difference is similar to the difference in temperature.

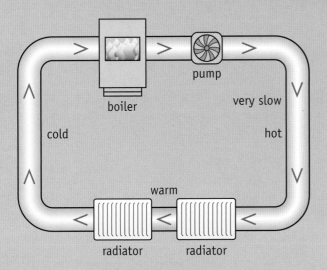

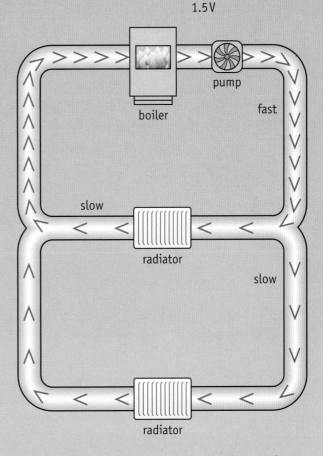

The light bulbs in the series circuit are not transferring as much energy as the parallel ones since the voltage across each is less. They also transfer the energy more slowly due to the smaller current. Both of these effects mean that increasing the number of bulbs in a series circuit reduces their brightness.

This happens in the hot water system too. Increasing the number of radiators in series means that each emits less heat energy. It is easier for the water to flow around the parallel system, so it flows faster. In the same way the electric current from the cell in the parallel circuit is larger than in the series circuit.

Heating and cooling

The hot chocolate in the polystyrene cup is gradually cooling down. It does this because it is losing energy. The energy transfers out of the hot liquid and into the surrounding room. Energy can transfer between objects when one object is hotter than the other – so there must be a difference in temperature. In this case the chocolate is hotter than the room.

A drink of cold milk would gradually warm up. This time the room is the hotter object, so the heat would transfer the other way.

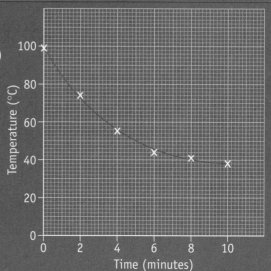

You could investigate how the temperature of the hot chocolate varies with time. Since temperature and time are both continuous variables (they can have any value) you should draw a line graph. The shape of the graph then helps you to draw a conclusion, for example about the time it takes to reach a safe temperature to drink.

When you carry out investigations you need to measure the variables as accurately as you can. This means that your measurements of temperature and time are close to the actual (true) values. Some measuring instruments are more accurate than others, but even a good quality measuring instrument can give inaccurate results if you make an error when you use it.

- Choose the best quality instrument available.
- Choose a thermometer with an appropriate range for your measurement.
- Remember to 'zero' the stopclock before using it.
- Remember to read the unnumbered marks in between the numbers that are marked on the thermometer's scale.

Energy transfers from hot things to cold things in a few different ways. In a metal rod that is heated at one end, energy transfers through the rod by conduction.

Where the temperature is higher, the particles have more energy and vibrate more vigorously. The energetic particles in the hot part of the rod collide with their neighbours. These particles then vibrate more vigorously. So energy is transferred to these neighbouring particles towards the cooler end of the rod.

This transfer of energy by collisions is what we mean by heat conduction.

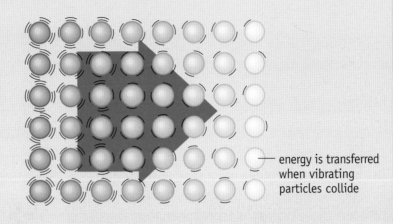

energy is transferred when vibrating particles collide

Materials, like polystyrene, that don't conduct heat very well are called insulators.

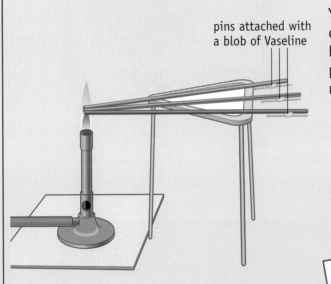

pins attached with a blob of Vaseline

You can investigate how well different metals conduct by heating one end of metal rods in a Bunsen flame. When the Vaseline melts, the pin falls. The pin will fall off very quickly if the material is a good conductor.

You need to be very careful when using a Bunsen burner. When you are not using it make sure you have a yellow flame that people can see easily. Hold objects in the flame using tongs and remember that objects remain hot for a long time after you've heated them.

Particles in solids are closer together than they are in liquids. Why do you think that solids are usually better conductors of heat than liquids?

Energy from the Sun

You notice the difference between light and shade very easily on a sunny day. Walk out of the shade and you begin to feel hot very quickly. Heat transfers between the Sun and your skin. However, heat can't transfer by conduction since the energy has to travel through space. Space is a vacuum and there are no particles to transfer energy by collisions. The only way in which heat energy can be transferred in a vacuum is by radiation.

The heat that we feel on a hot, sunny day is from the Sun's infrared radiation. Infrared radiation is also responsible for the heat that we feel when we are near a fire. Light energy is another way that the Sun and other stars transfer energy by radiation. Astronomers have studied the radiation from galaxies up to 13 billion light years away.

We use fossil fuels to heat our homes and to generate electricity. The three main fuels are coal, crude oil and natural gas. Crude oil can be separated into many different types of fuel such as gasoline for cars and kerosene for jet engines. Fossil fuels were formed very slowly from layers of dead plants and animals. These fuels store chemical energy. The ultimate source of this energy was the Sun.

Hundreds of millions of years ago, plants absorbed and stored energy from the Sun as they grew. Some of the energy stored in plants also passed up the food chain.

Most of the energy we use has originally come from the Sun. We can absorb the Sun's radiation directly to heat our homes using solar panels and to provide electricity using solar cells.

Plants can also absorb the Sun's energy and use it in photosynthesis. They convert the energy into chemical energy which they store as biomass (such as wood, leaves or seeds). We can use this energy resource by eating the plants. The Sun's energy passes up the food chain. We can also use biomass as a fuel or generate electricity by burning it.

The heat that you are currently receiving from the Sun took 10 million years to reach the Sun's surface from its core. It then travelled 150 million km in about 8 minutes to get to you by radiation.

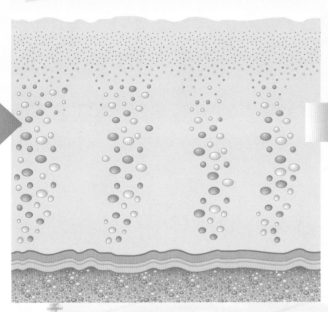

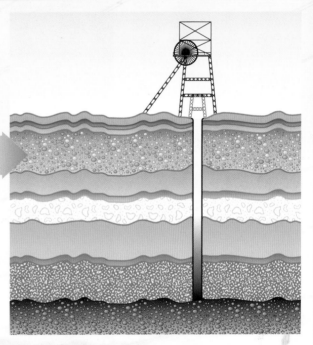

Dead plant and animal material collected at the bottom of swamps and oceans and layers of sediment built up slowly to form rocks.

Eventually the temperature and pressure grew so great underground that the fossil fuels began to form. Today we extract these fuels as a valuable resource.

197

Energy resources

An energy resource is something that stores energy in a form that we can easily use. Fossil fuels and biomass are energy resources. We can use their stored chemical energy to heat buildings, drive engines or generate electricity. Understanding different energy resources is very important. Some resources are quickly running out. Using some energy resources can also lead to environmental problems like global warming and acid rain.

Energy resources are either non-renewable or renewable. Renewable resources (like wind energy) never run out.

Most of our electricity currently comes from non-renewable resources. These include fossil fuels and nuclear fuel. Once we have used these resources they are gone for good, so we must use them responsibly.

The world's use of energy resources needs to become sustainable so that we will always have enough energy available for electricity, heating and transport. We will need to generate more of our electricity using renewable resources.

things to think about •

How would you feel if a wind farm like the one in the photo was built near your house?

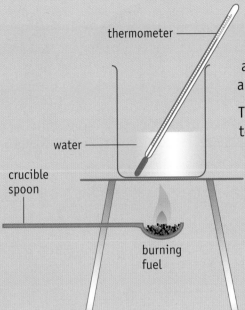

thermometer

water

crucible
spoon

burning
fuel

You can compare the amount of energy stored in different fuels by using this apparatus. To make it a fair test you should use the same amount of fuel each time. You should also control other variables – use the same amount of water and the same starting temperature.

The energy released from burning the fuel increases the temperature of the water. The fuel that releases the most stored energy will produce the largest temperature rise.

Unfortunately, lots of heat will be dissipated (lost) into the surroundings and so not all the heat is transferred to the water. This means the temperature rise may not be the true value. There could also be errors if the thermometer is not very accurate.

The measurements that you obtain from experiments are called data. In this experiment the data are not very reliable since somebody else carrying out the same experiment might get very different results. To support your conclusion you could check your results with other people's measurements. This is called secondary data.

Secondary sources for data or information can be books, websites and even the results tables from your classmates. Be careful when you use secondary data. It is important to check that the additional data give a valid comparison. A valid comparison must be based on measurements of the correct variable, taken from a fair test.

You should also check the data and any conclusions are presented in an unbiased way. A wind farm company's website might present data about available wind energy but omit other relevant data. A protest group might present the same data but make a different conclusion. A valid conclusion must be based on reliable data, and not just opinion.

Transfer of heat

The butter on the toast is melting – it is changing state from solid to liquid. To do this, it must gain energy. The energy comes from the hot toast. Heat can only transfer between objects if there is a temperature difference. So the toast must be hotter than the butter.

In this case energy is transferring by conduction. Particles in the hot toast have more energy and vibrate more vigorously. They collide with particles of butter and pass on some of their energy.

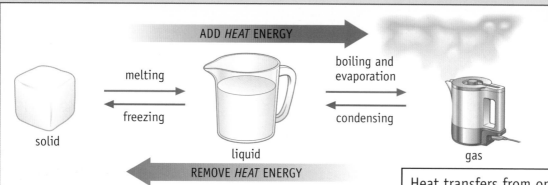

ADD *HEAT* ENERGY

melting

freezing

solid

liquid

boiling and evaporation

condensing

gas

REMOVE *HEAT* ENERGY

Heat transfers from one place to another by conduction, convection and radiation. Absorbing or emitting energy makes an object change temperature or change state.

The average human produces about 1.5 pints (0.85 litres) of sweat every day.

Liquids can change into gases by boiling or evaporation. Unlike boiling, evaporation can happen at temperatures lower than the boiling point.

Evaporation only occurs at the surface of a liquid. To get a high rate of evaporation, there needs to be a large surface area.

Evaporation happens because some of the particles at the liquid's surface are moving fast enough to escape as a gas (vapour). Since the fastest particles leave the liquid, the average energy of the remaining particles is less. The liquid's temperature drops. We use this effect to cool down when we produce sweat.

We feel heat from the Sun when we absorb some of its infrared light. Heat transfer through empty space is called radiation. Radiation transfers energy without particles – it is the only way that the Sun's energy can reach Earth through the vacuum of space.

Most of the energy transferred to the toast from this toaster is in the form of infrared radiation.

Convection is another way in which heat is transferred. Like conduction, in convection the energy is carried by particles. This time, the particles actually move from one place to another, rather than transferring energy by collisions between neighbouring particles.

Convection can only occur in liquids and gases. It is convection that makes hot air and hot water rise.

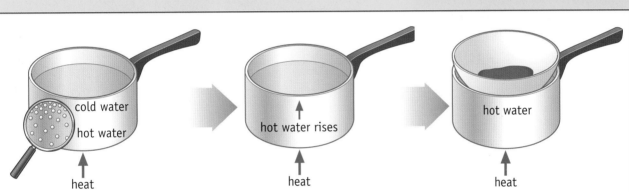

The water at the bottom of the pan is heated. This makes the water expand – its particles get further away from each other.

The hot water is less dense than the water above because it has expanded. The less dense water rises. The cold water above it is denser, so it falls.

Energy has transferred through the water by convection. The particles in the hot water can now heat the chocolate in the bowl by conduction.

Convection is very important in heating most homes. Water heated by the boiler is pumped to the radiators. Air in contact with the radiators heats up and swirls around the room due to convection. This ensures that the whole room is heated evenly.

You can see the convection currents in this beaker of water. As the water is heated, the water rises to the top and then swirls around. The colder water is moving down the right side of the beaker. The movement of the water is shown by placing a few crystals of purple dye at the bottom.

201

Reducing energy losses

It is expensive to heat large buildings like Buckingham Palace. This thermogram shows that a lot of heat is escaping. Different colours indicate different temperatures. The yellow windows are much hotter than the purple walls.

The energy emitted from the windows and the walls is wasted energy. It spreads out (dissipates) so it can't easily be reused. To save money and to conserve limited fuel resources all households need to find ways of reducing such energy losses.

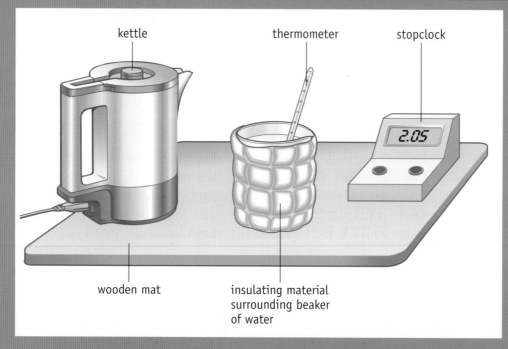

kettle   thermometer   stopclock

2.05

wooden mat   insulating material surrounding beaker of water

Control variables

- volume of water
- initial temperature of water
- thickness of insulating material

You can reduce energy losses from a warm object by using insulating materials. Insulating materials are poor conductors of heat. They slow down the rate of heat transfer by conduction and so keep the object at a higher temperature.

By measuring how slowly the water cools you can decide which insulating material is the best.

As well as the variable you are investigating, there are usually lots of other variables that will affect your results. To make the experiment a fair test and allow you to make a valid comparison, you need to keep these variables constant. These are called control variables.

Energy can be changed (transformed) from one form to another. However, the total amount of energy going in is always the same as the energy coming out. None is lost – we say that energy is conserved.

This diagram represents the energy transformations in a TV. It is called a Sankey diagram. The width of the arrows represents the amount of energy.

An efficient device wastes only a small proportion of the input energy. Devices can be made more efficient by reducing the wasted energy.

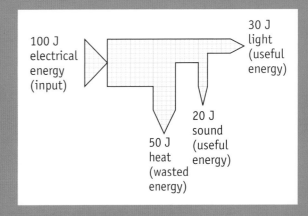

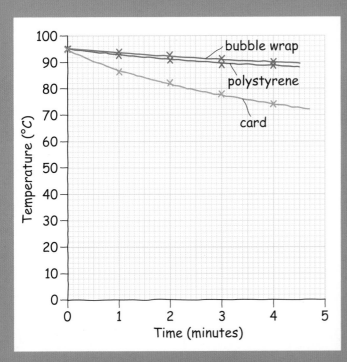

On this graph the line of best fit for bubble wrap is very close to the line for polystyrene. You wouldn't be confident in concluding that the bubble wrap is the best. You could conclude that the bubble wrap and the polystyrene are about the same, or that the precision of the measurements is not good enough to compare the two materials. Alternatively, you could modify your experiment. For example you could make measurements for a longer time.

Since heat rises, a large proportion of the wasted energy in your home passes through the roof. Hot-water tanks, walls and windows also need good insulation. Therefore, most new houses are built with cavity wall insulation, loft insulation and double glazing.

Most insulating materials trap air. Air is a very poor conductor of heat. Trapping air also stops heat transfer by convection.

things to think about

Heat is also lost from a warm object by radiation and convection. How does this affect the results of your insulation investigation?

203

Energy efficiency

If you could design the perfect light bulb, it would transform all the electrical energy supplied into light energy. Your perfect light bulb would be 100% efficient since it transforms all of the electrical energy into useful energy.

Unfortunately there are no devices that are 100% efficient – they all waste some of their energy in some way. In almost all devices, the wasted energy is lost as heat. Modern low-energy light bulbs produce much less heat than older bulbs do. They are more efficient. Using efficient devices helps conserve limited fossil fuel resources.

Since energy is conserved (the total energy remains the same) you can work out the wasted energy if you know the input energy and useful output

total energy in (J) = useful energy out (J) + wasted energy out (J)

$$\text{efficiency (\%)} = \frac{\text{useful energy out (J)}}{\text{total energy in (J)}} \times 100$$

energy. A light bulb might convert 100 J of electrical energy into 20 J of light energy. You know that it must have produced 80 J of heat, since the total energy out (20 J of light energy, 80 J of heat energy) must equal the total energy in (100 J of electrical energy). The efficiency of this light bulb (using the equation shown) would be $\frac{20}{100} \times 100 = 20\%$.

Are there any situations where the energy lost due to friction is useful?

The smoke produced by this dragster is caused by the heat produced by the tyres. They are spinning against the track and heating up due to friction. This heat burns the tyre rubber and causes smoke.

Friction is a very common cause of wasted energy. Whenever there are moving parts, friction transforms some of the energy of the moving parts into heat. To make machines more efficient you need to reduce the friction.

To calculate the efficiency of a device you need to understand which energy changes are useful and which are wasteful. For example, cars are devices that move. Their useful output energy is movement (kinetic) energy. The input energy is the chemical energy from the fuel and the wasted energy is radiated as heat. You can see some of the heat transferred away from a few cars in this thermogram of a car park. Which cars have recently arrived? The other cars have cooled down because their heat energy has dissipated (spread out) into the atmosphere. It is impossible to use this energy again.

Here are some Sankey diagrams for different devices. They show the energy changes for each device and a calculation of the efficiency.

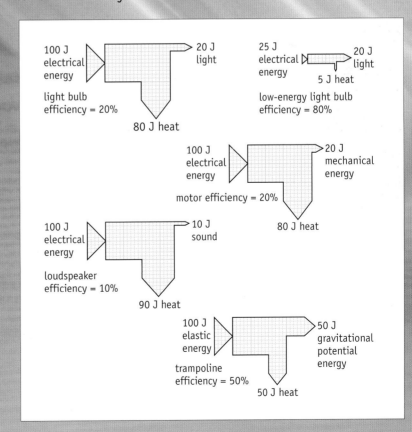

Energy for electricity

In this power station, burning fossil fuel transforms chemical energy into heat. Water absorbs the heat and changes into steam. The energy transferred to the steam increases the kinetic energy of its particles. The faster the steam particles move, the more force they exert. The steam turns large fans called turbines. These turbines turn a generator, which transforms movement energy into electrical energy. At every stage some energy is dissipated.

Fossil fuels are used because they are very reliable. Unlike wind and solar energy, their availability doesn't depend on the weather. However, burning fossil fuels produces carbon dioxide as well as other forms of pollution. Increased carbon dioxide emissions are thought to be leading to climate change.

Fossil fuels are a non-renewable resource. The current use of fossil fuels to generate electricity is not sustainable. We need to look at alternative methods of electricity generation and more efficient systems. People have lots of different views about the best method for their town, their country or the environment.

boiler

hot steam

turbine

generator

electricity

fossil fuel

cold water from cooling tower

to cooling tower

Hydroelectric power uses the kinetic energy of falling water to drive turbines. These power stations don't produce carbon dioxide and the resource will never run out – it is renewable. However, the large dams can flood habitats for people and wildlife.

The Energy Saving Trust has calculated that in the UK it takes about 14 power stations just to provide the electricity for our home entertainment gadgets such as TVs and games consoles.

Solar cells directly convert light energy into electrical energy. Energy radiated from the Sun is free and renewable. Solar cells are currently expensive and the output power depends on surface area so very large panels are needed. Also it isn't sunny all of the time.

Engineers are trying to extract tidal energy and wave energy from the sea. Although the tides and waves are renewable resources, these power stations are very expensive. The technology needs to develop before these resources can be used effectively.

Nuclear fuel will run out, but not as soon as fossil fuels. Nuclear power stations do not produce carbon dioxide. However, the radioactive waste is harmful and needs to be stored safely because it remains radioactive for thousands of years.

Wind energy is renewable and doesn't produce carbon dioxide. It isn't as expensive as solar power. Wind farms take up a lot of space and they make a lot of noise. Also, wind energy isn't reliable – it isn't windy all of the time.

In geothermal power stations hot underground rocks turn water into steam to drive turbines. The heat rises from deep in the Earth's crust and is renewable. Building the stations is technically difficult. There are only certain places on Earth that have a suitable geology.

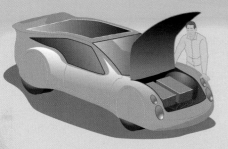

Fuel cells generate electricity from chemical reactions. They are like batteries but the chemicals can be replaced when they run out. Usually the waste product is just water. Fuel cells are currently very expensive, but could eventually be more widely used in electric cars.

Sun, Moon and the Earth

For about 50 years, astronauts and satellites have been able to take photographs of the Earth from space. These photos show that the Earth is not flat but a spinning sphere. However, people knew this for hundreds of years before we could take any photos. Astronomers were able to create a picture of the Earth by looking carefully at the sky.

When the Earth passes between the Moon and the Sun you can see the Earth's shadow on the Moon's surface. This is a lunar eclipse. The curved shadow shows that the Earth has a circular shape.

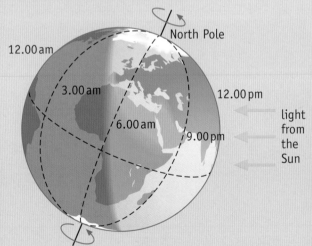

The Earth rotates around its north–south axis.

As the Sun rises and moves across the sky it looks as if the Sun travels round the Earth, but it is the Earth that is rotating. At night, you get the same effect. Due to the Earth's rotation, the stars seem to move slowly across the sky.

The Earth's rotation also gives us day and night. A point on the Earth's surface faces towards the Sun during the day and away from the Sun at night time.

The Sun is a huge sphere of gas. Its volume is over a billion times the volume of the Earth. The pressure and temperature at the Sun's core are so large that nuclear reactions take place, releasing lots of heat and light energy. Our Sun is a very typical star.

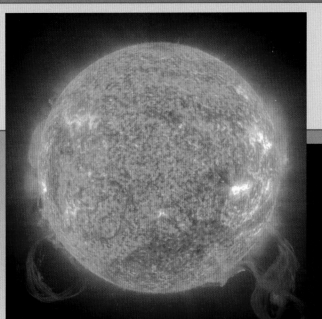

The Moon is a solid rocky sphere about a quarter of the size of the Earth. It has many craters because it was hit by lots of meteorites (rocks from space) in its early life.

Scientists think that the Moon was formed when a planet the size of Mars crashed into the Earth.

Shadows also change direction as the Earth rotates. The length and position of the shadow can be used to tell the time. Sundials show different times on different places on the Earth. The fact that countries have different time zones from each other is more evidence that the Earth must be spinning.

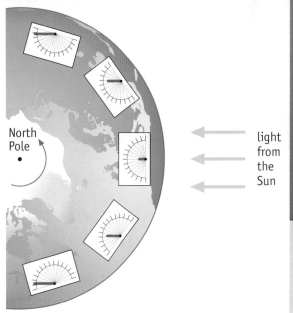

The time of day is related to the position of the shadow.

Seasons and years

We can use the idea that the Earth moves to explain how the days and the seasons change throughout a year. Scientists worked out how the Earth must move around the Sun before people could go into space to see for themselves.

This is a good example of a scientific model. A model is a picture about what is happening that seems to explain all of the known facts.

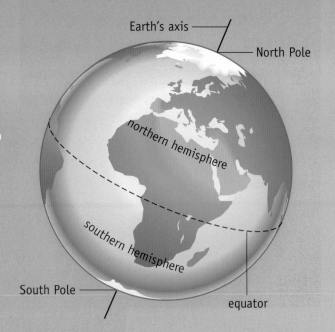

Earth's axis

North Pole

northern hemisphere

southern hemisphere

South Pole

equator

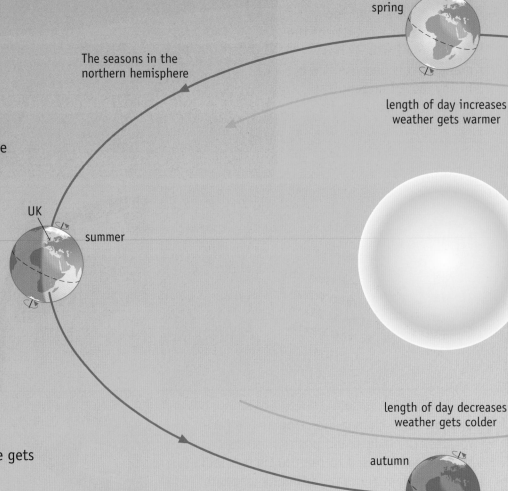

spring

The seasons in the northern hemisphere

length of day increases
weather gets warmer

UK

summer

length of day decreases
weather gets colder

autumn

Here it is summer in the northern hemisphere. The days are longer than the nights.

The tilt of the Earth's axis means the UK spends more time in daylight than it does in the Earth's shadowed side.

More of the Sun's energy is gained, by warming up the air and ground, during the day than is lost during the night.

The northern hemisphere gets warmer.

In the northern hemisphere's summer, a small part of the Earth near the North Pole is in permanent daylight. Although the Sun still appears to move across the sky, it never actually sets.

Here it is winter in the northern hemisphere. Due to the tilt of the Earth's axis the nights are longer than the days.

This time, the UK spends more time in the Earth's shadowed side than in daylight.

Since more energy is lost during the night than is gained during the day, the northern hemisphere gets colder.

winter

things to think about •

What would happen to the Earth's climate if the Earth wasn't tilted?

Due to the Earth's spin, people in the UK are rotating around the Earth's axis at nearly 1000 km/h. The Earth orbits the Sun at a speed of about 30 km/s. That's 108 000 km/h.

211

Stars and planets

You can see four planets in this photograph of the night sky. The two bright 'stars' are Jupiter and Venus. Venus is closer to the horizon. Below Venus and to the right is Mercury. Above Venus to the left are Mars (top) and Saturn (left).

Although in this photo the stars and planets look very similar, they are very different. The planets reflect the light from the Sun and they are much closer to us than the stars. Stars emit their own light. They are much bigger and brighter than the planets.

If you look at the planets through a telescope you can see that they are very different from the stars. In a telescope, stars still look like points of light, but the planets have a distinctive disc shape. You can also see the rings of Saturn.

If you want to take a photograph of the night sky using a telescope you need to mount it on a motorised platform. This keeps the telescope pointing the same way even though the Earth is rotating. If you don't do this then the stars will seem to move as you're taking the picture. Long exposures will give you a photo of the stars similar to the one on page 208.

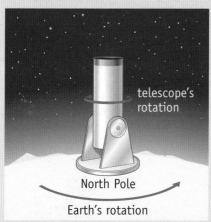

telescope's rotation

North Pole

Earth's rotation

The brightness (intensity) of the stars gets less the further they are away. That's why the planets and stars look quite similar. The stars are actually very bright but they are very far away.

Venus spins in the opposite direction to the Earth and most of the other planets. Scientists think a huge collision in the past almost flipped Venus right over.

You see the planets and the Moon by the sunlight reflected from them. You can also see satellites in this way. Satellites are much closer to the Earth and they move around (orbit) the Earth very quickly. Some of them pass across the whole sky in a few minutes.

You can see a satellite moving relative to the stars with the naked eye. The photograph shows how a satellite has moved in just a short time.

Asteroids and comets

Apart from the planets, there are many other objects that orbit the Sun. These include asteroids and comets.

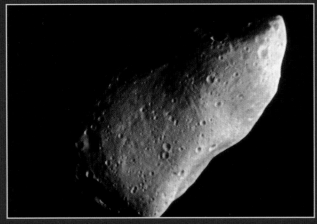

Asteroids are rocky objects that were formed at the same time as the planets. Most asteroids are very small but a few are as large as 800 km across. Asteroids mainly orbit the Sun between Mars and Jupiter in a region called the asteroid belt. However some asteroids orbit closer to the Sun and can come quite near to the Earth. We are keeping a close eye on these to make sure they aren't going to crash into us.

Comets consist of ice, frozen gas and rocky material. They were formed at the same time as the planets but much further out from the Sun. Comets have very different orbits to the planets. A comet's orbit is elliptical (oval shaped) with the Sun near to one end. Unlike the planets, comets can orbit the Sun at any angle and direction.

When a comet is near to the Sun it forms a tail. The tail is produced by the Sun evaporating some of the comet's gases and blowing them away. Sunlight reflecting off the comet and its tail provides a spectacular view from the Earth.

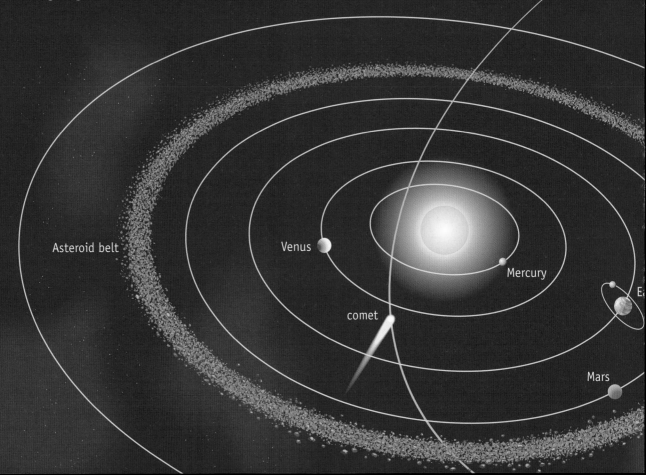

Asteroid belt

Venus

Mercury

Ea

comet

Mars

If an object larger than 1 km collided with the Earth it could cause a global catastrophe. Scientists are using telescopes to try and find any objects that might cause us harm. Once they have found them they work out where they will be in the future and how close they will approach the Earth.

Currently we are only worried about one asteroid. There is a 1 in 300 chance that it will collide with the Earth on 16 March 2880. Although the risk is very small, collisions have certainly happened in the past. We need to keep looking – there are still undiscovered objects out there.

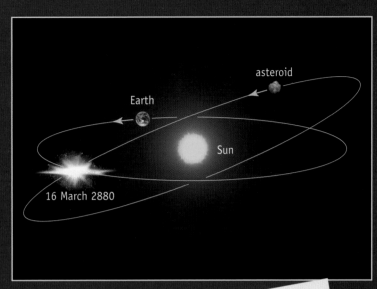

There is only one known case of an object from space injuring a human being. A man was hit by a meteorite in 1954.

In 1994 twenty fragments of a comet crashed into the planet Jupiter. The damage might not look much but each 'scar' is about the size of the Earth.

Such a collision on the Earth would throw dust into the atmosphere and block out the sunlight for many years. The resulting climate change could cause a mass extinction. We think a comet or asteroid similar in size to one of the fragments caused the extinction of the dinosaurs.

If we discovered that an object was actually going to collide with us, what action could we take?

Jupiter

Ideas about the solar system

In the year AD150 Ptolemy (an Egyptian astronomer) published his ideas about the solar system. How have people's ideas changed since then?

In Ptolemy's picture of the solar system all of the heavenly objects orbited the Earth, which was fixed and non-rotating. The planets moved in small circles (epicycles) as they circled the Earth. This picture was similar to earlier Greek ideas, but Ptolemy turned these ideas into a mathematical model.

Ptolemy's model was very complex, but centuries of data on the position and movement of the Sun, Moon and planets seemed to support his theory. His calculations could also be used to predict planetary positions.

Nicolaus Copernicus suggested that the planets orbited the Sun instead of the Earth, and used a mathematical model (also with epicycles) to describe their orbital motion. However, not many people believed his idea that the Earth actually moved, which disagreed with the teachings of the Church.

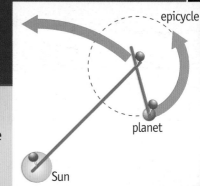

epicycle

planet

Sun

Johannes Kepler realised that Copernicus might be right. He worked for a famous astronomer called Tycho Brahe. Although telescopes had not yet been invented, Brahe had made very precise observations of the planets. Kepler tested Copernicus's theory and used mathematics to work out that the planets' orbits were simple ellipses (oval shapes). This was much simpler than the epicycles model.

Galileo studied the solar system with the newly invented telescope. He found further evidence that the Sun was at the centre of the solar system instead of the Earth. Many people found the evidence very convincing. Galileo got into a lot of trouble with the Church for publishing his ideas.

Newton's theory of gravity explained why the planets orbited the Sun rather than the Earth.

The line of the pendulum's swing on the Earth's surface changes slowly...

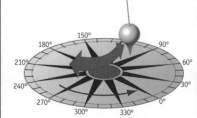

Foucault used a pendulum to show that the Earth is spinning on its axis. This evidence proved that Ptolemy's idea of the Sun orbiting the Earth every day must be wrong.

...as the Earth spins underneath

Timeline values: 100, 150, 200, 300, 400, 500, 600, 700, 800, 900, 1000, 1100, 1200, 1300, 1400, 1500, 1543, 1600, 1601, 1610, 1686, 1700, 1800, 1851, 1900, 2000

The Sun is nearly 100 times heavier than the mass of all the planets put together. Therefore the Sun's gravity is a dominant force, even at long distances. Newton showed mathematically that the inwards gravitational force from the Sun at the centre of the solar system keeps the moving planets in their elliptical orbits. Similarly a planet's gravity causes its moons to orbit it whilst the planet orbits the Sun.

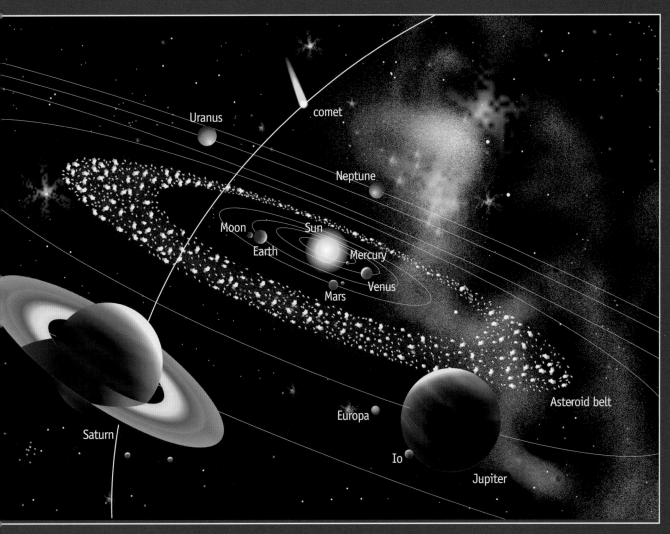

Newton's theory of gravity doesn't quite work. Even in Newton's day, astronomers noticed some anomalies when they made really precise measurements of Mercury's orbit. Einstein produced a new theory of gravity about 100 years ago. So far, all the measurements of the positions and movements of the Sun, Moon, planets, moons and comets agree with this theory.

How do you think ideas about the solar system will change in the future?

Einstein showed that gravity actually slows time down. Clocks on the GPS satellites are ticking slightly faster than clocks on Earth.

Space exploration

By sending robotic spacecraft to fly past or land on the other planets and their moons it is possible to study their surface and atmosphere close up. The photo below, taken by the Galileo spacecraft orbiting Jupiter, shows the plume of gas and dust from a volcano erupting on the left-hand side of Jupiter's moon Io.

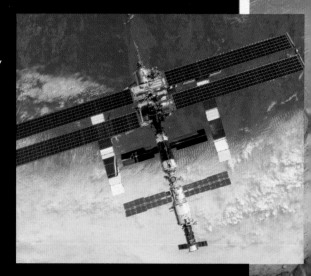

Spacecraft placed into artificial orbit around a planet can collect scientific data at a distance. Based on both images and data, scientists can produce a hypothesis of what the surface is like even if no probe has landed there. When probes land on a planet, moon or asteroid or pass through a comet's tail, they can actually take samples of rocks and gases to test these hypotheses.

things to think about • What are the benefits of observing Earth from space, and not just on the ground?

One of the main benefits of being able to travel into space is the development of artificial satellites. These allow almost instantaneous phone and TV communication around the Earth. GPS satellites make navigation easier.

Meteorologists use satellites to monitor the Earth's weather. This allows the prediction of natural disasters like hurricanes. On longer timescales, satellite images of changes to the Earth's surface can provide evidence to support theories such as plate tectonics and to answer questions about the impact of human activity on the Earth.

The International Space Station (ISS) is an orbiting research lab. At the orbiting distance the force of gravity is nearly as great as on the Earth's surface, but objects inside the ISS behave as if they are weightless. This is because the station is in continual free fall towards the Earth's surface.

In the ISS astronauts carry out experiments that are not possible on Earth, such as examining the effect of weightlessness on the growth of crystals or seedlings, and its effect on humans. Experience of living in the ISS also helps to increase our understanding about how to live safely in space.

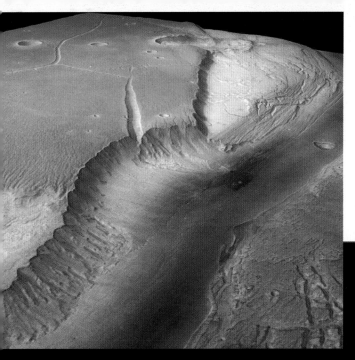

Many landers and orbiting spacecraft have been sent to Mars. Images of Mars show what look like gigantic channels eroded by flood water. This may be evidence that liquid water once existed on the surface of Mars. If water is still present below the surface then it is just possible that there is microscopic life. No probes have discovered any water yet but future unmanned (and possibly manned) missions will test for water and for the presence of life using more sensitive techniques.

The Hubble space telescope takes very clear pictures because it is above Earth's atmosphere. Images from Hubble have led to some very important discoveries about the formation of stars – such as in these giant pillars of gas and dust. Hubble has also found evidence for planets around stars other than the Sun.

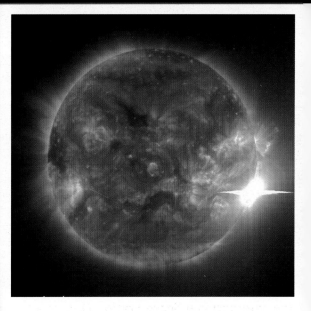

The Sun is the only star that can be studied close up. The SOHO satellite orbits the Sun and collects data about regions of hot gas inside the Sun. Solar flares can disrupt communications and electricity supplies but SOHO's pictures can give an early warning that a flare has erupted.

Earth's climate is affected by the Sun's brightness. Astronomers have observed sunspots for over 300 years. Changes in the number of sunspots may cause climate change, so it is important to monitor changes in the Sun's output.

Index

Acknowledgements

The Publishers would like to thank the following for permission to reproduce copyright material:

p.5 Science Photo Library; **p.4** © Dennis Hallinan/Alamy; **p.6** Du Cane Medical Imaging Ltd/Science Photo Library; **p.9** Mauro Fermariello/Science Photo Library; **p.10** Eye of Science/Science Photo Library; **p.11** Dr Y Nikas/Phototake Science/ photolibrary.com; **p.12***l* Dr Y Nikas/Phototake Science/photolibrary.com; *r* Dr G. Moscoso/Science Photo Library; **p.13***lt* James Stevenson/Science Photo Library; *r* GE Medical Systems/Science Photo Library; *lb* National Library of Medicine/Science Photo Library; **p.16** D. Phillips/Science Photo Library; **p.17***t* Microworks/Phototake Inc/photolibrary.com; *b* Claude Nuridsany & Marie Perennou/Science Photo Library; **p.20***t* Wellcome Photo Library; *b* Science Photo Library; **p.21***l* David Scharf/Science Photo Library; *r* NIBSC/Science Photo Library; **pp.22–3** Dr Kari Lounatmaa/Science Photo Library; except *b* Wellcome Photo Library; **p.24***t* Martyn F. Chillmaid; *c* Pascal Goetgheluck/Science Photo Library; *b* Ashely Cooper/ Alamy; **p.27***l* Science Photo Library; *r* DR Jeremy Burgess/Science Photo Library; **pp.28–9** © PhotoAlto/Alamy; **p.28** © PhotoAlto/Alamy; **p.28** © Jean-Yves Ruszniewski/TempSport/Corbis; **p.30***l* Sheila Terry/Science Photo Library; *r* Matt Meadows, Peter Arnold Inc./Science Photo Library; **p.31***t* CC Studio/Science Photo Library; *b* © Joao Luiz Bulcao/Corbis; **p.32** Steve Gschmeissner/Science Photo Library; **p.33** Mehau Kulyk/Science Photo Library; **p.34***t* Science Photo Library; *b* AJ Photo/Science Photo Library; **p.35***t* © Peter Jordan/Alamy; *b* Pascal Goetgheluck/Science Photo Library; **p.36***tr* Eric Grave /Science Photo Library; *tl* © Arco Images/Alamy; *b* Anthea Sieveking/Wellcome Photo Library; **p.37** Simon Fraser/Science Photo Library; **p.38***tl* Jerome Wexler/Science Photo Library; *tr* Eye of Science/Science Photo Library; *bl* Bill Longcore/Science Photo Library; *br* Libby Welch/ Wellcome Photo Library; **p.39***t* Adam Jones/Science Photo Library; *c* Walter Dawn/Science Photo Library; *b* © Bubbles Photolibrary/Alamy; **p.40** Becca Law; **p.41** Tay Rees/Riser/Getty Images; **pp.42–3** © Kevin Dodge/Corbis; **p.43***t* Margot Granitsas/Science Photo Library; *b* © Bettmann/Corbis; **p.44***t* FLPA/ Nigel Cattlin; **p.44***b* © Janine Wiedel Photolibrary/Alamy; **p.45** © Louise Gubb/Corbis Saba; **p.46** BSIP/Science Photo Library; **p.48***tl* Michael Abbey/Science Photo Library; *tr* Eye of Science/Science Photo Library; **p.48***b* Eric Grave/Phototake Inc/Photolibrary.com; **p.49** © Clouds Hill Imaging Ltd./Corbis; **p.50** Dr Yorgos Nikas/Science Photo Library; **p.51***l* Dr Yorgos Nikas/Science Photo Library; *r* Dr Yorgos Nikas/Science Photo Library; **p.52***t* Andrew Syred/Science Photo Library; *c* Pasieka/Science Photo Library; **p.52***b* Dr Tony Brain/Science Photo Library; **p.53** © Dennis Kunkel/ Phototake Inc/Photolibrary.com; **pp.54–5** © Herve Conge/Ism Ism/Phototake Inc/photolibrary.com; **p.54***t* © Herve Conge/Ism Ism/Phototake Inc/photolibrary.com; *b* © Dennis Kunkel/Phototake Inc/photolibrary.com; **p.56***t* Sinclair Stammers/Science Photo Library; *b* Steve & Ann Toon/Robert Harding Picture Library Ltd/photolibrary.com; **p.57***t* © Nation Wong/zefa/Corbis; *c* © Arco Images/Alamy; *b* Carolyn A. Mckeone/Science Photo Library; **p.59** Time & Life Pictures/Getty Images; **p.60** TEK Image/Science Photo Library; **p.62** Martin Land/Science Photo Library; **pp.62–3** Martin Land/Science Photo Library; **p.63** Jonathan Cook; **p.64***t* David Nunuk/Science Photo Library; *b* © Herve Conge/ISM ISM/Phototake Inc/photolibrary.com; **p.65** Maximilian Stock Ltd/Science Photo Library; **p.66***l* © Herve Conge/ISM ISM/Phototake Inc/photolibrary.com; *r* Andrew Syred/Science Photo Library; **p.68***l* Martin Bond/Science Photo Library; *r* Mark Edwards/Still Pictures; **p.69** NASA/Science Photo Library; **p.70** 1st left Peter Scoones/Science Photo Library; 2nd left INGRAM; 3rd left Georgette Douwma/Science Photo Library; 4th left Richard Ellis/Science Photo Library; 5th left Gary Meszaros/Science Photo Library; 6th left Photodisc; **p.71***b* 1st left Photodisc; 2nd left © Image Source/Corbis; 3rd left Bob Gibbons/Science Photo Library; 4th left Photodisc; 5th left Stephen P. Parker/Science Photo Library; 6th left Photodisc; *t* Peter Scoones/Science Photo Library; **p.72***l* Alexis Rosenfeld/Science Photo Library; **p.72–3** © Paul Souders/Corbis; **p.73***r* © David Muench/Corbis; **p.74–5** © Herbert Spichtinger/zefa/Corbis;

p.74*c* © Rolf Richardson/Alamy; *b* © Holt Studios International Ltd/Alamy; **p.75***t* © John Conrad/Corbis; *b* © Steve Bloom Images/Alamy; **p.76***t* William Ervin/Science Photo Library; *b* © blickwinkel/Alamy; **p.77***b* © Holt Studios International Ltd/Alamy; **p.78***t* Martin Bond/Science Photo Library; *b* © Photofusion Picture Library/Alamy; **p.79** © Christopher Pillitz/Alamy; **p.82***l* NRSC LTD/Science Photo Library; *r* British Antarctic Survey/Science Photo Library; *c* FEMA/ Liz Roll; **p.83** NASA Goddard Space Flight Center (NASA-GSFC); **p.84–5** Reto Stockli, NASA Earth Observatory; **p.84** Jim Varney/Science Photo Library; **p.85** SKYSCAN/Science Photo Library; **p.88***t* © By Ian Miles-Flashpoint Pictures/Alamy; *b* Martyn Chillmaid/Photolibrary.com; **p.89***lt* © Grant Farquhar/Alamy; *lc* © Robert Harding Picture Library Ltd/Alamy; *lb* © Klaus Hackenberg/zefa/Corbis; *r* © Owen Franken/Corbis; **p.90***tl* © Andrew Woodle /Alamy; *tr* © Tim McGuire/Corbis; *b* © Jon Bower/Alamy; **p.91***t* © Pavel Filatov/Alamy; *b* © Nordicphotos/Alamy; **p.92***b* © Gianni Diliberto/Jupiter Images; *t* © sciencephotos/Alamy; **p.93***l* © sciencephotos/Alamy; *r* © sciencephotos/Alamy; **p.94** Andrew Lambert Photography/Science Photo Library; **p.95***l* Andrew Lambert Photography/Science Photo Library; *r* Andrew Lambert Photography/Science Photo Library; **p.96** Martin Dohrn/Science Photo Library; **p.97** © Dbimages/Alamy; **p.100** Andrew Lambert Photography/Science Photo Library; **p.102** 1st top left Edward Kinsman/Science Photo Library; 1st top right Charles D. Winters/Science Photo Library; 2nd top left Charles D. Winters/Science Photo Library; 2nd top right Charles D. Winters/Science Photo Library; 3rd top left Claude Nuridsany & Marie Perennou/Science Photo Library; 3rd top right Martyn Chillmaid/Photolibrary.com; 4th top left © Kari Marttila/Alamy; 4th top right Russ Lappa/Science Photo Library; 5th top right © Phototake Inc./Alamy; 5th top left Maximilian Stock Ltd/Science Photo Library; **p.103** Joseph Stroscio; Robert Celotta/NIST; **p.105***t* Andrew Lambert Photography/Science Photo Library; *b* Martyn F. Chillmaid; **p.108** Charles D. Winters/Science Photo Library; **p.128***l* Andrew Lambert Photography/Science Photo Library; *r* Martyn F. Chillmaid/Science Photo Library; **p.129***t* Andrew Lambert Photography/Science Photo Library; *c* Andrew Lambert Photography/Science Photo Library; *b* Andrew Lambert Photography/Science Photo Library; **p.131** Andrew Lambert Photography/Science Photo Library; **p.132** Jonathan Cook; **p.134***t* © Glyn Thomas/Alamy; *b* Eye of Science/Science Photo Library; **p.135***t* NASA Kennedy Space Center ; *b* Cordelia Molloy/Science Photo Library; **p.137** © robert llewellyn/Alamy; **p.138***t* Jonathan Cook; *c* Jonathan Cook; *b* © Julie Mowbray/Alamy; **p.139***t* © Don Despain/www.rekindlephoto.com/Alamy; *c* © The Print Collector/Alamy; *b* © Stephen Bisgrove/Alamy; **p.140***t* Jonathan Cook; *bl* © Vanessa Miles/Alamy; *br* Colin Cuthbert/Science Photo Library; **p.141***b* Ron Chapman/Science Photo Library; **p.143** Jim Amos/Science Photo Library; **p.144–5** Peter Menzell/Science Photo Library; **p.144***t* Fredrik Fransson/Science Photo Library; *c* GeoScience Features Picture Library; *b* GeoScience Features Picture Library; **p.146** Image by Robert Simmon, SSAI/NASA GSFC, based on data copyright Space Imaging; **p.147***l* © Leslie Garland Picture Library/Alamy; *r* © mediacolor's/Alamy; **p.148–9** © Jacques Jangoux/Alamy; **p.149** Pat & Tom Leeson/Science Photo Library; **p.150–1** © Stephen Shepherd/Alamy; **p.150** Jerry Lodriguss/Science Photo Library; **p.153** © NASA/Roger Ressmeyer/Corbis; **p.155***r* © Todd Gipstein/Corbis; *l* © Alan Schein/Alamy; **p.156–7** David Nunuk/Science Photo Library; **p.157***r* Paul Silverman/Fundamental Photos/Science Photo Library; *l* © Alen MacWeeney/Corbis; **p.158–9** © Matthias Kulka/zefa/Corbis; **p.158***t* © Matthias Kulka/zefa/Corbis; *b* Annabella Bluesky/Science Photo Library; **p.159** © Jesper Jensen/Alamy; **p.160***t* © Tony Lilley/Alamy; *c* Richard Megna/Fundamental/Science Photo Library; **p.160***b* © Lebrecht Music and Arts Photo Library/Alamy; **p.161***r* © Ashley Cooper/Alamy; **p.161***lt* Hank Morgan/Science Photo Library; *lb* Edward Kinsman/Science Photo Library; **p.162** © keith morris/Alamy; **p.164** © Phototake Inc./Alamy; **p.164** © Phototake Inc./Alamy; **p.166** Hutch Axilrod/Photonica/Getty Images;

p.168 © Larry Lilac/Alamy; **p.170**c © John Terence Turner/Alamy; l NASA/ Sandra Joseph, Tony Gray, Robert Murray; r © Joern Sackermann/Alamy; **p.171**l Stephen Dalton/NHPA; r © www.gerardbrown.co.uk/Alamy; **p.172** Pascal Goetgheluck/Science Photo Library; **p.173** © KLJ Photographic/ Alamy; **p.176–7** Gustoimages/Science Photo Library; **p.176** © Dominic Burke/Alamy; **p.178**r © Leslie Garland Picture Library/Alamy; l NASA; **p.179** Erich Schrempp/Science Photo Library; **p.180**tl © blickwinkel/ Alamy; tr © Tami Chappell/Reuters/Corbis; b © StockShot/Alamy; **p.181**l © Kim Westerskov/Alamy; r © Transtock Inc./Alamy; tl © Rob Walls/ Alamy; **p.182**tr © paul ridsdale/Alamy; © Andrew Fox/Alamy; Sheila Terry/Science Photo Library; **p.183** © Ashley Cooper/Alamy; **p.184–5** TEK Image/Science Photo Library; **p.185**t Doug Martin/Science Photo Library; c Doug Martin/Science Photo Library; b © Tony Lilley/Alamy; **p.186**t © Rob Wilkinson/Alamy; b © Werner H. Müller/Corbis; **p.188** Alex Bartel/Science Photo Library; **p.189**l Andrew Lambert Photography/ Science Photo Library; cb Martin Bond/Science Photo Library; ct Andrew Lambert Photography/Science Photo Library; r © David Levenson/Alamy; **p.190**t Will & Deni Mcintyre/Science Photo Library; br Daniel Sambraus/ Science Photo Library; bl © Andrew Holt/Alamy; **p.191** © Purcell Team/ Alamy; **p.196–7** © David Robertson/Alamy; **p.198**t © Lester Lefkowitz/ Corbis; b © Chase Jarvis/Corbis; **p.200**t © lee hacker/Alamy; b © C. Lyttle/ zefa/Corbis; **p.201**t Mark Sykes/Science Photo Library; b © sciencephotos/ Alamy; **p.202** Tony Mcconnell/Science Photo Library; **p.203**l © sciencephotos/Alamy; r © Hugh Threlfall/Alamy; **p.204–5** © Libby Welch/Alamy; **p.204** © picturesbyrob/Alamy; **p.205** Ted Kinsman/Science Photo Library; **p.208**l © Richard Wainscoat/Alamy; r George East/Science Photo Library; **p.209**l SOHO (ESA & NASA); r NASA Marshall Space Flight Center (NASA-MSFC); **p.211** Doug Plummer/Science Photo Library; **p.212** John Sanford/Science Photo Library; **p.213**l © Roger Ressmeyer/Corbis; r Pekka Parviainen/Science Photo Library; **p.214**l © Corbis; r © Aaron Horowitz/Corbis; **p.215** Hubble Space Telescope Comet Team and NASA; **p.216** Sheila Terry/Science Photo Library; **p.218–9** Courtesy NASA/JPL-Caltech.; **p.218**t NASA; b NASA/Science Photo Library; **p.218–9**t EUROPEAN SPACE AGENCY/DLR/FU BERLIN (G. NEUKUM)/ Science Photo Library; **p.219**r Courtesy of SOHO. SOHO is a project of international cooperation between ESA and NASA.; bl NASA Headquarters – Greatest Images of NASA (NASA-HQ-GRIN)

t = top, b = bottom, l = left, c = centre, r = right

Every effort has been made to contact copyright holders but if any have been inadvertently overlooked the Publisher will be pleased to make the necessary arrangements at the earliest opportunity.